Political Economy, Concisely

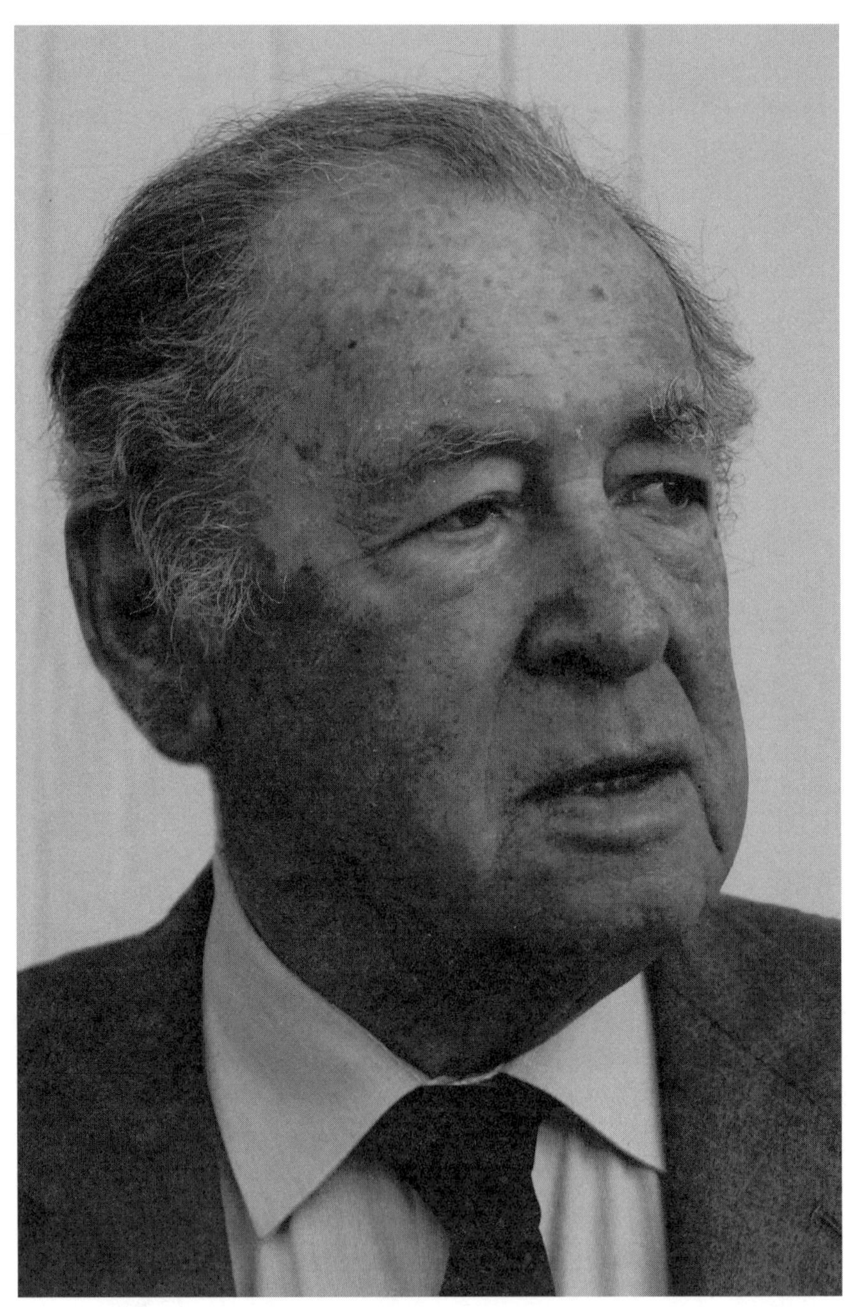

ANTHONY DE JASAY

Political Economy, Concisely

ESSAYS ON POLICY THAT DOES NOT WORK

AND MARKETS THAT DO

Anthony de Jasay

Edited and with an Introduction by

HARTMUT KLIEMT

LIBERTY FUND

Indianapolis

This book is published by Liberty Fund, Inc.,
a foundation established to encourage study of the
ideal of a society of free and responsible individuals.

The cuneiform inscription that serves as our logo and
as the design motif for our endpapers is the earliest-known
written appearance of the word "freedom" (*amagi*), or "liberty."
It is taken from a clay document written about 2300 B.C.
in the Sumerian city-state of Lagash.

Printed in the United States of America

C 10 9 8 7 6 5 4 3 2
P 10 9 8 7 6 5 4 3 2

Library of Congress Cataloging-in-Publication Data
De Jasay, Anthony, 1925–
Political economy, concisely: essays on policy that does not work
and markets that do / Anthony de Jasay;
edited and with an introduction by Hartmut Kliemt.
p. cm.
Includes bibliographical references and index.
ISBN 978-0-86597-777-8 (hc: alk. paper)
ISBN 978-0-86597-778-5 (pbk.: alk. paper)
1. Free enterprise. 2. Free enterprise—Europe. 3. Central planning.
4. Central planning—Europe. 5. Europe—Economic policy. I. Title.
HB95.D39 2009
330—dc22 2009005124

LIBERTY FUND, INC.
8335 Allison Pointe Trail, Suite 300
Indianapolis, Indiana 46250-1684

CONTENTS

INTRODUCTION

Anthony de Jasay may be seen in the role of a Frédéric Bastiat of our times. Like Bastiat, whom he admires (and credits with the discovery of opportunity cost, a cornerstone of economics), Jasay himself is a philosopher-economist with hard-won, practical experience. He displays an affinity for British classical liberalism, particularly for David Hume, but keeps his distance from the Utilitarians. A longtime resident of France, Jasay shares Bastiat's encounters with the perversities of the centralized state. Like his great French forerunner, he took (and still takes) to the pen to express his criticism. However, unlike Bastiat, who was a Frenchman, Jasay came to France from Hungary, his native country, with stops in Austria, Australia, and finally Oxford, where he taught economics.

As a philosopher-economist, Jasay continues the British Moralist tradition originating in the work of Hobbes. Although the British Moralists often sought to refute Hobbes, the themes he initiated persist to the present day. Jasay's first book, *The State,* is a paradigmatic case in point. Its first sentence asks, "What would you do if you were the state?" In response, Jasay spells out his version of what has been called the "Logic of Leviathan" but does not endorse the substantive Hobbesian claim that social order requires this dangerous animal as its creator. Quite to the contrary, Jasay claims, if individuals are left alone, they tend to coordinate their actions; conventional rules and social order will emerge spontaneously.

Always insisting on keeping key concepts in their proper place and not letting them get tangled together, Jasay draws a sharp distinction between freedoms and rights (and considers the "right to freedom" a confused notion). Freedoms are those feasible acts that fall within the spontaneous rules of the social order. Rights and their matching obligations evolve either from voluntary agreements (contracts) or "from above"—the rights being conferred and the obligations imposed by authority.

Drawing a distinction between freedom and rights leads directly to

Jasay's theory of property. He holds with Hume that property originates in finding, is transferred by consent, and is antecedent to society or the state; it is a freedom. He attacks the conventional view that property is a "right," let alone a "bundle" of detachable rights conferred by some collective decision, with the state carrying out the matching obligation of enforcing the right. According to Jasay, this widely accepted view of property rights, proclaimed even by such staunch defenders of freedom as Armen Alchian, implicitly conveys that property is held at society's pleasure, by its grace and favor. Society can withdraw any or all of the detachable "rights" to property just as it has conferred them. If, on the contrary, property is a liberty, the violation of this liberty is a breach of the ageless conventions that define what may and what must not be done.

Whether or not Jasay's view is correct, the basic distinction he makes is of the utmost importance: there exist at least two concepts of property. According to one concept, property is defined by social conventions that are not subject to public law and that precede public enforcement. The other concept emphasizes that a property right represents a public obligation enforced by the state. Using the first concept, it is incongruous to think of property in the context of distributive justice; using the second, however, such an understanding comes naturally. Many of Jasay's criticisms are based on this fundamental insight.

The state requires submission of some to the will of others. According to common wisdom, democratic procedures morally dignify a corresponding "rule of submission." Contrary to that notion, Jasay insists that legitimate obligations must be self-imposed by those to whom they apply or must result from conventions that emerged from unforced acts of individuals. The first of the two sources of obligation is widely accepted. But in Jasay's framework the second is crucial as well. Conventions that emerged in a spontaneous process bring about legitimate obligations. At the same time, conventions restrict that which can be legitimately accomplished through collective action, including law enactment.

Jasay's view of the normative force of conventions is obviously in certain aspects similar to Hayek's endorsement of common law, which is not the outcome of deliberate enactment. But, whereas in the Hayekian case the state is seen as an enforcer of order, Jasay conceives of the state as a source of distortions of social order. The state's claim to the exclusive use of coercive power will endanger property in particular. Individuals who manage to capture the state machinery will use it for their own exploitative purposes. Whenever conventions as coordination devices are substituted by less-benign commands of central authorities, the potential exists for an infringement on individual liberties. And, in Jasay's view, because of the ever-increasing growth and power of the state, these infringements nowadays abound.

Despite his criticism of state action, Jasay is too realistic to engage in the exercises of so-called anarcho-capitalist thinking. Rather, he accepts the realities of the state and collective action, knowing that his criticisms will not make the problems go away but believing that it is worthwhile to make us aware of the perversities of politics. Jasay's aspiration is not to exert an influence on politics by imposing his own policies. To borrow from the title of another of his books, he is "against politics." Because politics as such is a threat to liberty, the primary aim should be to contain it. In this context, the essays in this collection provide grassroots criticisms that make the follies of daily events at least more conspicuous and thereby containment, perhaps, more likely.

Political Economy, Concisely comprises fifty-eight essays that appeared in electronic form over a five-year period, from 2003 to 2007, on Liberty Fund's Library of Economics and Liberty website (http://www.econlib.org/library/), as well as several other short essays published during the last ten years from various journals and newspapers. Further, as this collection shows, the era of the printed word and, for that matter, the printed book, is not over. When collected in printed form and given a thematic rather than a chronological arrangement, Jasay's short essays become even more impressive, supporting one another like the stones in a Roman arch.

To supplement the shorter essays of this volume, the reader might turn to the more-extended essays in some of the companion volumes of this series. However, the essays in *Political Economy, Concisely* are not merely preparatory for the longer discussions. They have their own specific merits precisely because of the requirements dictated by brevity. The advantages of a concise format compensate for the occasional lack of elaboration. What is not in one will come up in another, complementary, essay. Although it is good economic common sense to insist that there should be no such thing as a free lunch, the essays herein challenge that maxim, at least to the degree that clarity and brevity can successfully coexist, with no hidden costs.

The ideas expressed in these essays reflect the wit and intellectual elegance of their author, challenging conventional wisdom in a subtle yet incisive manner. The editing in this volume has been kept to a minimum. Additions by the editors of the Econlib website, cross-references to essays that appeared earlier on the same website, and typographical errors have been eliminated. Some essay titles have been slightly changed, and in a very few instances subtitles to sections have been added. The assignment of the essays to categories corresponding to the seven parts of this volume seemed rather natural, whereas the particular sequence of parts, as well as the arrangement of the essays within each part, offered a great level of freedom that, it is hoped, has been used to provide a meaningful context for the reader. In the end, however, the essays can and do speak for themselves.

Hartmut Kliemt

PART 1

Rights, Property, and Markets

PROPERTY OR "PROPERTY RIGHTS"?

Economists who own their home or have other assets will regard them as their "property." When speaking in their professional capacity, however, they change their vocabulary and will invoke "property rights." Do these terms mean the same thing?—and does it matter which term is used? This essay argues that "property" and "property rights" mean different things and muddling them up presents an insidious but quite serious threat to the kind of social order wherein economic efficiency and individual freedom have the best chance to survive.

"A BUNDLE OF RIGHTS"?

Ironically, the author who has done the most to impose the term "property rights" on scholarly usage was Armen Alchian, an economist of irreproachable credentials both as a fine theorist and as a defender of the free society. In a seminal essay[1] that has become a foundation stone of "property rights economics," he explained that when you owned, say, a piece of land, what you had was the right to leave it fallow, to plough it, to grow wheat on it for your own use or for sale, to walk across it, to fly over it, to build a house on it, to grant an easement on it, to lease it to another party, to bequeath or to sell it. Property was such a "bundle of rights." It is tempting to hold that if you removed one stick from the bundle, it remained a bundle; if you removed two, it still remained a bundle. How many sticks can one remove without the remainder ceasing to represent property, and are some sticks more essential than others?

This concept of property opens the door to a kind of gradualist argument. If "society" or the government purportedly acting on its be-

First published by Liberty Fund, Inc., at www.econlib.org on December 4, 2006. Reprinted by permission.

1. Armen A. Alchian, "Some Economics of Property Rights," *Il Politico* 30 (1965): 816–29.

half removes from the bundle a stick here and a stick there, if it forbids the owner to build on his land, or subjects the growing of some crop to an acreage quota, imposes an easement or a public preemption privilege, the "bundle" that is left is still property of a sort. How many rights may the government remove from it for the bundle still to pass for property and the government to pass for its protector?

FREEDOMS AND RIGHTS DIFFER FUNDAMENTALLY

The "bundle of rights" concept gives rise to a dangerously weak theory of property. To find the root cause of the weakness, one must go "back to basics" and firmly grasp the difference between a freedom and a right.[2]

A freedom is a relation between *one person* and a set of acts. The person is presumed to be free to perform any act in the set that does not breach the rules against torts (offenses against person and property) and (a less stringent requirement) the rules of civility. A substantial obstruction of freedom (e.g., gagging or threatening to hit a person to stop him from speaking freely) is a tort or an incivility. As such, it is wrong. To say that a person has a "right to a freedom" is tantamount to saying that he has a right not to be wronged—a redundant and silly proposition. It also implies that he would not have this freedom if he had not somehow obtained a right to it—an implication that is at the source of much false theorizing. You do not need a right to move if your moves stay within the rules—this indeed is what it *means* to have rules.

In contrast to a freedom, a right is a relation between *two persons, the rightholder and the obligor,* and an act the obligor must perform at the rightholder's bidding. A right may be created by contract in which the obligor, in exchange for a consideration, surrenders his freedom to perform (or forbear from performing) some set of acts as he pleases, and agrees to perform (or forbear from performing) it as required by the rightholder. Here, both parties enter voluntarily into the right/

2. See Anthony de Jasay, "Freedoms, 'Rights,' and Rights," *Il Politico* 66 (2001): 369–97.

obligation relation. However, a right may also be created by some authority, such as the government acting on behalf of "society," *conferring* it upon rightholders and *imposing* the corresponding obligation on obligors of its own choosing. The conferring of welfare rights on some and the imposition of the corresponding taxes on others is a mundane example. The granting of civil rights to some minority and the imposition of the appropriate conduct on the rest is a perhaps less mundane one. The notion of "property rights," as used in current economic theory, conjures up the fiction that property is conferred by "society" upon the proprietors and the corresponding obligation to respect it is imposed by "society" on everybody. (It is worth noting that respect for property is part of the rules against torts. Violating property is a wrong that must simply not be done; and this interdiction is enforced by various private or public ways and means of enforcement ranging from reciprocity and retaliation to law courts and a police force. A separate obligation to respect or protect property, a corollary of the supposed "right to private property," is double-counting. Like any other double-counting, it obscures the view of what is owned and what is owed.)

PROPERTY RIGHTS, TRUE AND FALSE

There are, in fact, genuine property rights in the sense of two-person relations involving a right and a matching obligation. Leases, loan agreements, a shareholder's equity in net corporate assets, options and other equity and credit derivatives, insurance policies, and, in a broader sense, all outstanding contracts with the exception of contracts of employment, are property rights proper.

When you lease your house, we know where the tenant's right(s) come from. They arise from the surrender, for a given period, of your freedom to use your own house and your assumption of an obligation to let the tenant use it subject to certain conditions and in exchange for value received or to be received.

But where does your putative "right" to own the house come from? The standard answer is that it comes from your purchase agreement with the previous owner, or a bequest or gift he made to you. The previous owner's right to do this, in turn, came from an agreement with, or bequest or gift from, the owner previous to *that* owner, and so on. Such a regress, however, can only shift the problem ever further backward and does not resolve it.

The literature offers us two solutions, the Lockean and the socialist. In the Lockean solution, the chain of legitimate transfers of ownership goes on backward until it ends with the original owner who took possession. He had a "right" to do so if two notorious provisos were satisfied: he must have "mixed his labor" with what he appropriated, and he must have "left enough and as good" for those who came after him. These pious provisos have come in for much and deserved criticism on grounds of their contestable logic, and in this essay I will simply leave the reader to judge the Lockean solution for himself.

The socialist solution is to intimate that property is privately held only by the grace of society that could choose to change its distribution, or take it into public ownership, if it did not create a *right* to it and if it did not confer this right upon individual proprietors. The latter hold their property subject to any conditions by which society circumscribes the right to it. It may withdraw the right altogether if it deems it in the public interest to do so. Constitutional obstacles to this can always be got round, for society is not going to stop itself from doing what it wishes to do. In any event, if the right to property is in society's gift, it can always take back the right it has conferred and with that extinguish its own obligation to protect it.

THE PRESUMPTION OF GOOD TITLE

The contradictions and outlandish fictions of both the Lockean and the socialist solution disappear in thin air the instant we cease to maintain the arbitrary supposition that one needs a *right* to own valuable resources. This supposition originates in an atavistic belief that everything should belong to everybody or be shared equally, and any departure from this norm requires a justification, an *excuse* of some kind.

Not everyone believes this, and those who do believe it only in certain contexts. It is not a universal human trait, but only one of various extravagant ones. In no way does it place it beyond dispute that owning property is morally reprehensible and unjust unless it can be shown that a *right* to it exists.

Ownership is a fact of life whose origins are veiled by the mists of prehistory. By the elementary rules of debate, the burden of proof lies with those who claim that a *right* is needed to justify it. This claim must be made good either as regards the institution of ownership in general or, failing that, the ownership of a particular asset by a particular owner. As to the former, making it good is impossible, for a metaphysical proposition cannot be verified. As to the latter, the claimant must show that the owner does not have good title to the asset.

It is blatant nonsense to try and switch the burden of proof to the owner, and ask him to prove that his title is good; for he can never prove the negative assertion that there is no flaw hidden in it somewhere out of sight. It is he who wants us to believe that there is one, who must spot the hidden flaw.

Putting it concisely, challenges to property require to be verified by the challenger, for they cannot be falsified by the defender. It is this asymmetry that generates the presumption in favor of title ("possession is three parts of the law"). Property being analytically a freedom, it is no surprise to find the same logic yielding the presumption of title that yields the vaster and more inclusive presumption of freedom.

"DESIGN FAULTS" IN LOCKE'S THEORY OF PROPERTY TAINT OWNERSHIP WITH GUILT

Ownership is a relation between an owner and a scarce resource, such that the owner is at liberty to use and alienate it, exclude all others from access to it except by his consent, and thus also at liberty to grant various kinds of prior claims and use rights in it for those toward whom it assumes contractual obligations. It is doubtful whether ownership, even ownership by a collective entity, has any meaning without some element of exclusion that separates owners from nonowners of the resource in question. When everybody owns a thing, nobody owns it.

The crux of moral and political aspects in property theory is how an unowned object first becomes legitimately owned. Once the legitimacy of first acquisition is settled, all subsequent acquisitions by the saving of income, exchange, gift, or bequest of assets can be defended on the ground of mutual consent. If that test is met, the distribution of property cannot be condemned as unjust unless the voluntary transactions that gave rise to it are also condemned as either unjust or irrelevant to just ownership.

Some enemies of property ownership choose to attack initial acquisition, others the relevance for valid title of subsequent voluntary transactions. This article will treat the first of these two targets. Luck plays a large role in the history of ideas, and as bad luck would have it, the most influential theory of property to this day is that of John Locke.[1]

First published as part 1 of "Property and Its Enemies," by Liberty Fund, Inc., at www.econlib.org on August 4, 2003. Reprinted by permission.

1. See John Locke, *The Second Treatise of Civil Government* (1690); there have been many editions, but especially significant are John Locke, *Two Treatises of Government: A Critical Edition with an Introduction and Apparatus Criticus* by Peter Laslett, rev. ed. (Cambridge, UK: Cambridge University Press, 1963), reissued with a new introduction by Cambridge University Press in 1988; and *Political Writings of John Locke,* ed. David Wootton (New York: Mentor, 1993).

His starting point is ambiguous. Arguably, a clear and straightforward theory of how an unowned resource comes legitimately to be owned had to wait till Hume's *Treatise of Human Nature.*[2] In Locke, everything is, albeit in a vague way, already owned at the outset: God "has given the earth to the children of men," "given it to mankind in common" (chap. v, §25), "yet there must of necessity be a means to appropriate [the fruits]" to "a private dominion exclusive of the rest of mankind" (chap. v, §26). This suggests a passage from "common" to "private" ownership, though Robert Nozick[3] interprets it as dealing with establishing rights "in an unowned object." Locke's text tells otherwise, but one might take it that his "common ownership" of everything by everybody can be dismissed as a mere verbal flourish that cannot have any force. However, the fatal fault line in Locke's design runs elsewhere.

For Locke contends that the passage of an object into exclusive ("private") ownership will not harm anyone provided "enough and as good is left for others," and—more problematically—he seems convinced that this condition is satisfied with the greatest of ease. He has two scenarios in mind. One is the English enclosures, where village commons of rough, swampy pasture were converted into well-drained, well-tilled arable fields, yielding (as he put it) ten times the produce. The other was the clearing of the virgin forest by the American colonists of New England and Virginia. In both cases, a wide margin of abundance appeared to leave enough and as good for others. For the next three centuries, many theorists have taken it that Locke has established the legitimacy of private property and the state's duty to protect it.

However, a closer look reveals that the "enough and as good" proviso is in fact a sharp-edged weapon in the hands of the enemies of property. The "others" who are excluded by an act of first appropriation can suffer prejudice on two possible counts. One is loss of use, the other is loss of opportunity. Loss of use occurs when others, who used to hunt or graze animals on the land, or otherwise profited from

2. David Hume, *A Treatise of Human Nature,* ed. David Fate Norton and Mary J. Norton (Oxford, UK: Oxford University Press, 2000).

3. Robert Nozick, *Anarchy, State, and Utopia* (New York: Basic Books, 1974), 174.

free access to the resource in question without ever incurring exclusion costs to appropriate it for their private use, now find themselves excluded from it by the first appropriator. Two views could be held about this. The hard-nosed one is that since these free users had done nothing to ensure the perennity of their own access to the resource, they have no claim against the appropriator who excludes them. The other, less rigorous view is that the appropriator owes them some compensation. The question is whether he can possibly compensate them adequately for their lost way of life. Did the periodic free issue of beef cattle to reservation Indians compensate them for losing the buffalo hunts? Almost any answer to such questions is as contestable as any other.

Compensating for loss of use is awkward, but much, much more awkward is the problem of loss of opportunity in case "enough and as good" is not left for others to appropriate. The quandary bifurcates: one of its branches leads to known resources, the other to unknown ones to be discovered.

Known resources have all been appropriated long ago. None is left for the taking by today's propertyless "huddled masses." It is easy to see, and Nozick has nicely proved by backward induction (p. 176) that if there is not "enough and as good left" today, the most recent appropriation must have violated the proviso, and so have all the preceding ones including the very first. In vain do many defenders of the capitalist order argue that its prodigious capacity to create wealth allows today's propertyless to be as well off as if they had (some) property, so they have not really lost potential welfare. The fact remains that others who passed before them have preempted the opportunity to get property simply by taking possession of it. Becoming a well-paid employee of some owner may be no consolation for failing to become an owner. In a book of labored and often twisted arguments, the far-left philosopher Gerald Cohen[4] validly makes this point along with countless invalid ones. If the Lockean proviso is worthy of the respect accorded to it, all title is illegitimate and every owner is guilty of

4. Gerald Cohen, *Self-Ownership, Freedom, and Equality* (Cambridge, UK: Cambridge University Press, 1995).

crowding nonowners out of the opportunities Locke said they ought to enjoy.

However, perhaps there is "enough and as good" opportunity left hidden in the as yet unknown world, to be discovered? Nobody knows what the as yet undiscovered part of the world conceals, but it is likely to contain valuable resources nobody owns.

Alas, the proviso will not let go. If a prospector finds a new gold mine or the wildcatter brings in a rich oil well, the probability of other prospectors and wildcatters making equally valuable finds diminishes, however slightly. If Edison discovers electricity, every other inventor has lost the opportunity to discover it. Exceptional strokes of genius, unexpected technological breakthroughs, and lucky strikes remain possible. But on the average, every new discovery will raise the probable finding cost of the next comparable discovery. This trend is manifest in petroleum and minerals, as well as in most branches of applied scientific research. The burden of rising finding costs is aggravated by the fact that what is eventually found—subsurface resources or "intellectual" property—is as a rule not accorded fully owned status by the legislator as would be the case if the "finders, keepers" principle were respected.

The long and short of it is that "enough and as good" is never left for everybody who might wish to get it. Over time and over large numbers, known resources all pass into someone's ownership, and the finding cost of unknown ones must continue to rise as it has risen, irregularly but inexorably, through history. Locke's proviso, far from asserting that first appropriation is just, in fact tells us that ownership begins with an original sin. In a somewhat perverse way, he unwittingly lays the foundations for doctrines that profess that "property is theft."

There is a simple means of releasing Locke's stranglehold on property theory. It is politely to decline his opening gambit. Why does a person who takes an opportunity owe anything to others who might have taken it but did not?—and why is this debt forgiven if, but only if, there are "enough and as good" opportunities left for these others so they get a second chance? It would obviously be a nice and friendly physical world where one person could take his opportunity and there was in fact always another and as good left for another person. But if the physical world is not quite as nice as this, why ought the first person to abstain from taking his opportunity, and why is his resulting ownership illegitimate? Must society choose between "private" ownership and justice? The requirement is arbitrary and one should not allow oneself to be browbeaten by arbitrary demands.[5]

5. Another such arbitrary demand is made by Cohen (ibid., 83–84), who advances the moral postulate that all property is jointly owned, no one can unilaterally take out "his" share from the joint holding, and the latter should be managed by democratic consensus. We may note that the late lamented Soviet Union has come close to fulfilling these moral requirements. Their realization, however, was regrettably discontinued.

IS OWNERSHIP A MYTH?

Economists should take more interest in the theoretical defense of property than they presently do. The relevance of a sound defense of the freedom of ownership, to my mind, does not just spring from property being necessary for viable markets (though this is of course true). It is rather that if property is in some sense inviolable, it constitutes a barrier to redistribution, or at least makes redistribution look dubious from a moral point of view. Redistribution is at the heart of welfare economics and politics. The concept of politics as something that comes from some other source than the state's grace is nowadays vigorously attacked precisely in order to make redistribution look compatible with justice, the respect of "rights." As I argued in my previous article, Locke, without of course wanting to, has paved a royal road for these attacks upon the freedom to own. Some seriously taken academic work now treats our idea of "mine" and "thine" as a myth.[1] Why does it, and is it right?

Locke's theory of property, even in the weakened form proposed by Robert Nozick,[2] fatally condemns ownership to illegitimacy. If enough and as good must be left for others, no one must keep property exclusively to himself or herself.

The obvious way to avoid this trap is not to fall for the arbitrary judgment, bordering on the intellectual bluff, that in finding an object of value, the finder deprives others of the opportunity of finding it. This judgment would grant to everybody some claim upon every undiscovered resource and put the eventual owner into everybody's debt. The

First published as part 2 of "Property and Its Enemies," by Liberty Fund, Inc., at www.econlib.org on August 4, 2003. Reprinted by permission.

1. E.g., John Christman, *The Myth of Property: Toward an Egalitarian Theory of Ownership* (Oxford University Press, UK: 1995); Liam Murphy and Thomas Nagel, *The Myth of Ownership: Taxes and Justice* (New York: Oxford University Press, 2002); and (under a less bellicose title) Jeremy Waldron, *The Right to Private Property* (Oxford, UK: Clarendon Press, 1988).

2. Robert Nozick, *Anarchy, State, and Utopia* (New York: Basic Books, 1974).

"finders, keepers" principle, in sharp contrast, implies no judgment, but a statement of fact, namely that though others might have found the object, they did not, and the owner who did owes no debt to them. This is the underlying logic of David Hume's theory of property,[3] which begins with what he calls "first occupation" and to which he adds "long occupation" (p. 507). All viable theories of property down to our day fall into the Humean pattern, though most seem to be unaware of the fact.

Hume dismisses in a footnote (p. 505) Locke's attempt to justify ownership by the "mixing" of one's labor with an external resource, and pays no attention to the "enough left for others" clause. He creates his theory in two moves. The first establishes legitimacy. Society is formed by the "first assignment" of property to the "present possessor" (p. 505). This moment is decisive; the rest is all a matter of voluntary transactions. For "fitness and suitableness ought never to enter . . . the distributing of the properties of mankind" (p. 514). Judges of morals and efficiency are offered no role to play. Of course, the "stability of possession" is not inconsistent with its "transference by consent," i.e., by the classic means of sale, gift, and bequest. The distribution of property resulting from such exercises of the owners' liberty corresponds to the ideal of justice. This is all familiar and amounts to a reasoned explication of our ingrained sense of mine and thine.

His second move, however, is far from familiar; in fact, it quite astonishingly anticipates the last word in social theory, the convention as a coordination equilibrium by which benign rules of behavior are formed in a wholly uncoerced manner. Nearly everyone will voluntarily observe a rule of mutually agreeable conduct because nearly everybody else is doing so. He remarks that social disturbance mainly arises from the "looseness and easy transition" of goods (p. 489). Insecurity of property would be the result, were it not for the recognition by nearly all that mutual respect for property leads to prosperity while violation of this rule leads to misery in "solitary and forlorn condition" (p. 489). In modern language we would now say that a convention to respect property emerges as a superior equilibrium solution of an in-

3. David Hume, *A Treatise of Human Nature,* 2nd ed. (1739; reprint, New York: Oxford University Press, 1978), Book III.

definitely repeated noncooperative coordination "game." Unilateral expropriation of the property of others cannot perdure, while reciprocal violence is an inferior equilibrium, impoverishing all.

Hume's discovery of the convention as a self-enforcing means of safeguarding an orderly distribution of property molded by voluntary transactions is a master stroke. It establishes that order and wealth do not depend on government, for rules can emerge and regulate behavior without a rule-maker and enforcer. In his words that can never be quoted too often, "the stability of possession, its translation by consent, and the performance of promises. These are, therefore, antecedent to government" (p. 541).

The "ownership is a myth" school brushes aside as naive the notion that the wealth and income you acquire in voluntary transactions is yours. A recent, radical, often clever and occasionally too clever work of this school by Murphy and Nagel finds it quite natural to ask: "What is the moral basis for a right to hold on to one's earnings?" (p. 7). This is, of course, a "when did you stop beating your wife" kind of question. It would as a matter of course put the burden of proof on you to show why you should be allowed to "hold on" to your property. The authors call it a delusion that the burden ought to be on whoever seeks to deprive you of part of it, that there is good cause for doing so. The alleged delusion is the myth of property. The book sets out to dispel it.

Property "rights" for Murphy and Nagel are just one part of a "legal convention" and must be evaluated by "society" together with the other parts, notably with the fiscal requirements of order and "social" justice, upon which property is asserted to depend. It is not clear what is meant by a "legal convention," nor why this odd term is used in preference to plain language. In plain language, there are laws that require government to protect property from all except from itself, and other laws that allow it to take property (by means of income and other taxes) so as to pay for expenditure that yet other laws direct it to incur. All these laws are decided, directly or by proxy, by "social choice" which is inherently redistributive, favoring some at the expense of others in the raising of revenue, the allocation of spending, or both.

It is trivially true that as a matter of empirical fact, property in the hands of owners and income-earners is what is left to them after the levying of these taxes. Talking instead, somewhat nebulously, of a "legal convention" makes it seem that Murphy and Nagel are saying something more than this.

In reality, they do not. More precisely, what they do say beyond the trite fact that generally you are not allowed to hold on to all you earn, and particularly their copious references to how this squares with justice and freedom, is largely smoke-and-mirrors work. It relies on the tacit fiction that the tax treatment of income and wealth is the outcome of judging and evaluation done by a single mind, the mind of "society." The result is necessarily consensual and nonconflictual. Everybody wants property to be subjected to the same constraints, so as to create an agreed "framework . . . all find morally comfortable" (p. 42).

Post-tax property "rights," then, are either a matter of the will of a single imaginary actor, society, or a matter of an equally imaginary new convention that has supplanted the old one Hume was the first to identify.

It is unthinkable that the authors would use the word "convention" in bad faith, trying to put one over the reader. Their free and easy reference to it can only be due to ignorance, a lack of understanding of the concept of a convention. The latter is a strictly spontaneous outcome of autonomous individual acts of mutual adjustment. Legislation, choices imposed by political winners upon losers who are obliged by the constitutional rule of submission to comply, are alien to it.

Such inconsistencies and downright fudges are forced upon the "myth of property" school by the impossible posture it is trying to maintain. It wants redistribution. It also wants to affirm that justice commands it. If your property, the product of free transactions, is yours, then it is unjust to take some of it away. Therefore property, as seen in your deluded old-fashioned view, is affirmed to be a myth; the reality is a "legal convention" by which society judges what part of it you may morally keep. Thus is justice saved.

True to form, Little[4] cuts cleanly through this wall of fudge: "taking property away from some to give to others is an infringement of the former's freedom. . . . If every infringement of rights is an injustice, it follows that the state ought to be unjust for the purpose of some redis-

4. I. M. D. Little, *Ethics, Economics, and Politics* (Oxford, UK: Oxford University Press, 2002), 38.

tribution. This is an uncomfortable statement, but it is not a contradiction. It is what I believe myself."

There may well be overriding reasons for redistribution, though I have not found one and do not believe in them. However, if there are any, they are not reasons of justice. Rather, they override it. It would be healthier and intellectually more honest to face this and say so, than to try and emasculate the theory of property so as to make right the violations of ownership that "society" chooses to make legal.

HOW TO GET A FREE LUNCH?
JUST APPLY FOR IT

One of the great theorems of economics tells us that, in a competitive equilibrium and with constant returns to scale, income distribution is a function of the marginal productivity of the factors of production and their ownership. Buyers pay and sellers get the marginal product, benefits equal contributions, and "there is no free lunch." Much the same equality between factor rewards and products is explained by the exclusive nature of ownership. Exclusion bars access to resources except by the owners' consent. Productive resources are exchanged at the values of their marginal products. Once again, there is no free lunch; everything is fully paid for. Moreover, since all exchanges are voluntary between willing buyer and willing seller, the distribution of benefits and contributions is just if the initial appropriation of resources was just. One might say, alternatively, that the question of justice cannot arise.

The first breach in this clean-cut system is taxation. Under it, contributions are exacted, rather than voluntarily exchanged against benefits. However, it could be, and always has been, argued that taxes buy public goods and services, defense, civil order, the protection of property, and so forth, so that the contributor does get a benefit, even if not in proportion to his contribution, i.e., even if taxation is redistributive, which of course it cannot fail to be. Nevertheless, some element of exchange is present, albeit progressively weaker as the financing of the welfare state takes a larger share of tax revenues.

The "enemies of property" contend, by denying the reality of a prepolitical and therefore pretax concept of property, that taxation is not really a breach of ownership, for the latter does not begin until after "society" has collected the taxes it chose to impose. While this truism

First published as part 3 of "Property and Its Enemies," by Liberty Fund, Inc., at www.econlib.org on September 1, 2003. Reprinted by permission.

correctly describes the accomplished facts, it does nothing to square them with justice.

The second breach, if it were eventually driven through, would be potentially far more radical. It would give an avowedly free lunch, a guaranteed basic income to every adult resident "with no strings attached, no questions asked."[1] The scheme would be introduced gradually to adjust to political realities, but the objective would be to give every adult an unconditional grant high enough to ensure subsistence. One of its most active promoters, Philippe Van Parijs, believes the scheme would resolve the dilemma between what he sees as the European economic "model"—high unemployment but little poverty—and the American one—little unemployment but much poverty. This is as it may be, and the present article will not pursue this point. Partisans of the proposal are unanimous that the main argument for it is not economic expediency, but justice.

The authors of the volume cited here all agree that the proposal is at least feasible, and the decline in statistically measurable GDP that it would probably cause would be bearable. The likely reduction in labor force participation might be offset by greater willingness to venture into self-employment if basic income were assured. Feasibility, then, is reduced to taxability. As Emma Rothschild puts it with engaging serenity, where the average income is higher than subsistence, the project can be realized.[2] All it takes is to tax everyone at a rate that need not even reach 100 percent of their earnings.

Even the most eminent contributors to the volume, such as Robert Solow who takes a fairly cautious view of the fiscal implications, show little doubt that the fiscal burden of a universal basic income for all at or near subsistence level would be peacefully borne by taxpayers and lead to no major perverse effects. Significantly, the very Milton Friedman who coined the dictum about there being no free lunch has advocated a negative income tax, which is an unmistakable free lunch and a first cousin of the universal basic income.[3]

1. Philippe Van Parijs, "A Basic Income for All," in *What's Wrong with a Free Lunch?* ed. Joshua Cohen and Joel Rogers (Boston: Beacon Press, 2001), 14.

2. Emma Rothschild, "Security and Laissez-Faire," in Cohen and Rogers.

3. Milton Friedman, *Capitalism and Freedom* (Chicago: University of Chicago Press,

While feasibility is merely the absence of a certain "argument against," the "argument for" on everybody's lips is freedom and justice. Van Parijs claims that society must ensure both formal and real freedom. Formal freedom implies the protection of property and personal liberty, while real freedom requires resources to let everyone use his or her formal freedom. Since resources cannot be redistributed without violating property "rights," it is clear that Van Parijs must regard these as a "myth" and must have some new kind of "rights" in mind. Others, too, call into question the distribution of property and income that results from voluntary transactions. Edmund Phelps[4] simply dismisses it as arbitrary, apparently on the ground that there is no such thing as a free market—a ground that is made to bear a weight that looks a little excessive.

However, by far the most ambitious argument for the justice of taking resources from existing owners and distributing them evenly is by an appeal to the Giant Externality. It is a perennial that keeps cropping up in a variety of guises in the antiproperty literature. In the *Free Lunch* collection of essays, Herbert Simon[5] asserts that at least 90 percent of the GDP of wealthy nations is due to this externality and less than 10 percent is genuine factor product and factor reward. By rights, the 90 percent should be "returned to the real owners" (p. 36). If all incomes were taxed at a flat 70 percent rate, the original recipients would still be retaining three times their due, and there would be ample revenue both for basic income for all and ordinary government expenditure.

Simon is of course right that accumulated knowledge, sensible institutions, and "social capital," taken together, represent a large positive externality, though it is guesswork to put a number on the difference it makes to GDP. For all we know, Simon's guess may be as good as anybody's. However, in reasoning from this starting point, he seems twice to take a wrong turning.

First, the Giant Externality is not owed to "society," but to countless specific actions of its members, each of whom acted the way he did for

---

1962). See chap. 12, "The Alleviation of Poverty," 192–93, where Friedman advocates "an arrangement that recommends itself on purely mechanical grounds."

4. Edmund S. Phelps, "Subsidize Wages," in Cohen and Rogers.

5. Herbert A. Simon, "UBI and the Flat Tax," in Cohen and Rogers.

sufficient reasons. An externality is a passing or lasting consequence of a human action that benefits or harms third parties and that was not part of the actor's reason(s) calling forth that action. Each individual who added his bit to the store of knowledge, who took up a trade and enhanced the division of labor, who fought against the curse of bad government that is the chief cause of poverty and waste, who taught her children a sense of duty and honor, helping to build "social capital," was doing so for good reasons of his or her own, no matter whether egoistic or altruistic ones. His or her actions had already earned the reward that it took to call them forth. Praise may be given, but no second reward must be exacted. None is due; all accounts have been squared. The Giant Externality is the sum of a myriad of small externalities, by-products of a myriad of individual actions that have all been "paid for" in some way. It does enhance factor productivity, no doubt by a great deal. But it is not, for all that, itself a factor of production.

The second wrong turning is to use the Giant Externality as the reason for an egalitarian distribution of property. Simon believes, perhaps rightly, that due to social networks and privileges, access to the Giant Externality is unequal. As a result, some factors are more productive and their owners get higher rewards than their due, and a high flat-rate tax whose proceeds are handed back in equal grants to everyone, would correct this.

However, privileged access to positive externalities is merely a roundabout way of saying that opportunities are unequal. The standard argument for remedying or compensating for inequalities, for what it is worth, is a moral one. It stands or falls with the intrinsic badness of inequality. If this argument fails, the purported unequal access to externalities is not a wrong and needs no remedy. If it succeeds, some remedy is required, and it makes no odds at all whether or not the externality "belongs to society." It is not its supposed "real ownership," as Simon puts it, that justifies the redistributive measures. In fact, it is not property and belongs to nobody.

It is perhaps incongruous, after contending with the attacks on property of some very distinguished theorists, to take note of what Robert Goodin[6] has to say. However, he offers tactical advice on using the "so-

6. Robert Goodin, "Something for Nothing," in Cohen and Rogers.

cial" impulses of conservative political regimes for luring them step by step into granting universal basic income. Unwittingly, he tells us much about our times and about his own constituency. Conservative regimes are already prepared to pay people for socially useful activity, such as looking after other people's children and infirm or elderly parents. The next step could be to pay them for looking after their own children and their own parents, cooking their meals and making their beds. The step after that, though Mr. Goodin stops short of it, is to pay them for making their own beds rather than leaving them unmade, a mess that one could deem socially undesirable. State salaries could be paid for more and more kinds of socially useful work. We are then well on our way to universal basic income. "All we then have to do"—concludes the streetwise Mr. Goodin—"is persuade people to apply for it" (p. 97). Just put in for it! This simple battle plan is probably as effective against property as sophisticated arguments showing why it is not legitimate.

THE PROBLEM OF CONTRACT ENFORCEMENT

Received wisdom advances two broad reasons why government is entitled to impose its will on its subjects, and why the subjects owe it obedience, provided its will is exercised according to certain (constitutional) rules. One reason is rooted in production, the other in distribution—the two aspects of social cooperation. Ordinary market mechanisms produce and distribute the national income, but this distribution is disliked by the majority of the subjects (notably because it is "too unequal") and it is for government to redistribute it (making it more equal or bending it in other ways, a function that its partisans prefer to call "doing social justice"). However, the market is said to be deficient even at the task of producing the national income in the first place. Government is needed to overcome market failure. A society of rational individuals would grasp this and readily mandate the government to do what was needful (e.g., by taxation, regulation, and policing) to put this right.

I claim that at least some, if not the whole, of the market failure argument fails to prove its case. There have been other writings using related arguments to the same effect, but one more such will not be too many.

1. ONE-OFF CONTRACT EXECUTION

The division of labor implies exchange and exchange is the execution of a tacit or overt contract. In standard theory, if one party to a contract executes his part by delivering as agreed, the other party's optimal course of action is to take the delivery and walk away without delivering his part. The first party knows this and correctly concludes that his best course of action is not to deliver. The second party knows that this is the case. Therefore the parties will not contract and the

First published as part 1 of "The Failure of Market Failure," by Liberty Fund, Inc., at www.econlib.org on October 2, 2006. Reprinted by permission.

mutually advantageous exchange of deliveries will not take place. (The well-rehearsed model of this interaction is, of course, the notorious prisoners' dilemma which has been a cornerstone of arguments for political authority from the 1950s to the 1980s, though it has since been somewhat eroded by the widening understanding of game theory.)

If circumstances permit the two parties to execute simultaneously, the problem disappears, since each delivery is contingent on the other, so that both parties are best off if each delivers. Plainly, however, it is not always convenient or efficient to insist on cash-on-the-barrelhead dealings. A modern economy is inconceivable without the bulk of exchanges being nonsimultaneous. Do contracts involving credit or other nonsimultaneous execution require a third party, such as the state, to see to it that both parties fulfil their commitments?

It used to be thought that in a small-scale, "face-to-face" society, say the village cattle market, no third-party enforcer is necessary, because no party to an exchange could risk to default and face loss of reputation and even retaliation in some unpleasant form. In large groups of "faceless" contracting parties, on the other hand, each could default with impunity. Hayek, for one, strongly argues that in the "great society" where anonymous dealings prevail, a firm legal framework was needed to underpin the free market, which could not function at all without it. His "spontaneous order" emerged inside this (nonspontaneous) framework.

This type of "market failure" argument, that comes strangely from a Hayek who is widely venerated as a champion of classical liberalism, fails mainly by getting the facts wrong. The most obvious one is the unworldly idea of contracts between anonymous parties who can walk away from the contract without delivering their side without anyone knowing who they were. *There are no anonymous contracts.* Where thousands of faceless customers stream through the checkout counters of a supermarket, they have a contract with the bank who issued their credit card, and the card company has a contract with the supermarket, each party to each contract being duly named and identified. In wholesale trading dealers in the same trade know a good deal about their counterparties half a world away and if they do not, their bankers and brokers do. Default risk is shifted, often to specialized intermediaries, to whoever will assume it at the least cost because best able to minimize it. For relevant purposes, the wide world is a face-to-face society, or at any rate functions much like one.

The other fact of life that standard market failure theory does not get right is that while many market exchanges are done in the form of one-off contracts that are fully executed once each party has made one delivery, many more—probably the greater part of aggregate market exchanges—are not. They are run on continuing contracts providing for repeated executions, often an indefinite number of times.

2. REPEATED EXECUTIONS

The example that first springs to mind is the labor contract, where the employee agrees to render some service week by week, month by month, and the employer agrees to pay him at regular intervals, for a period or until either party terminates the contract by giving due notice. Similar contracts with repeated delivery often govern the supply of parts and materials to manufacturers and the supply of finished goods to commerce. They typically run for an indefinite yet uncertain duration.

Unlike the one-off kind, such contracts do not obey the logic of the prisoners' dilemma where "take the money and run," i.e., deliberate default, is the best strategy. Defaulting on any given delivery at any link of the chain of deliveries breaks the chain and normally wrecks the contract. Therefore it pays only if the gain made by defaulting on a single delivery outweighs the present value of all future gains that would accrue if the contract went on to its indefinite term.

The balance in favor of continuing to deliver as agreed (or pay as agreed) will be vastly strengthened if the potential defaulter loses, not only the anticipated gains from the contract he would break, but also the potential gains from other contracts that third parties would decline to conclude with him after they learned that he was a defaulter. The forgone gains from potential contracts, added to the forgone gains from the contract the defaulter has actually broken, create a strong conjecture that carrying out commitments under the system of repeated contracts is a *self-enforcing convention.*

This conclusion parallels the deduction, made by numerous theorists and therefore known as the Folk Theorem, that mutual cooperation through a series of indefinitely repeated games, each of which has the structure of a prisoners' dilemma, is a possible equilibrium.

3. FREE-RIDING

Little is left, then, of the market failure argument which holds that the market cannot spontaneously generate the contract enforcement required for its own functioning. If this argument were valid, a really free market would be a logical impossibility. "Real existing" markets would all depend for their very existence on the scaffolding of an enforcing apparatus.

It so happens that most "real existing" markets do make some use of the enforcement service provided by the legislature, the courts, and the police. Why is this the case if the market failure argument is invalid and there are adequate incentives for rational economic agents to adhere to a self-enforcing convention of contract fulfilment?

The short answer is that punishing and hence deterring default is rarely costless. Even passively boycotting the defaulter involves some cost in inconvenience, even though incurring the cost may be the means of preventing a greater loss. If much the same result can be got without incurring any cost, that method will be preferred.

Once legislatures, courts, and police—in one word, the government—are in place, maintained by the taxes it has the power to exact, firms and individuals will rationally prefer to entrust the task of enforcement to it and enjoy the illusion of getting something for nothing, instead of making the effort themselves. They perceive this as a chance to free-ride on the taxes paid by everybody else, and do not perceive that ultimately their own taxes must increase to cover the cost of all the free-riding others will also prefer to do. The tendency fits nicely into an important objective of every government, namely the goal of discouraging private enforcement and vesting in the state the monopoly of all rule enforcement.

4. THE ENFORCEMENT AGENCY

It is a long way from putative market failure to the risks of overwhelming political power, but that long way must nonetheless be travelled.

Textbook theory rather blithely teaches that since contracts are inherently default-prone, their binding force must be assured by the services of a specialized enforcement agency (such as the state). However, if the agency is to be bound by tacit or overt contract (such as a constitution) to a best-effort service in the interest of all bona fide economic agents, *that contract itself needs enforcement,* for why else should the agency not go slack or biased or otherwise abusive? Plainly, however, the enforcement agency cannot be entrusted with enforcing such a contract against itself. The supposed remedy could well be much worse than the disease. Perhaps herein lies the ultimate failure of the market failure thesis.

THE PUBLIC GOODS DILEMMA

Public goods are freely accessible to all members of a given public, each being able to benefit from it without paying for it. The reason standard theory puts forward for this anomaly is that public goods are by their technical character *nonexcludable.* There is no way to exclude a person from access to such a good if it is produced at all. Examples cited include the defense of the realm, the rule of law, clean air, or traffic control. If all can have it without contributing to its cost, nobody will contribute and the good will not be produced. This, in a nutshell, is the public goods dilemma, a form of market failure which requires taxation to overcome it. Its solution lies outside the economic calculus; it belongs to politics.

1. EXCLUSION COST

Access to a private good is controlled by its producer or owner by a variety of devices ranging from shop counters, safes, walls, and fences to measures against theft, robbery, fraud, illicit copying, and breach of contract. The cost of these devices and measures is the exclusion cost of the good. Every good is private or public according to whether exclusion cost is or is not incurred in making it available. A public good is distributed freely to all comers from a given public, avoiding the exclusion cost that would keep it private. This saving is the "productivity of publicness."

Given sufficient imagination and clever technology, every good can be excluded at *some* cost. Arguably, some would be very awkward to exclude, but none is intrinsically "nonexcludable," i.e., *doomed* to be a public good. By the same token, every good, whether private or public, has many more or less imperfect substitutes that may also be private or public. Thus, contrary to received theory, a more general view tells

First published as part 2 of "The Failure of Market Failure," by Liberty Fund, Inc., at www.econlib.org on November 6, 2006. Reprinted by permission.

us that while no good is intrinsically public, the higher is its exclusion cost and the more imperfect are its substitutes, the more efficient it is to provide it publicly.

2. SOCIAL PREFERENCE FOR NONEXCLUSION

There is one type of exclusion cost that is more important by far than all the rest in putting a good in the public category: it is social preference. It is intangible and is only revealed by the choices it inspires. A pure example is a children's playground. Access to it is excludable at low cost by a fence and a ticket collector at the gate. However, society would suffer deep moral embarrassment if rich children could use the playground but poor ones could only watch them from the outside. Therefore real exclusion cost would be unbearably high, and children's playgrounds are provided as public goods.

There are other, less pure but quantitatively far more important examples. One is free universal education. Most countries provide it to age sixteen, some to university degree level. In this case, technical-logistical exclusion cost would be quite low (indeed, in a broad sense negative as exclusion would permit student selection, and that would in turn lower production cost), but social ethics would not tolerate the exclusion of poor, dumb, and subscholarship standard pupils. With education becoming a public good affording free access, the share of public goods in the national product expands vastly. Organizing health care in the form of a free-access public good on the pattern of the British National Health Service expands the domain of public goods even further and multiplies the gravity of the public goods dilemma.

However, it is perverse to argue that this is a true case of market failure. The dilemma presents itself, not because the market cannot cope, but because society does not choose to entrust the matter to it. It may have quite worthy moral reasons for doing so. But it must not be overlooked that since public goods can be consumed at zero marginal cost, a tendency is created to their chronic overconsumption. This, in turn, involves an encroachment of the public upon the private sector and a cascade of adverse indirect consequences.

3. FREE-RIDER OR SUCKER

Received "market failure" theory has a false perspective not only in characterizing some goods as intrinsically public rather than *made* public by social choice reacting to intangible exclusion costs. It also mistakes the public goods dilemma for a version of the prisoners' dilemma. It then finds that like the prisoners' dilemma, the public goods dilemma has only a noncooperative equilibrium solution.

Individuals, unless forced to pay taxes, have two choices with regard to a public good: to contribute or not to contribute to its cost while enjoying its benefit. The noncontributor gets a free ride, the contributor is a sucker. For the standard theory, the conclusion is easy: there will be few or no contributors. The market will fail to produce the public good, particularly if it is indivisible or "lumpy," so that a minimum number of contributors is needed to produce even a single "lump" of it (e.g., if the public good "education" comes in "lumps" no smaller in size than a schoolhouse and teacher).

Consider, however, the would-be free-rider who must weigh the attraction of a free ride against the risk that by withholding his contribution, he will cause the total of contributions to fall short of the minimum outlay needed to render the good really "public" freely accessible to all and satisfying the accepted criterion of publicness, namely "nonrivalry in consumption." This criterion means that consumption of it by one person does not reduce the amount available to any other person.

Consider likewise the hesitant sucker who must weigh the opportunity cost of contributing against the chance that his contribution will be the one needed to raise total contributions over the threshold of the minimum required for the "lump" of public good needed to permit access to it by the marginal consumer.

In the face of these two pairs of possible outcomes, neither is the free-rider strategy unquestionably the best, nor the sucker strategy unquestionably the worst. Which of the two is the rational choice depends on the subjective probability each potential contributor attaches to others going for the free-rider or the sucker choice, as well as the value he attaches to having the public good instead of resorting to private substitutes.

The critical values of these variables depend on a complicated set of factors that cannot be detailed in a brief essay. However, it is intuitively fairly clear that there is nothing foredoomed about public goods in general. Whether a good can be "made public" by voluntary contributions depends on how rational calculation and anticipation of the behavior of others leads to a division within a group between free-riders and suckers. Each of the two possible social roles, the free-rider and the sucker, leads to a pair of uncertain alternatives. For the free-rider they are the free ride (the best) or failure of the public good (the worst). For the sucker, it is that he contributes like everyone else (the second-best) or that he contributes when some others do not (the third-best). In the standard theories of market failure, the free-rider strategy is "dominant"—it is always the best whatever anyone else may do. In effect, however, the pair "best or worst" is intrinsically neither superior nor inferior to the pair "second-best or third-best." Rationally, one pair is chosen depending on the probability that one member of the pair rather than the other member will in fact turn out to be the case. The problem becomes simply a case in the theory of risky choices.

Public goods can thus be brought back under the calculus that guides *homo oeconomicus*. The provision of public goods does not presuppose collective choice that overrules individual ones by the brute force of politics. Those who instinctively mistrust collective choices and trust that reasonable solutions emerge from free individual choices need not feel browbeaten by the "market failure" argument.

TRYING THE FREE MARKET

Introducing her recent book[1] devoted mostly to contesting certain ethical defenses of the free market, the young Cambridge philosopher Serena Olsaretti (a little resignedly, it would seem) remarks that the market in its diverse variants is now accepted across the whole political spectrum. For the foreseeable future, the question "should we have a market?" will not seriously arise. Is not this all the more reason to question the morality of what she calls the "unbridled" form of the market?

1. PRESUMED GUILTY

Anyone challenged to justify his conduct has very nearly lost the battle if he starts to demonstrate his rectitude. "When did you stop beating your wife?" is the schoolbook example of the question best met with silence by both the innocent and the guilty.

The arguments about the justice of the free market, like other adversarial arguments, have a definite logical order. Initially, the free market enjoys the benefit of the doubt. It is presumed innocent of violating justice. The burden of proof that it does violate it lies with the accuser. Until at least some solid evidence is brought, the defense has no case to answer. "Evidence" in a trial of morality cannot, however, very well come in the form of ascertainable fact. If it comes at all, it does so in the form of support built on a strong moral theory.

Related to the presumption of innocence, though resting on somewhat different grounds, is the presumption for the status quo. It is up to those who think it should be changed to marshal sufficient reasons why the change would be a change for the better. The market, in a de-

First published as part 1, "Presumed Guilty," and part 2, "Unacceptable," of "Trying the Free Market," by Liberty Fund, Inc., at www.econlib.org on April 4, 2005, and May 2, 2005. Reprinted by permission.

1. Serena Olsaretti, *Liberty, Desert and the Market* (Cambridge, UK: Cambridge University Press, 2004). Originally an Oxford doctoral dissertation prepared under the aegis of G. A. Cohen.

bate about the just or the good society, figures as the status quo or at least closer to it than the proposed reform. It is for the reformers to press home the charge that it ought to be changed.

Neither the case that the free market is unjust (though perhaps still worth preserving—a claim that is independent of whether it is just), nor the case that it should be transformed or abolished altogether, has ever been successfully established. The last significant attempt to establish the charge of injustice, that of Rawls, was at best inconclusive and has since subsided. The second, drawing mostly on socialist inspiration, did get actual occasions to change or abolish the market, and these occasions have, if anything, vindicated the status quo. So far there is still no case of either kind to answer.

The apparent failure by foes, but even more so by friends, of the free market to grasp the role of the burden of proof, and what it takes to shift it from the challenger to the defender, is one of the puzzles in recent intellectual history. There is a widely shared commonsense perception that the free market generates inequalities of income and wealth. Since the market is not an agent and does not generate anything, it would be more illuminating to say that the world being what it is, and people's luck, resources, talents and characters being distributed the way they are, the effects of exchanges among people will be reflected in their wealth and incomes being unequal. It is the facts of life that cause the inequality, not the market. Either way, however, the very word "inequality" suffices to set off a knee-jerk reaction in the defenders, making them feel that a substantial case against the market has therewith been made. It is now presumed guilty and defenses need to be deployed.

The reaction, however, is gratuitous. Creating inequality is not a charge that needs any answer unless inequality is a wrong of some kind—such as injustice. If the market or, more narrowly, its morality is really to need defending, it must at the very least be made plausible that inequality is unjust.

Instead of waiting for this to be shown, the defenders of the free market have rushed to argue that, regardless of inequalities, it was indeed just. Like most social theorists who would rather write about what other social theorists have said of a thing than about the thing itself, Olsaretti seems more concerned with the coherence of these defenses than with the thing they defend. She divides them into desert-based and rights-based ones. Much of her critique is worth serious consideration, despite her firm habit of making her points by what George Stigler called the surest method of academic persuasion, namely relentless repetition. Her positive contribution, as distinct from her analysis of the mistakes of others, is slim and brief by comparison.

Of the two main lines of defense, she seems more combative when tackling the rights-based one. In fact, there is not a great deal to discuss in the desert-based one because (though Olsaretti does not make this point) the relevant arguments are so thoroughly subjective that at the end of a short chain of just a few links, the reasoning rapidly reaches the dead end where it is "my say-so against your say-so" and debate is a waste of time. Olsaretti confines the desert argument to personal labor and effort, leaving the reward accruing to capital out of consideration. Even so, she reaches the obvious conclusion that rewards cannot all be imputed to compensation for pains or contribution to product, for "brute" luck enters into rewards and must be "neutralized." Someone ("we") must tell what adjustments will achieve neutrality, i.e., purge the system of rewards of the influence of luck. However, the sole means of separately identifying the parts due to pure compensation, to contribution, and to brute luck is subjective judgment, leaving us with your say-so against my say-so. If it were the case that luck makes market outcomes unjust—a proposition that would be important if it were compelling, rather than an unsupported assertion that can be countered by other similarly unsupported assertions—then we might still be unable to say by what adjustments we could make them just. In other words, even if the desert theory of market justice appealed to one moral intuition (among others), it would still be little more than a useless form of words.

The "rights-based" defense of the free market has a startling element in its very foundation which most academic opinion, including Olsaretti's sharply critical one, seems never to question, let alone reproach. In its starkest form, it appears in the famous first sentence of the preface of Robert Nozick's much-quoted vindication[2] of libertarian ideals: "Individuals have rights, and [etc.]." Alternatives might have

2. Robert Nozick, *Anarchy, State, and Utopia* (New York: Basic Books, 1974).

read "Individuals ought to have rights, and . . ." or perhaps "If individuals had rights, and . . ." and would have been unobjectionable, though they might not have conveyed the same message. As it is, this starting point devalues much that follows it and makes Nozick's defense of the free market wide open to a flank attack. The fault is important because Nozick is probably the most influential libertarian defender of feasible freedom, and Olsaretti takes his book as the representative text her critique targets above all others.

We do not in fact know that "individuals have rights" and nothing entitles us to pretend that we do. Characteristically, authors now frequently refer to rights "we have assigned," from which one could infer that rights are created by somebody somewhere and are then conferred upon individuals (while the correlative obligations are imposed in some unspecified distribution). Nozick tells us that the rights he asserts individuals to have are boundaries that segregate their person, property, and contracts. Once again, we wonder how he knows. However, if these particular rights have somehow been "assigned" to them, what is to stop an anti-Nozick, moved by moral concern for the well-being of individuals and for what is due to them in respect of their dignity and autonomy, from assigning additional rights to them—rights that are rights-of-way, easements cutting through the Nozickian boundaries? Is this not the rights-based model of "social market economy" or some other hybrid?

Nonlibertarian believers in rightsism, notably Rawls and Scanlon, are less bold than Nozick and seek to find consent-based explanations of why they believe that individuals have certain rights rather than simply alleging that they do. Either way, however, the introduction of putative rights, not arising from contracts individuals conclude with one another, offers great facility for sculpting the just, i.e., rights-respecting, order in the desired form.

Defending the "unbridled" market by asserting Nozickian rights repeats the same strategic mistake as defending it as if it were presumed guilty. This defense relies on the outlandish Lockean fantasy of self-ownership to derive the proposition that people are entitled to the wages of their labor and the product of their endeavors. Though it is perhaps a side issue, it is worth pointing out that self-ownership is a category mistake: ownership is a relation between owner and thing owned such that the owner is free to dispose of what he owns. It is nonsense to talk of a relation between you and yourself. Nor can you dispose of your own self, exchanging it for another's as you could exchange a thing you owned for another thing. In any event, reliance on this misfit idea is not necessary. The whole "entitlements" theory of justice is going about it the wrong way round. The point to prove is not that each individual is entitled to the fruits of his efforts (or to what he has exchanged them for), but that somebody else is entitled to take such fruits away from him. This and the implicit presumption of good title unless it is proved to be vitiated, is the proper logical order for conducting a trial of the market.

2. UNACCEPTABLE

When they defend the free market that is presumed to bring about unjust outcomes, libertarians contend that transfers of rightfully acquired "holdings" preserve rights provided they are not coercive. In seeking to refute this defense, Serena Olsaretti is largely unconcerned with the justice of first acquisitions (often taken to be the more controversial half of the defense) and constructs a case for the prosecution in which the trickle of coercion as the sole source of rights-violation is swallowed up by the broad river of "forcings." Voluntariness, rather than freedom, is the criterion of legitimate transactions, and forcings exclude voluntariness. Voluntariness presupposes the acceptability of option(s), though the author's exact position on this is so involved as to defy a simple summary (including her own that she provides in her Conclusions). We shall look at it presently.

In dealing with coercion and forcing, she is not interested in the different nature of these acts. (In fact, forcing in her scheme takes place without anyone having to do any forcing, while for coercion someone must coerce.) What matters is the effect on the victim: "What makes choices carried out under coercion non-voluntary is exactly what also makes other types of *limited choices* non-voluntary. The alternative faced by the man who hands over the money when threatened with a gun is to be killed; the alternative of a worker who sells his labor power at whatever price is to remain unemployed and suffer severe hardship.

The relevant condition (in both cases) is the absence of an acceptable alternative" (p. 151, my italics). Note that the choice is "limited" not only in these types of cases, but in literally every choice, but let that pass.

At this stage the argument runs into a conundrum. "Unacceptable" defines an option that cannot be accepted. A person in any given position has accepted the option of taking that position. It was an acceptable option. It appears that it could have been taken voluntarily, even though there were no acceptable alternative to it.

The author explicitly states that "although no choice among several alternatives is involved, the individual nonetheless does the thing he does voluntarily" (p. 140). If the option actually taken was indeed the sole one on offer, all other acceptable options must have been accepted by the other participants in the market, and none is left. Supply equals demand and the market is cleared. It has stood its moral trial if all these acceptable options, despite each being de facto the only one available to the person who took it, were taken voluntarily. Where everyone finds his own position at least acceptable and where there are no available options left is a situation where there are no unacceptable ones either, i.e., where the free market is just in the way the author conceives justice.

She very decidedly contradicts her own idea of voluntariness without alternatives, however, by laying down in several places that voluntariness hinges on the availability of acceptable alternatives; in her Conclusion she goes a little further and stipulates that everyone must "face a *sufficient* range of options" (p. 164, my italics) for their choices to be voluntary. This seems to be her last word.

Can one infer anything further about the "sufficient range"? It turns out that an offer may be too good to refuse and thus is tantamount to "forcing" (p. 147); it does not fit into the range that guarantees voluntariness of choice. Offers that are not good enough may pass for unacceptable. What can one say, though, about options that are all acceptable but not equally good? It could reasonably be argued that choosing any but the best is counterpreferential and could only be motivated by a fit of mental disorder. The best must be chosen despite the availability of acceptable but inferior others. Is the best then chosen really voluntarily? The case differs only in degree from the offer that one cannot refuse.

If a given gap between the best option and the next-worse one is too large for the choice of the best to qualify as voluntary rather than a "forcing," should one try little by little to narrow the gap—and if so, how narrow must it get for truly voluntary choice between the topmost pair of options? Rigorous reasoning would seem to allow only one conclusion: the gap must be infinitesimal, with preference being replaced by indifference. The free market would satisfy the requirements of justice if everyone faced at least a pair of equally good options and there was not a better one topping them. It would take only a couple of further refinements for the free and just market to resemble an egalitarian Nirvana.

This, to be fair, is not what Olsaretti is driving at and she would hardly concede that this is the way her own argument is drifting. She is, however, content to stop at the condition where acceptable options for everybody are guaranteed by some nonmarket redistributive mechanism. She is well aware of the twistability of the word "acceptable." Average opinion may consider a certain minimum income just acceptable in a rich Western country and a tiny fraction of it acceptable in a poor sub-Saharan one. A person may honestly judge an option open to him as unacceptable because he did not like it or found it too steep a step down from his actual position. Fear, pride, and mistaken expectations of the future might weigh as much in judgments of acceptability as material welfare. Above all, acceptability, like such other sensations as liking, satisfaction, or deprivation, cannot properly be represented in absolute, yes-or-no terms, but only in relative ones. Acceptability is, for all we know, a continuous variable. Graphically, it is a scale along which options are ranged between the very sweet ones at the top and the very bitter ones at the bottom. Beneath the bottom, there is nothing but unfeasibility that is simply outside the choice set. Nothing is really unacceptable if it can be chosen.

Perhaps made uncomfortable by some subconscious awareness of this logic, the author can do little more than protest her good intention to steer clear of the more obvious of the threats that using this concept poses to her thesis. She wants to "avoid *complete* subjectivity" (p. 153, my italics) and believes that she attains objectivity by declaring an option acceptable if it suffices to satisfy "basic" human needs.

However, we are no nearer to objectivity if we qualify the quintessentially subjective term "need" by adding that it must be "basic." She seems a little uncertain herself about the adequacy of the idea of basic needs, and with a curtsey to A. K. Sen, tentatively attaches to it the designer labels of "functioning" and "capability," making her groping for an objective threshold of acceptability a good deal more uncertain and her predicament a good deal worse.

She would be better off by postulating an arbitrarily fixed minimum income for all and a corresponding "bridling" of market outcomes on the well-trodden and equally arbitrary ground that things would be more equal and therefore nicer that way. Such a less ambitious project would have spared her a number of difficulties. One she grapples with is the distinction between freedom and voluntariness and whether the first is a necessary condition of the second. Another has to do with the responsibility for "forcings" where nobody is doing any forcing. We must, it seems, accept that injustice can arise spontaneously (but there is no hint whether justice, too, can do so). There is a lack of awareness that in looking for justice, we want the facts of the case to be ascertainable. Olsaretti, one is forced reluctantly to find, seems to feel that where the facts are not really ascertainable, judgments will do as well.

Her honest and conscientious try at finding an original reason for morally condemning the free market, developed from a critique of its libertarian defense, was, it seems to me, self-defeating. She sought to derive a criterion for the market's justice from voluntariness, and for voluntariness from acceptability. But she had to fit the continuum "acceptable" to the binary "just-unjust" and that was bound to upset her design. She needed the binary pair "acceptable-unacceptable" to get a proper fit with "just-unjust," but that pair was just not there.

THE STATIST LEGACY

One of our many lazy mental habits is glibly to take it as read that economic activity is, and indeed must be, carried out "within a legal framework" which largely conditions how people behave. The law says that they must respect each other's person and property, fulfil their obligations, pay their taxes, and care for their dependents. They will by and large do these things if the law is enforced. The state is there to enforce it. As rivalry in enforcement would lead to a shambles, society entrusts to the state the monopoly of law enforcement and willingly shoulders its cost. Despite occasional causes for grumbling, it is broadly agreed to be money well spent, for where would we be without the law?

The double trouble with this line of soothing tale, which nearly everybody accepts and recites, is that it is not altogether true, and that even if it were, it would fall far short of an explanation of why broadly comparable legal systems are consistent with vastly different economic behavior in different societies. To begin with, it is not even certain that the "legal framework" really acts the way imagined in standard economic and social theory. The state guards its lawmaking and enforcing monopoly with ferocious jealousy. The fact that it is an effective monopoly should lead us to expect that it will maximize some kind of net result, achieving some high degree of compliance with the law, and do so economically. In reality, because it is a monopoly subject to a popular mandate and must not arouse dread, fear, and hatred, it is restricted in what it may and what it must not do. It must produce compliance and serve up justice in white gloves on a silver platter—a demand it is most of the time quite unable to meet. It must be sensitive to shifts in public opinion between novel shades of political correctness and human-rightsism, as well as to pressures from single-issue groups and special interests. As a result, it must become a law factory, pouring out

First published as "Misbehavior, Punishment, Prosperity: The Statist Legacy," by Liberty Fund, Inc., at www.econlib.org on August 6, 2007. Reprinted by permission.

an ever broader stream of new and complex legislation. Perhaps more important, it is financed from taxes imposed on people according to criteria that have little to do with what these taxpayers, taken individually, obtain from the state by way of law enforcement services. Like any other tax-financed service where contributions are divorced from benefits, the "legal framework" is an open invitation to free-riding. Individuals will unload (or at least have a good try at unloading) onto the state responsibilities that in a well-ordered society they could and would themselves carry on their own behalf or for neighbors, partners, and peers.

Here we reach the nub of the problem of why people in some societies behave mostly well, while in others they so often misbehave. Law even at its best controls only a small part of human behavior. At its worst, it aspires to control a great part, but largely fails. Vastly more important than the legal system is the much older and more deeply rooted set of unwritten rules (technically, spontaneous conventions) barring and sanctioning torts, nuisances, and incivilities that together define what each of us is free to do and by the same token what no one is free to do to us. If these rules are kept, everyone is free, property is safe, and every two-person transaction is mutually beneficial (though third persons may be exposed to negative externalities—for the rules are no bar to competition or the general rough-and-tumble of ordinary life).

How well these rules are kept depends on how well children are brought up, on war or peace, and on other ultimate causes that are not hard to divine. The proximate cause, however, is the effectiveness of sanctions. To mete out punishment for misbehavior always involves some cost to the well behaved who take it upon themselves to administer it. He and those he cares for benefit if misbehavior is punished and hence deterred, but he would benefit even more if the punishing were done and the cost borne by someone else. Rational calculus may tell him that given the likelihood of others undertaking what he would not, his best course is to undertake it himself.

If all or most calculate the same way, all or most will contribute to discouraging misbehavior and the cost to each will be correspondingly lower. Punishing the breach of the rules by individual or joint action, particularly within peer groups, will also have become a convention, one of the basic rules whose breach, in turn, will itself tend to be sanctioned by punishments that may range from reproach and the cold shoulder to ostracism and business boycott.

There are a number of ways in which the peoples of the northern half of Europe seem to be better behaved than their southern counterparts. Dependability, punctuality, respect for the given word, steadiness of effort, greater discipline at work, and lesser need for close supervision seem to be some of them, though this is but an impressionistic judgment that it is hard to document by statistical evidence. These are not traits that make life in northern societies necessarily more fun, more cheerful, or less boring, but they do make for efficiency and prosperity despite the handicaps of climate. A brute fact that seems to bear this out is that most manufactured goods and some services originating in Northern Europe are more expensive than their close substitutes made farther south, but sell just as well.

North and South have contrasting mentalities with regard to punishment for certain types of misbehavior. In the North, self-dealing, conflict of interest, and corner-cutting are punished by serious social sanctions if they are not outright crimes punished by the state. In addition to the punishment, the perpetrator is considered dishonorable, covered with shame. In the South, though perpetrators may well be detected, they are in puzzling ways quite often allowed to get away with impunity and are not even ostracized, but rather regarded with envy and reluctant admiration. Even stealing from the public purse may be regarded as a bit of a joke. Elected officials jailed for corruption are often triumphantly reelected when they are released. It is not too rash a generalization to say that while northern society may be priggish, the southern one is amiably and cynically indulgent. Needless to say, the prevailing impunity further encourages corrupt practices, which in turn act as significant handicaps to efficient resource allocation.

One aspect of behavior whose economic significance towers above all else is the attitude to property. It is distinctly different in Southern from Northern Europe. Beginning with land, the monarch in Spain, Portugal, France, and the Papal States had greater latitude to dispose of the property of his subjects and in terms of security of tenure, there was little equivalent in these countries of the freeholder so widespread in Northern Europe. Moreover, Southern European society was deeply (and it would seem lastingly) influenced by the egalitarian streak in the New Testament, the severity of Jesus toward the rich and the money changers in the Temple, and, nearer modern times, the teachings of the Catholic Church regarding what has come to be called "social justice." Property, especially moneyed property, let alone "finance capitalism," is distinctly unpopular in Catholic culture but is a fairly well tolerated fact of life in the Protestant one. We could see the reasons why even if we had never heard of Max Weber.

Unpopularity of property, shading into hatred and moral condemnation, immensely strengthens the hand of the state, for it is the sole seat of redistributive power that can legislate property and income away from some and to the benefit of others. The stronger the state, the greater the role assigned to the "legal framework" whose dynamics push it to encompass and regulate more and more aspects of personal and social behavior. As a corollary, the *raison d'être* of the unwritten, conventional rules is undermined, the private punishment on which they depend is discouraged by the monopolist state, and the practice of civil society to look after its own interests and concerns withers away in some places though it persists in others, and its roots can probably never be quite eradicated.

YOUR DOG OWNS YOUR HOUSE

Did you know that your dog owns your house, or rather some portion of it? If this is not immediately obvious to you, you will find it helpful to consider some aspects of the ethics and economics of redistribution.

Your dog is alert, plucky, and a fearsome guardian of your property. For all we know, without his services, you would have been burgled over and over again. Your belongings would be depleted, and the utility you derived from your home would be much reduced. The difference between the actual value of your home and its unguarded value is the contribution of your dog, and so is the difference between the respective utilities or satisfactions you derive from it. We do not know the exact figure, but the main thing is that there is one.

More thought is needed fully to unravel the question of who owns your house, and indeed the question of who owns anything. If there were no fire brigade, the whole street might have burned down and your house would no longer stand. The fire brigade has contributed something to its value, and some figure ought to be put against their name. The utilities should not be forgotten, for how would you like to live in a house without running water, electricity, and so forth? Some tentative numbers had better be credited to them. Surely, however, you cannot just ignore the builder who erected the house, the lumberman, the brick factory, the cement works, and all the other suppliers without whom the builder could not have erected it. They too must have their contribution recognized, even if it must be done in a rough-and-ready fashion.

Is it right, though, to stop at this primary level of contributions?—should we not go beyond the cement works to the builder who built the kiln, the gas pipeline that feeds the fire, the workers who keep the process going? Tracing the ever more distant contributions at level after level, we get a manifold that is as complex as we care to make

First published by Liberty Fund, Inc., at www.econlib.org on April 22, 2002. Also published in *Economic Affairs* 22 (2002): 46–48. Reprinted by permission of Blackwell Publishing.

it, with a correspondingly complex jumble of numbers that purport to place rough-and-ready values on the contributions. We can count them moving sideways as well as backward as far as the mind can reach, starting with that of your dog and ending (if you finally lose patience and decide to stop there) with the Founding Fathers or Christopher Columbus.

At this point, you give up and say that your house, and any other holdings you thought you owned, really belong to society as a whole, and so do the holdings of everyone else. Everybody has a rightful stake in your holdings and you have a rightful stake in everybody else's holdings. Society, that is, "we," are alone entitled to decide how big everybody's stake ought to be. "We" are the rightful owners of everything, the masters of "our" universe. As such, "we" are entitled to take from Peter and give to Paul, as well as to regulate what Peter and Paul are allowed to do in matters of production, commerce, and consumption.

A less thoroughgoing version of this argument, instead of crediting everyone for their direct and indirect contributions to the creation of everything of value, simply states that the security of tenure of all property depends on society maintaining public order. Without it, there would be "jungle law," and no one could enjoy their holdings. It follows that it is really society which lets you have them on a grace-and-favor basis. Society, that is, "we," can revoke such grace and favor partly or wholly. Property can be reallocated between grace-and-favor holders as "we" see fit in the public interest, promoting efficiency, equality, or some judicious mix of both.

Objections to such arguments, except when they were just angry and indignant outcries, have generally tended to be uneasy and often downright lame. The reason is probably the great intellectual weakness of our ideas about the legitimacy of property, rooted as they are in the Lockean provisos about first possession. One proviso states that you may freely take possession of unowned resources if "enough and as good" is left for others. However, there are countless millions of "others" today who should be pleased to take possession of quarter sections of rich meadow or of a handily located oil well, but cannot find unowned meadows and oil fields any more. Even if their great-grandfathers could still find such unowned pieces of property, it is clear that they have failed to leave "enough and as good" for their descendants. Under this ill-conceived proviso,[1] all original titles are invalid, hence all present, derivative titles are defective, too. One might as well concede that only collective ownership of everything by "us" is legitimate.

Surely, however, you feel fully entitled to what you currently produce?—even if holdings of property are contentious. For it is hard to accept that what you earn by the sweat of your brow is at best only partly yours, even if that might imply that what others earn by the sweat of their brows is partly yours, too. The legitimacy of redistributive taxation (and ultimately there is no other kind) hinges on this. The standard argument is that under complete autarchy, you might claim that you own what you produce, but under division of labor the contributions of everyone to everything must all be considered. Only if your own effort represented the sole input could you claim the output as entirely yours. In fact, the rise of redistributive policies, and our growing acquiescence in them, is sometimes explained by the ever broader spread of the division of labor.

Modern redistributive doctrine tells us, reasonably enough, that no output is ever produced by a single input. For even if you make something single-handed, you owe your capacity to do so to teachers who taught you, doctors who kept you alive, policemen who protect you from malefactors, and supermarket operators who feed you. This is exactly where we came in when we found that your dog owned a portion of your house. Current output and current earnings are subject to the same reasoning about the multiplicity and untraceability of contributions as are holdings. To sound the depths of contemporary thinking on the matter, consider the following text: "A medical researcher might make a discovery of great commercial value. He might have worked

1. The physical world being finite, every appropriation of land, minerals, oil, timber, or other resource by a would-be owner raises the risk that a future would-be owner will not find "enough and as good" without incurring higher finding costs, if at all. Arguably, the supply of unowned resources today is inelastic, hence the proviso of enough and as good being left was not satisfied yesterday, and therefore it was not satisfied the day before and the day before that. First possession under the proviso was therefore illegitimate even if it had satisfied the other Lockean proviso, the "mixing of labor" with it.

terribly hard to bring it off. But even so, who trained him? Who moved the subject to the point where the discovery became possible? Who built the lab in which he worked? Who runs it? Who pays for it? Who is responsible for the enduring social institutions that present the commercial opportunities? One who cleverly exploits the social framework has both his cleverness and the framework to thank."[2]

How soon, in reading the above, did you spot the underlying, crucial fallacy? Its course is a mixture of the plausible and the preposterous, and any reader who gets a little lost in the backing and filling between such opposites has an excuse of sorts for being bemused. However, clearing away the muddle is fairly straightforward provided we refuse to be impressed by verbiage, but stick doggedly to common sense, hard as that may sometimes be to do in the face of the massive browbeating that seeks to enthrone the verbiage.

There is a minor and a major point to recognize. The minor point is that the "framework" is not a person, natural or legal, to whom a debt can be owed, "institutions" do not act, "society" has no mind, no will, and makes no contributions. Only persons do these things. Imputing responsibility and credit for accumulated wealth, current production, and well-being to entities that have no mind and no will is nonsense. It is a variant of the notorious fallacy of composition.

Once this is understood, we can move on to the major point. All contributions of others to the building of your house have been paid for at each link in the chain of production. All current contributions to its maintenance and security are likewise being paid for. Value has been and is being given for value received, even though the "value" is not always money and goods, but may sometimes be affection, loyalty, or the discharge of duty. In the exchange relation, a giver is also a recipient, and of course vice versa.

In the broad scheme of things, all this is part of the universal system of exchanges. Some of these exchanges may be involuntary. Such is the case where redistribution, a coercive act, is taking place. We then lose the trace, the precise measure, and the assured reciprocity of contributions to wealth and income, but this circumstance can hardly serve

2. James Griffin, *Well-Being: Its Meaning, Measurement, and Moral Importance* (Oxford, UK: Clarendon Press, 1986), 288.

to justify the very redistribution that has caused it. However, where exchanges are voluntary, tracing and measuring become, in a strong sense, otiose and irrelevant. For in a voluntary exchange, once each side has delivered and received the agreed contribution, the parties are quits. Seeking to credit and debit them for putative outstanding claims is double-counting.

All that is left then for the redistributor to argue is that value received and value given are not necessarily equal. Some, perhaps most, transactions are inequitable, leaving behind them unsettled moral claims that tax-and-transfer policies are fully entitled to square. This is a far weaker claim than the one that would have everything paid for twice, but it is still effective because it is open-ended and beyond the reach of empirical disproof. Who can falsify the allegation that an exchange has unduly favored one of the parties, that one of them was "exploited"?

It is always possible to affirm that voluntary exchanges are seldom if ever equitable, for the parties have unequal "bargaining power." This term is wide open to abuse, and is in fact widely abused. It is so easy and so irrefutable to brand a bargain as "unequal" that it is doubtful whether the expression is anything more than the speaker's say-so that can be just as irrefutably opposed by an adversarial say-so. All we can safely say of any voluntary exchange is that either party would rather enter into it than not. This is the classic case of "if it ain't broke, don't fix it," for few social arrangements have more solid foundations in manifest agreement.

It is wrong to "fix it" not because "it works"—though it undeniably "works" better than other arrangements "fixed" by well-intentioned social engineers. Social democracy in today's Europe, stricken by chronic unemployment, and socialism in yesterday's workers' paradise, are eloquent enough examples. But the decisive, argument-stopping argument against "fixing it" is quite different and has little to do with property. It has everything to do with agreement.

Most modern theories of how society ought to work rest on some idea of agreement. Almost invariably, however, the agreement is fictitious, hypothetical, one that would be concluded if all men had equal "bargaining power," or saw things through the same "veil" of ignorance or uncertainty about their future. Or felt the same need for a central authority. The social contract, in its many versions, is perhaps the best known of these alleged agreements. All are designed to suit the normative views of their inventors and to justify the kind of social arrangements they should like to see adopted. Yet the only agreement that is not hypothetical, alleged, invented is the system of voluntary exchanges where all parties give visible, objective proof by their actions that they have found the unique common ground that everybody accepts, albeit grumblingly, but without anyone being forced to give up something he had within his reach and would have preferred. The set of voluntary exchanges, in one word, is the only one that does not impose an immorality in pursuit of a moral objective.

PART 2

The Common Sense of Non-Economics

THE YAKOUBOVICH SYNDROME, OR LIES, DAMN LIES, AND ECONOMIC POLICY

"Lies, damn lies, and statistics" expresses the widespread, though not quite justified, belief that a series of numbers can be made to convey just about any message. Mendacious promises about what wonders various economic policies can do have a different but equally striking capacity to mislead not only the wide public, but the very perpetrators of the false promises, too. I fondly remember a story that makes this point.

Back in 1970, I spent a few days in Israel. One object of the visit was to find out a little about economic prospects and policies. Inflation was accelerating. I was being briefed by two intimidatingly bright bankers. Talk came round to a highly visible bankruptcy of a well-known businessman—let us call him Yakoubovich. I expressed disbelief that anyone can go bust in an inflationary environment by piling up debt.

"Normally," I was told, "it would not occur. But if you knew Yakoubovich, you would see how it can happen all the same." And they told me a number of anecdotes about the gentleman in question to illustrate the point. One of them, I found, teaches a great lesson about economic policy and much else besides.

Yakoubovich is sunning himself in a deckchair by the pool in the gardens of a Jerusalem hotel. In the pool, children are splashing each other, shrieking, jumping in and out, and making a nuisance of themselves. Yakoubovich calls out to them:

"Children, run round to the dining room, they are handing out cookies and sweets!"

The children run off and calm reigns around the pool. In a little while, Yakoubovich gets up, wraps himself in his bathrobe, and shuffles off.

First published by Liberty Fund, Inc., at www.econlib.org on September 4, 2006. Reprinted by permission.

"Yakoubovich, where are you off to?"

"I am going to the dining room, they are distributing cookies and sweets."

In the Yakoubovich syndrome, someone—typically, a political or financial operator—tells a lie or makes a fraudulent promise that is meant to earn him support. A significant part of his public is gullible and believes the lie. Seeing this, the perpetrator then comes to believe it himself and tries to act on it. The end is disappointment for all.

PURCHASING POWER

A characteristic promise setting off the Yakoubovich syndrome is to "give purchasing power to the masses." The setting is one where the economy is sluggish, crawling along below its potential. The space between the actual and the potential performance is, so to speak, wasted. If actual production were to rise to its potential, untold billions could be distributed to worthy recipients, the wants of the needy could be met, and projects serving the public interest could be promoted.

A beguiling promise is then made to bring about this rise in output by "giving" people the purchasing power to buy it. In his mighty effort to pull the Brazilian economy up by its bootstraps, President Kubitschek (1956–61) simply ordered all wages and salaries in the country to be doubled. Needless to say, prices doubled with wages, and production did not. Today, politicians in and out of government try to boost purchasing power by legislating higher minimum wages, more generous unemployment and retirement pay, and by inciting labor unions to make aggressive wage claims and bullying industry to meet the claims. The implicit argument is that if industry paid higher wages, demand for its products would increase and allow the higher wages to be paid. However, if wage costs increase all round, it is prices that will increase, not output. Demand would then just suffice to purchase the old, unchanged level of output, but not a higher one. If this were not the case, it would be because the old level of output was not in equilibrium and would have increased anyway of its own accord. The idea that higher costs amount to greater purchasing power springs from confusing demand and output at current prices with demand and output in real terms.

Unlike the "purchasing power" promise that boils down to conjuring up something out of nothing, another Yakoubovich lie that promises to squeeze the rich to help the poor does involve real resources and is not devoid of all logic. But it is fraudulent in misrepresenting the resources involved. The only part of the income of the rich that can be taken from them and safely given to be consumed by the poor without upsetting the saving-investment balance of the economy is the amount by which the rich reduce their consumption as a result of the higher tax meant to "squeeze" them. If they maintain their consumption and cut their investment instead, the poor can consume more only at the expense of fewer resources being devoted to investment. The actual result of the higher tax will no doubt be a reduction in both consumption and investment by the rich, with investment being cut more—not a result that would help the poor beyond the shortest of short runs.

DEVELOPMENT AID

A corruption-laden form of the Yakoubovich syndrome is the advocacy of development aid. A small minority in the economics profession is acting as part-time consultant either to donors on matters of development aid or to the governments of the countries asking for such aid. Some quite prominent economists do this as a full-time business, even forming their own corporations to carry it on. We can only guess whether a particular "development economist" is really convinced that aid will not be stolen or wasted and debt forgiveness will not result in the piling up of new debt. Many are no doubt genuinely convinced. But all are interested in aid flows being maintained and increased. Almost inevitably, for the simple reason that few people feel comfortable in pleading day in, day out something they know to be a lie, the interest in aid will in due course generate a belief that aid is in fact a good thing

Both the recipient governments and the donors must be persuaded that the charade of submissions and project appraisals, leading to transfers of vast sums, will in fact yield the cookies and sweets of economic development. In convincing them, development economists convince themselves, too, and are more inclined to act on their wishes than on the evidence provided by the often sad or sordid history of development aid.

One special twist in this reciprocal make-believe calls for attention. Europe is getting seriously alarmed by the rising streams of illegal immigrants entering it by landing in Spain, Italy, and Greece and moving northward. Underdeveloped countries and their advocates now argue that if they were helped to grow out of poverty, their peoples would be content to stay at home and the threat of illegal immigration would ease or cease. The idea is plausible over a time span of several decades, but implausible within our lifetime. Pumping in aid, notably into education, would induce some thousands to stay at home but make hundreds of thousands all the more eager to leave and reach more civilized shores.

WINNING POLICY BATTLES BUT LOSING THE WAR AGAINST ECONOMIC REALITIES

When the economic history of Europe in the last third of the twentieth century comes to be written, one of its most important threads will tell of the long series of battles in which governments fought against economic realities in order to satisfy the wishes and pander to the illusions of electoral majorities. The period is one where government spending expanded relentlessly from under 40 to over 50 percent of gross national product in the largest countries of continental Europe. (Last year, it reached 53.6 percent in France, provoking solemn promises by the powers-that-be that this time they will *really* start controlling spending and bring it down to 51 percent by 2010.) Piece by intricate piece, the machinery of the welfare state was put together. An ever more elaborate system of "workers' rights" was promoted until the labor code grew to several thousand pages—a happy hunting ground for labor lawyers, a minefield for enterprises. Trade union power came to be based, not on workers recognizing that union membership may serve their interests, but on legislation, government sponsorship, and the patronage afforded by the immense administrative machinery of the various social insurance schemes.

The forward march of politics across the domain of economics was widely accepted as justified, mainly for two reasons. One, expressed in such mantras as "Man matters more than the market" or "In democracy, it is ballots that decide, not dollars," was based on the delusion that markets and dollars have one will, man another, and the two pull in opposite directions. The other reason for welcoming the invasion of government into the economy was, and remains, the conviction that redistribution of income through taxation and targeted expenditure is an act of "social justice," a good deed and a moral duty.

First published by Liberty Fund, Inc., at www.econlib.org on February 6, 2006. Reprinted by permission.

"THEY DO NOT TALK BACK"

The future historian of these apparent triumphs over economic reality will very likely single out two phenomena that loomed more and more ominously and in fact began to signal that no matter how the battles went, the war was beginning to be lost. One was the growing severity of job protection policies that made firing employees so difficult and expensive that employers were frightened away from hiring them in the first place. New job creation fell to levels last seen in the Great Depression, for offering employment except on short-term contracts has become an act of reckless audacity. (One small but significant breach in job protection came just the other day when the highest French court of appeal ruled that terminating employees may be permitted not only when the enterprise is making losses threatening its survival, but also when terminating employees is necessary to *prevent* such losses.)

The other ominous phenomenon was that the high level of unemployment, which would have seemed abnormal a decade ago, has come to be seen as a fact of life. It has resisted the multitude of attempted therapies governments of both Right and Left tried to apply to it. The diminishing band of diehard defenders of the "European social model" still mutter that unemployment is high because the model is not "social" enough, or not European enough, and all will be well when it is made more social and more "harmoniously" European. Meanwhile, it is starting to be noticed that chronically high unemployment has almost wholly drained away the bargaining power of labor in the private sector. Union militancy is now confined to the public sector—essentially, to public transport workers, teachers, and government clerks. Thirty-odd years of socialist economic policies have reduced the mythical, red-flag-waving "working class" to passive impotence.

An anecdote bears eloquent witness to how workers "benefiting" from the "special model" now stand compared to those who are exposed to the "caprice of the market." Two years ago Toyota set up a car assembly plant in the industrially derelict region of northeast France. More recently, the president of Toyota visited the plant, expressed his satisfaction, and explained that the company has chosen to locate in France rather than in England (which was the runner-up candidate location) because "English workers can afford to talk back, but French workers cannot."

In fact, under the "European social model" real bargaining has practically ceased. Labor addresses its demands not to the employer, but to the government that may or may not be able to bully the employer into making concessions. Increasingly, the latter is unable to achieve much in the face of the risk that capital and operations will be moved out to central and eastern Europe, Asia, or Mexico. In actual fact, the volume of such movements is fairly modest, but their public echo is deafening and wreaks havoc in politics and the labor movement.

DISCREETLY, BACK TO BASICS

In current labor union language, bargaining hardly exists. In its place have come "meaningful negotiation" in which the employer meets union demands, and "blackmail" in which the employer obtains concessions.

Over the past year, there have been a number of high-profile cases of "blackmail" by European, chiefly German, flagship companies including Siemens, Opel, Bosch, Conti Gummi, and Volkswagen, usually involving the lengthening of the work week and in some cases lower pay for new recruits, in exchange for commitments by the employer not to reduce the labor force or limiting the reduction to a minimum, as well as undertakings not to move production abroad. These cases obviously had a bad press and made much political noise. Unions agreed to them under protest, stressing that the cases were exceptional, involving a small fraction of wage-earners, while for the vast majority industrywide collective contracts remained in force.

In the meantime, there was a mostly unreported groundswell of "blackmail" agreements between small and medium enterprises and their employees that departed from the official industry contracts. They involved longer hours, more flexible working arrangements, wage freezes, or lower pay increases than the industry norm. They were concluded between the enterprise and the works council, whose members were labor union officials who forbore from wearing their union hats. According to some estimates by industry associations, between 50 and

70 percent of enterprises with fewer than five hundred employees have concluded such agreements. Their cardinal feature was a promise of maximum discretion, so as to let labor organizations lose as little face as possible. Apparently, there was little opposition by the wage-earners themselves. Manifestly, there is more understanding and acceptance of realities in Germany than in France and Italy, where labor and the parties of the Left still seem to believe that the basic facts of life can be made to go away if you call them "unacceptable" loud enough.

In 2000, German labor costs were about 25 percent higher than French ones. By last year, the gap had practically disappeared. German forward economic indicators have been perking up since last spring, and unemployment has started to fall significantly even before the "Merkel effect" has come into play. It will be interesting to watch how the other "core" countries of the euro-zone will position themselves over the next year or two. Will they go on winning the policy battles and lose the war, or will they permit a gradual and discreet return to basics?

PAYING OURSELVES MORE OF THEIR MONEY

Politics has always held the ultimate whip hand over the economy simply by virtue of its power to make laws and its command of the police and the armed forces. However, there were long periods in history when it exercised the whip hand very little. Under oligarchic governments such as the Italian city-states during the Renaissance (and Venice for much longer), or during Holland's "Golden Century" (the seventeenth), one might even say that politics was used in the service of economic prosperity, rather than the reverse. There was the "brilliant episode" of liberal government in much of the nineteenth century where the most advanced Western governments left the economy almost wholly alone. These periods, though, were the exception rather than the rule. In our own time, with universal suffrage, competitive politics exploits to the utmost the lure for a majority of being able to bend the economy to its purposes. A democratic electoral program is now overwhelmingly an economic program having to do with taxes, trade policy, welfare "rights," labor law, the regulation of industry and commerce, subsidies, and so forth. To say that most of this is no business of the government would be as sacrilegious, and as sure an election-loser, as to say that the people's livelihood is none of the people's business.

MIXED-UP ROLES, MIXED-UP INCENTIVES

By one of those laws that have set the course of Germany after her defeat in World War II, corporate government had to be a two-tier one: the managing board was meant to run the business on behalf of the owners, and above it the supervisory board hired and fired the managing board, determined its pay, and approved or vetoed its major decisions. So far, this was straightforward and in no wise perverse, though it could become a little cumbersome. It was no more fertile ground

First published by Liberty Fund, Inc., at www.econlib.org on September 8, 2005. Reprinted by permission.

for cronyism and self-dealing than the single-board system of Anglo-American corporate organization. However, the German system was to be more democratic. The supervisory board was (and still is) a mixed body, with half its members representing the owners, the other half the workers. In practice, the worker representatives are usually, though not necessarily, union officials.

In other words, half of the managers' own bosses are representatives of the workers the managers are supposed to manage. This is an idyllic state of affairs, and could hardly be more democratic, but it only works in fair weather. It is quite unfit for crises, conflicts, and hard times, when painful, unpopular management decisions are called for but do not get past the supervisory board.

A funny case—if funny is the right word—that bears this out is the scandal at Volkswagen that has been entertaining Germany most of this summer. The management board has bribed a couple of worker representatives on the supervisory board to vote for unpopular measures the representatives' constituents, the workers, would presumably wish them to veto. For the system to work, responsible people had to be corrupted.

A more general case of mixing up the roles of employer and employee is the state enterprise. The state in many countries owns and runs enterprises in public transport, power generation and distribution, mining and metals, as well as in some unexpected odds and ends. Their tariffs (prices) are a prime subject of democratic politics; raising them is usually no vote-catcher.

From time to time, preferably ahead of some important election, wage claims arise. It is the employees' role in a market economy to push these claims, and it is the employer's role to resist them, until a bargained solution reflecting the supply and demand for labor emerges, with or without resort to a strike. However, the state as employer cannot behave like any ordinary employer. After all, its employees are the voters who are its democratic masters. The settlement of the wage claim is an eminently political matter, no less so than the fixing of public transport and utility tariffs. The politically most feasible solution is to bow to the will of the voters, grant the wage claim or most of it, and not pass the extra cost on in higher transport or utility prices. Along the line of least resistance, democracy triumphs, and state enterprises merrily pay out to wage-earners and public transport and utility customers the money of the unknown, invisible taxpayer. That money is all the more impersonal, coming out of nobody's pocket, as state enterprises first run up deficits for a few years before their depleted resources have to be replenished from the public purse. Very few people see clearly enough, or at all, the relation between the democratic fixing of public-sector wages and prices and the level of taxation.

In all such situations of role reversal and role usurpation, "we" by virtue of our democratic voting power pay ourselves more of "their" money, instinctively feeling good about the result, for we seldom identify "them" as being ultimately "us."

SQUATTING THE JOBS

It is a perfectly normal aspiration for every wage-earner to be free to leave his job without much ado, but for his employer not to be free to lay him off except with much ado, if at all. The wage-earner wants to own his job, or at least to "squat it."

Bit by small bit, nearly a century of "socially minded" labor legislation has added various "squatter's rights" to the employment code, concerning notice, unfair dismissal, and severance pay. The employee has come a little closer to "owning his job." In the last couple of decades in Western Europe, adding more and more valuable "rights" of this kind has mounted to a paroxysm, and every new step in this direction was naturally sure of majority support. Opposing apple pie and motherhood would be a less certain method of political suicide than opposing job protection.

Obviously, the more securely a worker "owned his job," the riskier and the less profitable it appeared to employers to offer employment. Thus, ever more comprehensive job protection became one of the prime causes of ever more endemic unemployment.

However, one of the perfectly natural and predictable effects of chronic unemployment is that labor cannot afford to be militant except in the public sector where wages and employment continue to be determined by politics. This is glaringly manifest in France, where strikes and strike threats flourish in public employment, education, and the railways and wages in these sectors keep creeping up, while in the private sector there is dead calm with workers keeping their heads down as they are bereft of nearly all bargaining power. They are relatively content to squat on what they have, grateful for job protection, and utterly oppose any step toward what is politely called "labor market flexibility." The primacy of politics over economics creates for them a perverse incentive to freeze hiring and firing, though they would no doubt be better off in an "old-fashioned" labor market where movement was free both ways. But then what would be the use of casting and counting ballots?

THE DOCTRINE OF "UNEQUAL EXCHANGE"
THE LAST REFUGE OF MODERN SOCIALISM?

Socialist intellectuals squirm when reminded of such basic tenets of Marxist economics as surplus value, the iron law of wages, and the declining rate of profit, tenets that were sacred in the glory days of advancing socialism but that are now kept under glass in the museum of strange ideas.

While the old stuffing of Marxist economics has been knocked out of socialism, two major attempts have been made to replace it with some alternative intellectual content. One was to upgrade the vague and emotional notion of "social justice," and underpin it with the idea that since "veils" of ignorance or uncertainty hide the future, the rational individual must opt for an egalitarian social order for his own safety ("society as mutual insurance").

It was then the obvious move to infiltrate the redistributive demands of "social justice" into the capitalist system, which may in other respects remain intact. Germs of this attempt can be traced back to mid-nineteenth-century English thought. It came to full flowering after World War II in the American brand of liberalism and in European social democracy. However, as a positive theory it is feeble. It needs bolstering by normative judgments condemning inequalities except if morally justified. But if we accept these judgments anyway, then we can safely throw away the theory. It is redundant and cannot salvage socialism's intellectual respectability.

At first sight more promisingly, the other major salvage attempt starts off as a non-normative economic theory (though it does not end like one). The starting point is that though total income is equal to total product, we cannot say that individual income is equal to the individual's contribution to the product. Each contribution is ren-

First published by Liberty Fund, Inc., at www.econlib.org on September 6, 2004. Reprinted by permission.

dered possible, or is "owed" to, countless past and present contributions by others. Society owes its product to itself. Given that it owns it, it may distribute it among its individual members in any way it chooses by switching on some recognized collective choice mechanism, such as democracy. It can bring about the chosen distribution either by taking the means of production and exchange into "social" ownership or, the more modern way, by using the tax code. The latter proceeding is supposed to preserve the principle of voluntary exchange and the essentials of the capitalist system. Paradoxically, this is a socialist theory of income distribution that states, in effect, that there is no theory of income distribution; it is always what society chooses it to be.

The idea that "every contribution depends on, and is owed to, every other" is a trivial truth. It is tantamount to saying that since you could not work and earn an income if you did not eat, you owe your income to the farmers, processors, and retailers of food. You also owe it to all who helped make you what you are and who in various ways help to keep you going.

You may object mildly (you might indeed object indignantly) that you have squared all these debts when you paid for the food and all the other commercially provided goods and services you used, and when you paid the taxes to finance the goods and services the state provided for you. The distribution of incomes was what it was because the prices of these goods and services, and the taxes, were what they were. Ultimately, all these things (except the taxes—but believers in the social contract would not allow even that exception) were matters of voluntary exchange. Voluntary exchange is a positive-sum game in which there are no losers, no debt is left unsettled, and no room is left for any other distribution that would make everybody better off. Is there anything left for socialism to complain about?

Here, the retreating defender of socialism is driven to the last resort. Exchange may well be voluntary, free of duress in any strict sense, and both parties may well be gainers. Admittedly, the positive theory stops short at this point. Nevertheless, all is not well, and for the socialist it seems imperative to inject a normative judgment into the argument. For even if both parties to a voluntary exchange gain, are their gains equal? Surely, under capitalism there is no mechanism, but under socialism there should and would be one, to restrain the freedom of contract and "correct" exchanges that are "unequal."

Careful thought is needed to make sense of this claim. In talking of the gains from exchange, are we talking of "utilities" or sums of money? If the former (as economists, at great cost to their discipline, often do), asking whether A's gain is greater than B's is as meaningful as to ask which is greater, birdsong or the color yellow. Since the two utilities are quantitatively no more comparable than a tune and a color, any comparison must be made in terms of the values someone entitled to judge such matters would attribute to the two gains. "Society" may or may not be entitled to make such judgments. Under socialism it would, under capitalism it would not be entitled to make them.

The matter is less straightforward if we try to look at gains in terms of money or goods. Suppose that in an economy using two factors of production, labor and capital, the distribution of income is the result of exchanges of one against the other, so that capital is able to use labor, or labor is able to use capital. "Equal" exchange does not mean that the share of wages in national income works out at 50 percent and that of interest and profit also at 50 percent. The reality is more like 80–20, and few socialists complain that the share of wages is unfairly high.

The socialist claim, instead, is that in most voluntary exchanges the poorer party concedes a greater part of the gain to the richer party than he would do if their "bargaining powers" were equal.

It is far from sure that one can define bargaining power, or compare the bargaining power of two parties independently of the bargains they in effect reach. Such comparisons are vacuous unless they can be related to some independent benchmark. For instance, if the going rate for a certain type of job in a certain region is $11 an hour and illegal immigrants are only paid $7 for the same job, it is not nonsense to ascribe the shortfall to their weaker bargaining power compared with that of their employers. The converse could be said of wage bargains at, say, $15 an hour that may occur in the face of excess demand and labor shortage. In both cases, we are supposing the benchmark rate of $11 to represent "equal" exchange and equal bargaining powers—a supposition that is grounded in nothing except perhaps some idea of normalcy under competitive conditions.

There is, however, a set of "abnormal" conditions where the commonsense view would not hesitate to hold that the "bargaining power" of workers is uniformly and permanently weaker than that of the employers. This condition is that of the chronically high unemployment that has prevailed in "core" Europe, notably in Germany and France, with only brief interruptions for three decades. For while under full employment the worst that can happen to a worker if he holds out for better conditions or refuses to accept worse ones is that he has to look for another job, under chronic unemployment the worst that happens to him if he loses his job is arguably very bad indeed.

The irony of it all is that chronically high unemployment is the unmistakable product of the very policies, pursued ever more intensively over the last thirty years, that socialist governments of all hues have put in place to make income distribution more equal, protect the workers, achieve "social justice," and banish "unequal exchange." It is thanks to these policies that "globalization," the export of jobs and the flight of enterprise, has come to present a genuine menace to the ordinary worker. Not for the first time, his avowed advocates are proving to be his worst enemies.

CORPORATE MANAGERS
ARE THEY GOING TO KILL CAPITALISM?

Mr. Claude Bébéar does not sit on the board of every major French corporation, but where he does not, friends of his probably do. He is now the most influential man in French business. Entirely self-made, successful, rich, he is a proven practitioner who does not shy away from theoretical reasoning. Shrewdly and boldly exploiting some grossly erroneous valuations, he has traded a small provincial mutual insurance company through a succession of ever more ambitious mergers to end up with an international insurance giant now named Axa, of which he is chairman and a major shareholder. In outlook, he is a manager first, a capitalist second, and equally sure of himself in both roles.

Written in the form of a friendly debate with Philippe Manière, one of the brightest French economic journalists, he recently published a widely commented-upon book somewhat startlingly titled *They Are Going to Kill Capitalism.*[1] Its central idea is that capitalism today is gravely menaced by the often irresponsible, ill-advised, or perversely motivated conduct of those upon whom it largely depends—corporate directors, investors, security analysts, fund managers, auditors, rating agents, bankers, and lawyers—all of whom are "saboteurs" of the system that nurtures them.

Mr. Bébéar thinks that radical socialism that seeks to do away with the capitalist order is no longer a likely threat. But he considers, no doubt rightly, that even right-of-center governments which try to help the system by well-meaning intervention generally end up doing more harm than good. Politicians do not understand the economy, and their clumsy interference cannot help it. The only real remedy is for the

First published as "Capitalism and Virtue: Politicians Do Not Understand the Economy, but Do Managers?" by Liberty Fund, Inc., at www.econlib.org on June 2, 2003. Reprinted by permission.

1. Claude Bébéar and Philippe Manière, *Ils vont tuer le capitalisme* (Paris: Plon, 2003).

unwitting, selfish, or even mindless "saboteurs" of capitalism to come to their senses, conform to the dictates of ethics, and assume their responsibilities. With the characteristic social piety of the French intellectual, he also calls for a "spirit of solidarity" to ensure that the wealth produced by capitalism should be "equitably shared" (p. 2). He wants less opportunism and more virtue.

Lest we forget, let us spell out clearly that of all types of economic organization, capitalism is the most economical on virtue. Its main strength is precisely that it functions, if not ideally well, at least better than its rivals when people are allowed to pursue their individual interests. Systems that need to rely on people being virtuous, "socially responsible," and more mindful of the common good than of their own will at best bring about mediocrity and stagnation, at worst disappointment and grief.

Politicians have a hard time understanding this, and French ones are more impervious to it than most. But do managers grasp it? If anyone does, a man of Mr. Bébéar's record ought to. Yet some of his critique of the selfish and the foolish must leave the reader wondering whether capitalism is meant to serve managers, or the other way round.

SHORT-TERMISM AND OTHER VICES AND FOLLIES

Short-termism, we are told, is one of the bad habits leading modern capitalism astray. A quarter is nothing in a company's life: quarterly earnings statements are irrelevant or misleading, and investors who react to them are doing themselves and the market no good. Their folly exposes companies to market shocks and may force them to sacrifice the future for the sake of prettier numbers in the next quarterly report. Shares should be bought for the long term. Long-term shareholders should be rewarded with more voting rights and higher dividends.

The logic of these suggestions leads to strange conclusions. The stock market could just as well close down. Shares would only be bought when companies wished to raise fresh equity capital, and they would never be sold. Any stray buyer would push the stock price sharply up and any stray seller sharply down. Markets are narrow enough now, but they would be many times narrower if holders reacted neither to earnings news nor to price movements. Improving prospects in one industry and worsening ones in another would not be reflected in relative price movements and would not promote the flow of capital from one industry to the other. Mr. Bébéar deplores the growing use of derivatives in fund management, because they "artificially boost" (p. 124) the volume of transactions in the underlying stocks. But this is precisely one of their benign side effects over and above their usefulness in redistributing risk from unwilling to willing takers.

Analysts are rightly castigated for their gullibility, poor judgment, and herd instinct. Mr. Bébéar recognizes that they cannot have the experience of seasoned business executives, but still blames them for their reliance on mechanistic analytical tools, when they should be backing the quality of management instead. However, while analysts may be a shabby sort of channel of communication between companies and investors, there is not a better one. Without them, investors would be even more in the dark than they are anyway, and more dependent on rumor.

Speaking as a true manager, the senior author is quite hard on rating agencies and bankers. Standard & Poor and Moody's only look at numbers and ratios, and far too readily downgrade reputable companies when the numbers temporarily swing the wrong way, instead of regarding the solid worth of the men who run them. Bankers no longer use their personal judgment and knowledge of a client's business in extending credit and setting interest rates, but rely on the rating agencies. Loan agreements may even include a clause of immediate repayment upon a certain downgrading by the rating agency, possibly precipitating a company's ruin. Here, Mr. Bébéar is really protesting against the division of labor between rating agency and bank, while his plea for judging persons rather than just numbers could be read as a plea for special treatment for members of the club that would surely provoke accusations of cronyism.

He does not spare lawyers who are "castrating capitalism" (p. 110)—which they probably do. But aren't corporate officers also to blame for their great deference to the lawyers?—a product of their anxiety about "cover"? It is hard to see how this could be overcome without changing both the managers and the lawyers.

THE WHIRLWIND OF SPECULATION

Nobody seems to like speculators. A defender of capitalism, however, ought to like them, rather than accusing them of generating vicious spirals. A speculator in stocks or currencies hopes to anticipate what the next man, and the one after that man, will do, and seeks to beat them to it. If he thinks there will be a buying spree, he will buy now, and if he expects a selling spree, he will sell now. He will sell what he has bought before the buying spree is exhausted, and buy back what he has sold before the selling spree is exhausted. If his anticipations were right, he will make money, and he will lose money if they were wrong. Obviously, however, if he was right and has made money, by beating the next man to both the purchase and the sale, he will have lifted the price when it was still low and lowered it when it was already high. In other words, if he was successful, he will have smoothed down the swing in the price that would otherwise have taken place. A market with active and successful speculators will be less volatile than it would otherwise be. Contrariwise, if he anticipated wrongly, he will have accentuated the swing and "destabilized" (forgive the trendy word) the market. As Nicholas Kaldor, no apologist for capitalism, has shown in a famous paper, speculators are benign if they make money and harmful if they lose it; but if they lose enough, they are wiped out and the harm stops. There is no vicious spiral, and the Tobin tax is otiose.

In Mr. Bébéar's book, however, the speculator does not anticipate a movement that is going to take place. Instead, he initiates and causes it. He sells (as a typical manager Mr. Bébéar dislikes bears more than bulls), and his selling sets off an avalanche of other selling, driving the price down to a level where he will buy back low what he has sold high. A man of vast experience of the securities markets seems really to believe that speculators, or at least some of them, have this magic power over the expectations of other market participants. However, if even a single one had such a power, his every move would set off moves by hordes of others in the same direction. The more he speculated, the more slavishly would others follow his infallible lead, the more money he would make, and the more powerful would be the next whirlwind he could set off. Before long, he would own the world. But this is not how the economy really works, and Mr. Bébéar must know it.

THEY WON'T KILL CAPITALISM

The rogue's gallery of "saboteurs," fools, cowards, opportunists, and other normal specimens of the human race won't kill capitalism. Perhaps they won't enhance its reputation, but capitalism never enjoyed a very high reputation in the eyes of the general public. It always deserved a higher one than the one it did have, if only because no rogues' gallery could ever stop it from performing reasonably well its basic function of delivering the goods.

It would indeed be nice if all whose job it is to keep the capitalist system going became more virtuous, more wise, more competent, and more responsible. We may wish and even work for this. But, *pace* Mr. Bébéar and others, let us by no means spread the altogether false belief that capitalism's survival depends on this wish coming true.

WHEN THE ECONOMY NEEDS MORALS

Like the road to hell that (as all know) is paved with good intentions, the road to economic stagnation and relative poverty (as all do not know), is paved with policies. Some, such as the "legal" work week, price and rent controls, or "job protection," are counterproductive, wrongheaded if not downright asinine. Others, such as compulsory social insurance or the sharply progressive taxation of income and inheritance, serve purposes that well-meaning public opinion thinks are both rational and just, that help build voting coalitions the government needs, but whose true economic cost is so pervasive and diffuse that it is never really perceived. Finally, there are policies aimed at mitigating the unforeseen side effects of other policies or at achieving particular results in, say, regional development, research, the pattern of foreign trade, or the support of certain industries, that may look quite reasonable if regarded in isolation, but whose cumulative weight disturbs and distorts the work the price system is to do in keeping the economy on an upward path tolerably close to its potential.

The sum total of all the policies in being is a cause of general underperformance. Even if every policy had a positive effect on its own limited target (which may be too much to hope), there would still be a negative diffuse effect on the economy as a whole due to deviations from the path of least resistance. But that would little by little weigh down activity without most people having much insight into why this should be happening. There will be a frenzied and increasingly desperate piling up of social policy, employment policy, industrial policy, energy policy, transport policy, measures for the young, for the long-term unemployed, for the unskilled, for small business, and for any number of other worthy causes. Little or nothing will be achieved.

Those who have followed the history of the French "social model" since its origins after 1975 are familiar with the details of such pro-

First published by Liberty Fund, Inc., at www.econlib.org on June 14, 2007. Reprinted by permission.

cesses. Italy, Germany, and the Scandinavian countries provide similar, albeit less stark, examples, though with one major difference: each, in its own manner, has recently at least tried to reverse the process and dismantle part of its towering policy edifice. European countries of the former Soviet bloc have also done some good demolition work. If this dismantling persists and gathers momentum, all may yet be well. The present article deals with the opposite scenario where no dismantling has started, or where it fails to gather momentum.

Generally, the trouble begins with public opinion waking up to the near-absolute primacy of politics over economics that characterizes advanced countries since World War II or so. In the nineteenth century and the first decades of the twentieth, public opinion was convinced that there were iron laws no government could transgress without risking catastrophe. Property belonged unconditionally to whoever held title to it, and could not be violated without the social order collapsing. Budget deficits could not be allowed to persist in peacetime, for printing money meant inflation and the spoliation of small savers. Wages and profits had their own natural levels and could no more be fixed by decree than the weather. These beliefs did not provide complete protection for benign economic equilibrium, but they helped.

Partly as a result of the widespread teaching of vulgarized economics, it came to be understood that none of these iron laws had actually to be respected, except perhaps in the very long run when we are all dead. People saw that everything that was politically feasible or indeed necessary could be done to the economy without the sky crashing down on them. A democratic government always had the whip hand over business. The freedoms of property and contract could always be curtailed by appeal to the public interest.

The proliferation of policies that seemed a good idea at the time was to shape the economy to perform as politics dictated. The objective was to establish "social justice" by redistributing the income once the economy has obediently produced it. Policy proliferation and redistribution are the obvious consequences of the primacy of politics. After a lapse of time that is quite short by historical standards, the result is clear. Each policy works to some extent, but their sum total brings overall failure.

At this point, the realization is dawning that, like a sick body saturated with an array of wonderful drugs to which it can no longer respond, the economy will not improve by subjecting it to a further overdose of remedial measures. Above all, historically high unemployment seems to have become chronic. It threatens the whole social order and, more importantly, the political survival of whatever shade of government happens to hold office. Desperate measures are suggested: the "available" work must be shared by ordering everyone to work shorter hours; business must be allowed to hire but forbidden to fire; it must be obliged to invest its profits rather than distribute them to fat cat shareholders; it must also be forbidden to delocalize to lower-cost countries; indirect taxes must be used to penalize imports; the state must pay the wages of young people in their first year of employment; and so forth. Some of these harebrained ideas are actually tried out, but either prove unenforceable or just do not work.

In the last resort, the cry then goes up for more social responsibility, more morals. In a normally functioning capitalist economy not pulled and pushed off balance by the politics of policies, the need for morals is at a minimum. Most economic agents are called upon to do only what is "incentive-compatible." This jargon term, regrettably part of the language of economics, means that the butcher and the baker best fulfil their role if they maximize their profit (or otherwise act in their best interest). The exception is the principal-agent relation, such as that between the employer and his employee, the owner and the manager, or the citizen and the state. Such relations are only partly or not at all incentive-compatible and leave a need for supervision and ingenious incentive-creating contracts. Egalitarian arrangements and command economies are both almost totally incentive-incompatible.

Instead of having to rely on morals, a normal capitalist economy works well if, and because, "honesty is the best policy"—namely it pays best. Deviation from the honest norm—shirking, free-riding, short-changing, making shoddy goods, stealing, or embezzling—might pay even better, but may trigger legal, economic, or social retribution. The best policy is the honest one if the expected present value of retribution is greater than the gain from any dishonest option. (The expected present value of retribution depends on the agent's subjective probability of being caught, on the pain of the punishment, on how soon it may be suffered, and the rate at which the agent discounts the future. Unsettled social conditions favor the dishonest option, as does slow justice and a high personal discount rate. Dishonest people are believed to discount the future at extravagantly high rates.)

Unlike a healthy capitalist economy, the near-bankrupt welfare state requires morals in the strict sense. It asks many of the most decisive economic agents to act against their own interests. Wealthy families or ambitious entrepreneurs must not emigrate to reduce their tax burden—doing so would be a betrayal of solidarity with their fellow countrymen. Top executives must not accept salaries and bonuses that would make them as rich as pop singers or football stars, but should limit their earnings to some moderate multiple of what their workers get. Firms must maintain the payroll and not throw their employees on the dole as long as the company is still profitable; only serious loss could justify laying off defenseless workers. Managers must manage in a "socially responsible" manner and not in the sole interest of the owners. (Interestingly, this demand is made in the name of morals, though if the manager does not run the business in the owners' sole interest, he is betraying his mandate and is in effect a thief who steals on behalf of "society.")

It is perhaps obvious, but it will do no harm to spell it out, that none of these alleged moral imperatives are pertinent in an economy that runs freely and has not been nearly suffocated by ill-advised attempts to use politics for improving economics. Workers, above all, are not menaced by chronic unemployment which strips them of bargaining power and leaves them to the mercy of a largely imaginary and axe-grinding moral code of economic conduct.

THE POLITICAL ECONOMY OF FORCE-FEEDING

In Mauritania, many parents caring for their girls' future well-being send them at a tender age to board with women specializing in fattening them up by amiable but relentless force-feeding. Like most African men, Mauritanians prefer them well rounded, and a girl who frankly bulges has a good chance of finding a rich husband, while a slim girl may have to content herself with being found by a poor one. Money may not make the girl happy, but the parents are nevertheless following a kind of economic rationale in having her force-fed. One does not know whether the rich husband will be nicer or on the contrary nastier than a poor one would be. With even chances of either outcome, rational choice must opt for the rich husband, for happy or unhappy, the girl will at least be more comfortable in the rich household.

There is a remote analogy between parents force-feeding their daughters with food and states force-feeding the children of their subjects with compulsory education. In both cases, compulsion is motivated by benevolent paternalism, though one might think that there is more excuse for parents acting paternalistically than the state doing so in loco parentis. However, the analogy stops here anyway. In particular, the results are not analogous at all.

According to statistics compiled by the European Commission, public expenditure on education by the twenty-seven member states amounted to 5.09 percent of the area's gross national product, with private expenditure by families and nongovernment institutions adding a mere 0.64 percent. The corresponding figures were 8.47 and 0.32 in Denmark, 5.12 and 2.32 in the U.S., 6.43 and 0.13 in Finland, 5.29 and 0.95 in Britain, 4.60 and 0.91 in Germany and 4.25 and 0.61 in Spain. The low proportion of money freely spent on buying education compared to public spending on force-feeding it to captive consumers is striking.

First published by Liberty Fund, Inc., at www.econlib.org on November 5, 2007. Reprinted by permission.

There is a wide enough consensus in Europe that public expenditure on education, on a rising trend in nearly every country, must go on rising and is never high enough. Most people believe that more spending means better education and do not see any clear link between their taxes and more public spending. Nobody feels the marginal cost of more education, and many do not realize that the marginal return, in terms of better-educated young people, may be very little indeed. Except perhaps in the case of Finland where high expenditure goes hand in hand with Europe's best average scholarly performance, there is no significant correlation between spending and educational results.

The sums involved are huge. Only "ill care" (euphemistically and misleadingly called health care, though its agenda is the treatment of illness rather than the preservation of health) absorbs a greater share of national incomes. The return on this vast outlay is poor and shows little or no improvement with time. Functional illiteracy among school-leavers in the state-run sector runs at around 15 percent. Many countries, with France in the lead, forbid selective admission at secondary and at university entry level as inegalitarian (though some selection is taking place surreptitiously). The result is that in each class, a number of hard cases prevent the rest from learning and the teacher from teaching. British education is good at the top end, thanks in large part to the 160 grammar schools that were spared in the devastating postwar reforms to bring in equality of opportunity, and that practice selection, but below that level standards are abysmal. State schools not only fail to teach their conscripted pupils basic knowledge but also fail to educate them to habits of regular work, discipline, and civilized conduct.

In defense of the schools, it is said that parents no longer do their share of educating children as they used to do. This is undoubtedly true, but then taxpayers did not use to pay five percent of national income to maintain schools in order that compulsory education should accomplish both what parents no longer do and what privately financed schools used to do in the past.

School attendance in most European countries is mandatory and free of charge from between five and seven to fifteen or sixteen years, usually with a further two years that may be mandatory, optional, or a part-time mixture of the two. In a recent speech Britain's prime minister Gordon Brown announced plans to extend the general school-leaving age to eighteen, though it was not clear whether this would be mandatory. University education is still optional everywhere in Europe, but there is a tendency to transform it into a "right" the young "ought to" exercise and to have the general taxpayer bear most of the cost.

More and more, education is taking the form of a "nonexcludable" public good that has the peculiarity that a certain age group is not only free, but actually compelled, to consume it. Moreover, this age group tends to be extended as the school-leaving age is prolonged. This is done in the firm belief that it will do a deal of good both to the young personally and to the national economy as a whole, making the cost well worth bearing and the force-feeding justified. However, a suspicion is spreading that this belief is illusory and that the material and moral payback may in fact be nil or negative.

Who, or what, is at fault? Everybody, and everything, is probably the right answer. One obvious structural fault springs, paradoxically, from the virtual shutting off of the normal producer-consumer conflict in the state sector. In private schools the producers, namely the teachers, must willy-nilly exert themselves to satisfy the customers, namely the pupils' parents. In state schools, the customers are captive. They do not pay (or so it seems to them at the level of each particular school) and must either consume what is provided or passively resist it. Whether they do one or the other, the jobs of the teachers are little affected. Teachers' unions behave accordingly and fight tooth and nail against attempts to inject some producer-consumer conflict and competitive effort into education by the use of school vouchers. In Europe, school vouchers have been and remain out of the question. Some teachers' unions, especially in France, also combat and seek to restrict apprenticeship for being a form of "child labor" that would reduce school attendance. They just succeeded in reversing a government decision that would permit apprenticeship from the age of fourteen; the age limit is now back at sixteen.

However, the root cause of failure lies deeper than teacher indifference, left-leaning prejudice, and bureaucracy. It lies in universal compulsory enrollment in a system that cannot educate under the same roof both the willing and the unwilling, the hopelessly dumb and the downright hostile. Probably no system can really do so, but if there is one that has a chance, it is one that demands only voluntary effort from the young and guides those unwilling or unable to make it, to channels that call for different kinds of endeavor and aptitudes. In one word, education as an obligation does not work, or at any rate does not work well enough to make it worthwhile. It needs gradually to be turned into a privilege provided only for those willing and able to draw from it all the benefit it offers, but withdrawn from those who abuse it or prove unable to use it.

The late James Coleman, an eminent Chicago sociologist, used to teach that it is good for children to be raised within mixed age groups and dangerous to have them grow up within same-age peer groups. For him, the small farmer family where young and old worked at their different tasks on the same farm, and the community of master and apprentices in the workshop, were the ideal educational environments. Adolescents thrown together in the school and "hanging out" together after school ran a high risk that too much of each other's company would coarsen them and make them form gangs where outrageous behavior earned them peer admiration.

This is perhaps the right juncture to remember the sinister story of compulsory social regrouping on a wildlife reservation in East Africa. The elephant population was growing too dense. To relieve the pressure, substantial numbers of young elephants were captured and placed several hundred miles away in an area where only a few elephants lived. After a while game wardens in that area began to find corpses of rhinoceros crushed to death by unexplained blows or pressures. The mystery of these deaths was solved when gangs of up to a dozen young elephants were observed chasing rhinos at full gallop. Catching up with one, they overturned and stomped it to death. It was concluded that being forcibly taken out of their family environment and thrown together with their peers had turned them into coarse, wanton hooligans.

I will stop short of insinuating that force-feeding the young with education some of them are unwilling or unfit to assume, and extensions of the school-leaving age that divert many young people from timely apprenticeship and natural transition into working life, are turning them into replicas of rogue hooligan beasts. Things are not as bad as that, but very much worse than the advocates of ever more, ever longer, and ever more expensive compulsory education keep on imagining. Their dream of turning out well-behaved and highly knowledgeable young people destined to have a better life than their parents, while by the same stroke creating a huge positive externality in the form of a "knowledge-based" superproductive economy (such as was set as the medium-term objective for the European Union at its 2003 Lisbon summit) is proving to be just that, a dream. Awake to reality, less paternalistic and less coercive means may be adopted, whose use runs into less resistance.

HOSTILE TO WHOM?

"ECONOMIC PATRIOTISM" TO RESIST "MARKET DICTATORSHIP"

Over the last year or so, cross-border bids for the control of high-profile corporations in one country by interests in another have multiplied. An unusually high proportion of such bids have been unsolicited by the directors of the target corporation. They have either been rejected by them to start with, or have bypassed them altogether and were addressed over the directors' heads directly to the shareholders. With a mixture of naïveté, cynicism, and hypocrisy that leaves sensible people breathless, such bids are called "hostile." Though seldom if ever asked, it is surely pertinent to ask: hostile to whom?

When the state-controlled Chinese oil company CNOOC tried to buy Unocal and the all-cash offer looked attractive enough to make it likely that the requisite proportion of shareholders would accept it, the furious noise in Congress and the media reached a pitch quite out of proportion to the intrinsic importance of the affair. China was going to undermine U.S. national security, divert "essential" energy supplies from the American consumer, and so forth. The political climate became so stormy that CNOOC was frightened away and Unocal was picked up at a somewhat lower price by Chevron. Some cool heads have reckoned that the Chinese offer overvalued Unocal, but happily American economic patriotism saved the Chinese from overpaying.

When the Dutch bank ABN Amro tried to buy the Italian bank Antonveneto in the face of board opposition, wheels within wheels started to spin, submerged power networks were activated, and the prolonged legal and financial battle ended with a resounding scandal and the forced resignation of the governor of the Bank of Italy. Some took the subsequent buyout of Banca Nazionale del Lavoro by the French bank BNP Paribas for a capitulation of the Italian national interest.

First published by Liberty Fund, Inc., at www.econlib.org on March 6, 2006. Reprinted by permission.

When all too audible stage whispers expertly spread the word that Pepsico was preparing to make a "hostile" bid for the French yoghurt and mineral water firm Danone, a "national champion," President Chirac, personally vowed to "resist the attack" and defend the brave French yoghurt against the brazen invader—though the bluster had little substance in it for lack of any clear legal power to stop Pepsico from making the offer and the Danone shareholders from accepting it. The prime minister solemnly appealed to "economic patriotism," called upon French companies to "padlock their capital structure" to make changes of control less easy, and initiated legislation giving the government powers to ban control passing to foreign hands in eleven "strategic" sectors of the economy.

Among a handful of other examples of "hostility," Mittal Steel's offer to buy Arcelor is creating the most emotion. Mittal, the world's biggest steel producer, is legally European but is 85 percent controlled by the Indian Mittal family. Arcelor, the world's No. 2, is European in legal domicile, management, and ownership. Mittal is downmarket, Arcelor is upmarket and proud of it. Its shareholders may choose to sell out to Mittal all the same, which the French and Luxembourg governments deem an intolerable "dictatorship of the market" and are angrily trying to block. The attempt is mainly bluster, but the rhetoric accompanying it is as ugly as it is confused.

Objectively, "hostile" offers are hostile only to the sitting management and related vested interests. However, when they are cross-border, they are invariably styled as attacks upon the host nation of the target company. When Dubai Ports is trying to buy the worldwide port installations of Peninsula & Orient, including those in five U.S. east coast ports, it is threatening American national security and must be stopped, though Dubai Ports would not replace American customs and port security personnel by Arab terrorists, and could not if it would. Likewise, when the Italian power utility Enel sounds as if it were planning to make a "hostile" offer for the Franco-Belgian power and water utility Suez, Paris quickly rushes through a shotgun marriage that preempts the possible Italian bid in the name of French "energy security." Presumably, there was a danger that Enel would pay big money for the Suez power stations in order to shut them down and plunge France and Belgium into darkness. However, the most inane pretext will do to brand perfectly bona fide transactions "hostile," especially if the widely hated stock market is involved in it.

PROTECTING THE PRINCIPAL-AGENT DILEMMA

The result of "economic patriotism" is to curb the liberty of owners to use their assets as they see fit within agreed liability rules. This includes the liberty of selling assets to the highest bidder who thinks he can make more productive use of them and will bet money on his belief. The cost of curbing this liberty is best understood by considering the principal-agent dilemma.

There is a general presumption that it is efficient for principals to delegate certain functions to agents and pay them for carrying out the tasks so delegated. The archexample is owners of corporate equity confiding management to professional boards of directors. In democratic political theory, the citizenry is supposed to confide to the state the task of managing society. In any principal-agent relation, the incentives guiding the principal partly overlap but in part also conflict with the incentives pursued by the agent. The corporate director and the shareholder both prosper when the company's profits rise and its prospects improve. However, the director is also interested in getting the most fabulous compensation package, the most secure tenure, the least stress and conflict, and also in empire-building that puts sheer size ahead of profitability. Analogous contradictions can be found between the interests of citizens and their state when the observer takes off the rose-tinted spectacles of democratic theory.

These are the costs of agency, and the dilemma of the principal-agent relation consists in this: you cannot reap the efficiency gains of agency without bearing its costs. The balance between the two depends in large part on the agency contract. The principal may seek contract terms that will minimize the conflict between his incentives and those of his agent. In politics, constitutions are attempts to frame such a contract, and we know from modern history how successful they have been. In business life, the great shift in managerial compensation from fixed salary to stock options in the last two decades of the twentieth century was another such attempt. Despite much and gross abuse and self-dealing, stock options have had some success in bringing owner and manager interests closer to each other. The recent accounting reforms have put a brake on such tendencies. In any event, it is logically impossible to frame an agency contract which would completely eliminate agency problems without effectively transforming the agent into the principal and losing the efficiencies yielded by the allocation of special tasks to specialists.

It is this dilemma that the "hostile" bid is designed partially to resolve. "Economic patriotism" is unwittingly combating this design, especially if carried out by foreigners or other outsiders not recognized by the domestic establishment of "cozy crony capitalism" which would, if it could, perpetuate the principal-agent dilemma.

THE MARKET FOR CORPORATE CONTROL

It is of course the height of absurdity to term offers made by buyers to sellers as "hostile" or "friendly." They are neither. The seller is free to accept or reject them. They may be hostile, though, to the sellers' agent who may lose his tenure if the seller accepts the bid. He can protect himself against this risk in two ways. One is by populist appeals to public opinion, legislative and regulatory maneuvers, "poison pills," and the like. The other is by brilliant managerial performance that gets so close to the ideal of long-run profit maximization that no one thinks he can make much better use of the assets by wresting control of them from the sitting directors.

The branch of theory dealing with the value of corporate control was grafted onto the theory of the firm by Henry Manne.[1] It would be impertinent to try and give a capsule summary of his short, seminal article here. Suffice it to say that the control premium offered by a bidder will lie in a gap, if any, between the company's market capitalization under its sitting management and the present value of all future earnings the bidder expects the corporate assets to yield under the best management he can appoint. The bigger the gap, the bigger must the agency problem be. Equally, however, the bigger the gap, the stronger is the incentive potential bidders have to try and buy the corporate

1. Henry Manne, "Mergers and the Market for Corporate Control," *Journal of Political Economy* 73 (1965): 110–20.

control. If potential bidders are not deterred by regulatory twists, poison pills, and appeals to patriotism or good manners, the sitting management must strain to "increase shareholder value" (as the current jargon has it) by better performance as well as by inspired rumors of impending bids so as to reduce the remaining gap between the current value of the company and its expected value to a rival, i.e., the control premium the rival would be willing to pay. Discouraging bids is to encourage sloth and inefficiency. Until this is better understood, agents will rise high on the backs of principals.

MANNESMANN'S COURTESY COULD PROVE RARE

Now that the Mannesmann-Vodafone contest is behind us it might be a good time to pause and consider what just took place and what the implications are for Europe. Many see in the outcome a watershed event. Mannesmann, a large German engineering concern that has grown into a spectacularly successful multinational telephone business, was after all the indisputable champion among continental Europe's giant corporations. By conventional wisdom, it should have been invulnerable to takeover attempts. Yet late last week, its management ended a three-month battle for control with Vodafone Airtouch by extracting terms beyond which Vodafone could not have gone.

According to the deal, the Mannesmann owners will walk away with 49.5 percent of the future Vodafone-Mannesmann. In exchange, the Mannesmann board renounced all recourse to the abundance of obstructive tactics it could have used, and recommended the Vodafone offer to its shareholders.

The first point I'd like to raise deals with language. The vocabulary used in the media was about what we could have expected. Throughout the long contest, journalists routinely spoke in terms of Mannesmann "falling victim to a hostile bid" if its board accepted any alternative that did not preserve Mannesmann as an independent corporate entity. It seems extraordinary that this language again passed unchallenged. But then it always does whenever a bidder addresses a corporation's shareholders without first securing, by golden handshakes and reassuring undertakings, the consent of its management and sometimes of the labor unions and the government as well.

First published in the *Wall Street Journal Europe,* February 10, 2000. Reprinted by permission.

HOSTILE TO WHOM?

In what way or to whom were this and similar bids *hostile?* Who exactly was the victim? Some of the managers, possibly, and some of the employees, if the transfer of the company's control is to improve efficiency and increase total wealth rather than merely pander to the vanity and megalomania of the bidder. But the idea that managers own their offices and employees own their jobs, to such effect that they are "victims" of "hostile" acts if they lose them, is surely strange.

Stranger still is the fact that so few in the media and among the broad public find it strange. Jobs are matters of contract; if they are to be protected, the protection must be embedded in the terms of the contract, not added later by lobbying and the propagation of spurious claims of rights of tenure. A corporation is owned by its owners. An offer for their shares is no more hostile to them than is the offer for any other piece of property to its rightful proprietor. What is indeed hostile is any claim to the contrary.

Perhaps the negotiated acceptance of the Vodafone offer is a first portent that things are no longer seen in Europe in the confused fashion that confused language promotes. Linguistic obfuscation on the part of mostly leftist journalists may have (let's hope) reached its limit. Perhaps owners, even in continental Europe, and even of large prestigious corporations, will now be allowed to own.

But this is far from certain. The second-largest "hostile" bid after Vodafone's was last year's three-way fight for supremacy in French banking. The managers of Société Générale and Paribas wished to merge the two banks; Banque National de Paris, or BNP, the same size as either of the others, tried to impose a merger of all three under its leadership. The contest took several months and provided classic examples of how corporate boards and governments now pay lip service to free capital markets, while doing their best to thwart them.

The management at the two defending banks, Société Générale and Paribas, showed pained astonishment and anger at having BNP appeal over their heads to the shareholders. They tried to have BNP's offer set aside, an action they knew was lost in advance but one that it took the courts months to deal with. The French government, for its part, set in motion one of the civilized world's most involved and opaque regulatory machineries to ensure that they would end up with the kind of three-way merger it wanted.

Paris sought to create one of the world's biggest banks, an idea that had irresistible appeal to the national ambitions of the French bureaucrats. The highest mandarins of the Ministry of Finance did little to conceal their determination to see BNP through to victory. They even tried to force the governor of the Banque de France, Jean-Claude Trichet, to browbeat the protagonists into agreement on the ground that a contested takeover threatened the stability of the nation's banking system.

The objective was to forestall shareholder self-determination by securing a deal among the respective managers. They were to deliver "their" banks to a tripartite superholding. The French government therefore fiercely warned off Banco Santander Central Hispano from supporting SocGen by buying its shares in the market.

When all else failed to deliver the solution that national grandeur demanded, the government froze the whole process, expecting the "victims" to get the message and comply. In response to warnings that investors were getting disgusted with his high-handed treatment, the then finance minister Dominique Strauss-Kahn (who, facing corruption charges, has since resigned) confidently and grandiosely declared: "The French state is not quoted on the stock exchange!"

In the end, bewildered shareholders sold Paribas to BNP while Société Générale stayed independent. There is of course no telling what the outcome would have been had managers and government not tried to usurp the owners' role. It is unlikely, though, that the result would have been exactly the same.

QUEENSBERRY RULES

The novelty of the Mannesmann case was that right from the outset the chief executive, Klaus Esser, said he would fight by Marquess of Queensberry rules, and throughout he did what he said he would do. He declined to use the tempting opportunities he had to restrict shareholder sovereignty. He could no doubt have provoked government interference, nationalist attacks in the media against the foreign invader, and labor-union agitation. He also had strong weapons in Mannesmann's by-laws.

Above all else, Mr. Esser could have invoked an obscure provision of German company law which offered every chance of leaving an uncompleted Vodafone-Mannesmann merger indefinitely mired down in the courts. This provision, untested and hard to interpret, fitted this particular case like a glove. It would have been ideal both to keep the lawyers of the two parties profitably employed for many years and to keep Mannesmann independent even if a majority of its shareholders had wanted it to merge. In the end, falling in with part of his supervisory board, Mr. Esser made peace and settled with Vodafone, getting a rather better price for his shareholders than the original, "hostile" offer. At no time did he try to stop them disposing of their property the way they saw fit.

Until the next test case and the next after that, however, we can only guess whether he could have done so if he had been prepared to use foul means as well as fair. Time will tell, because there are plenty of European managers only too willing to use legal subterfuges, appeals to the national interest, and local welfare to put across the notion that owners have no more say, and perhaps rather less, than anybody else connected with the business. It is too soon to feel confident, but perhaps one could start hoping that the Mannesmann case does indeed mark a turning in this road.

PART 3

French and Russian Tragicomedies

CAN PUTIN BUILD A REAL ECONOMY FROM OIL AND RIGOR?

Vladimir Putin is embarking on his second presidential term with a new prime minister whose profile may be telling us something about what he means to do in the next four years for Russia—as well as to it. Mr. Fradkov looks and acts as if he were a rather ungainly and somber early-model robot programmed to perform standard tasks reliably enough but with neither capacity nor intention to pursue ideas of his own. He leaves thinking and deciding strictly to his master, whoever the master happens to be. His career of safe mediocrity included the foreign trade ministry, an economic post at the Russian embassy in New Delhi, the direction of the tax police and the post of Russian representative at the European Union's Commission in Brussels. As an international negotiator, he distinguished himself by never answering a question of substance off the cuff, but instead searching in his files for the right cue card and reading off a prepared reply. He can be expected to carry out Mr. Putin's every wish with exemplary loyalty and rigor.

What is Mr. Putin planning to do? He has an approval rating that is exceptional even by Russian standards, and he is riding on a tide of oil and gas revenues that make his dirt-poor country suddenly look affluent and eager to turn its back on the humiliation of the Soviet fiasco. The national mood lends itself more than it ever did to a make-or-break try to lift the Russian economy out of its old rut and make it function like the much-envied economies of the Western bourgeois world.

For the moment, the numbers say that Russia resembles an oil sheikdom rather than a developed Western economy. With a population of

First published as "Third Time Lucky in Russia: Can Putin Build a Real Economy from Oil and Rigor?" by Liberty Fund, Inc., at www.econlib.org on April 5, 2004. Reprinted by permission.

142 million, it is about one-eighth the size of the German and one-fifth of the French economy, and as far as the USA is concerned, it is best to look the other way. Since the financial catastrophe of 1998, national income has admittedly grown quite briskly, the growth rate last year reaching 5.7 percent and in the latest quarter 7 percent. However, if the numbers can be trusted, more than the whole of recent growth was due to sharply higher oil prices and the 10 percent output rise these prices have called forth. Valuing their often heavy and high-sulphur oil at $20 a barrel f.o.b., one reaches the startling conclusion that as much as one-third of Russian national income is accounted for by hydrocarbons.[1] (Valuing Russian hydrocarbon output, including home consumption, at world prices admittedly overstates their contribution to national income; but even a much-reduced figure should worry their economic policy-makers.)

The broad result is that Russia today is suffering from what has become known as the Dutch disease. In the 1970s, Holland was a very large exporter of natural gas. Export receipts pushed up domestic incomes and costs, and brought in a flood of imports with which Dutch industry could not compete. Likewise, today's visitor to Moscow or Saint Petersburg sees hardly any Made in Russia goods in the shops; imports are everywhere, from cars, furniture, and clothes down to such humble items as bread and milk. Oil is generating plenty of income, while productivity is often abysmal and the quality of local products repellent. The major cities look prosperous, though the countryside is just as stagnant and miserable as it has always been; 38 percent of farmland is still state or municipal property.

Should the world price of crude slump in the near future, Russia would be in deep trouble. For the time being, she has a lease on life by courtesy of Saudi Arabia's price leadership at the head of the oil cartel. Mr. Putin must use the good times and the easy money to re-equip industry, rebuild the railways, and renew the country's decrepit infrastructure. Above all, he must create confidence in the rule of law,

1. Oil production so far in 2004 is running at 9 million barrels a day with exports at 3.7 million barrels a day. Gas production is comparable in energy equivalent but somewhat lower in value. Oil, and in particular gas, are still underpriced on the internal market, which leads to wasteful consumption.

whose lack, combined with an autocratic state, has always been the fatal obstacle to organic economic development.

This will be the third attempt in Russian history to reform society and allow a real, self-equilibrating economy to grow up. The first two, that we may ascribe to Piotr Stolypin and Boris Yeltsin, have largely failed. The current Putin attempt may be a case of third time lucky, though the chances are probably no better than even.

The first attempt goes back to the liberation of the serfs in 1861, a measure that for complex reasons has generated more resentment than satisfaction. The social climate was becoming tense, the state poured resources into its repressive apparatus, but the more the political police spied on them, the more the radicals and nihilists flourished. Grudging concessions by the court were taken as signs of failing strength. After the minirevolution of 1905, Stolypin was put at the head of the government and embarked on thoroughly intelligent liberal reforms. Grassroots development took off, an independent peasant class rose out of serfdom, and in the cities the beginnings of an entrepreneurial middle class started to show. The nihilists began to panic that the Stolypin reforms might succeed too well and make their movement irrelevant. They assassinated him in 1911. A bellicose turn in foreign policy, the outbreak of World War I, and the Bolshevik takeover in 1917 finally put Russian society back in the Stone Age.

The second great try was made under Boris Yeltsin's presidency after 1991. Its core was the handiwork of Anatoly Chubais, who wanted to get as much state property into private hands as possible as fast as possible before either the Communists could rally and stop him or some other of those nasty turns occur that Russia specializes in. The ensuing fire sale, in which insiders, bazaar traders, and mafiosi bought up the country's natural resources for a song, created immense fortunes of murky or worse origin, established the class of "oligarchs," and made "privatization" and "Chubais" the bitterest hate words in the language.

The putrefying carcass of the state was the ideal food for corruption of all kinds. The regulated ruble price of oil was about $2 a barrel and an export permit turned that into $20 or so; no prizes for guessing how export permits came to be procured. Because all this was too good to last, extreme short-termism became the rule of prudence, investing in long-lived assets would have been foolhardy, and profits were simply smuggled out. In a peak year, illegal capital flight reached $30 billion, a drain Russia could not really afford. Playing at capitalism without capital, or more precisely without the least assurance of secure ownership, could not achieve the decisive transformation the liberals of the Yeltsin era were hoping for.

Putin is putting heavy reliance on the *siloviki,* like himself middle-level graduates of the KGB and other security services who are ruthless but not arbitrary, rigorous, rule-bound, and not corrupt. If they manage to reduce theft, graft, and tax fraud, popular hatred and rejection of property and profit might be mitigated and capitalism might gain a degree of social respectability and acceptance. Such a regime of rigor will not foster democracy; Putin's Russia will be more like a police state than that of Yeltsin, let alone the ideal Western-style state the best intellectuals of the post-Soviet era are dreaming of. However, first things first: let capitalism truly take root, and then perhaps we shall see.

RUSSIA AND THE NEW EUROPE
GROWING APART

In 2005, Russia's GDP increased by an impressive 6.1 percent. It sounds churlish, but it happens to be perfectly reasonable to say that this performance was on the poor side. Oil, natural gas, and primary metals prices were all at or near unprecedented highs, and Russia's economy is now much like that of some underdeveloped one-crop country that is swinging wildly up or down with the prices of a couple of commodities. With oil brushing the $70 level, Russia should have been getting rich at a double-digit rate, and has not done so. The three Baltic states that regained independence from Soviet backwardness in 1991 have all hit double-digit rates, with Latvia in the lead at 13.1 percent p.a. in the first quarter of 2006, and none of these states produces any oil or gas, nor mines any metal ore worth speaking of. The rest of what Donald Rumsfeld, treating history in a somewhat cavalier fashion, named the "New Europe" is not doing quite as well as the Baltic countries, but its performance is respectable—and owes nothing to any commodity boom.

Despite appearances, Russia is proving to be a huge disappointment to those who believed that having shaken off socialism, it will restart the diversified, capitalist, and bourgeois development that was twice aborted, in the 1860s and in 1905. The Yeltsin years, especially after the loans-for-shares privatization wave of 1995, notwithstanding the mind-boggling corruption and thieving that accompanied them, were marked by a retreat of the state, decentralization of power, and the rise of a "robber baron" class that bore some resemblance to its American counterpart between 1890 and 1914. Despite its ugly features, this could have been the foundation of a viable, self-sustaining capitalist evolution.

First published by Liberty Fund, Inc., at www.econlib.org on July 7, 2006. Reprinted by permission.

The Putin era started off in 2000 as if it were a more orderly and less undignified continuation of this trend, but soon veered off in a new direction. Autocracy was restored, all political power was again concentrated in the Kremlin, the autonomy of regions was abolished and the big-money oligarchs cowed, driven to exile in London or put in prison in Siberia. Their places were mostly taken by Putin loyalists, recruited from the last generation of security service or army officers, grim men in their 40s and 50s who regard running a business as a kind of patriotic service to promote the greatness of Russia. In the last three years of the Putin regime, privatization was put in reverse gear and the state's share in the economy has started to rise again, moving from 30 to 35 percent, though of course still much below the Soviet-era level.

German Gref, the liberal-minded economy minister who now seems to be bereft of any influence, once said that the scarcest factor of production in Russia was the rule of law. It looks like it's getting scarcer. To the extent that they bestir themselves at all, the Russian courts are following in the footsteps of Justices Brandeis, Frankfurter, and the Warren Court in subordinating the force and freedom of contract to the "public interest" except that the Russian judges call it the "interest of the state," which is defined by Mr. Putin and his few dozen ex-secret-police colleagues and friends. The result is arbitrary resource allocation and declining productivity. For what such forecasts are worth, the government has abandoned its 7 percent medium-term growth target and is now expecting a declining growth rate.

Meanwhile, the "New" Europe is briskly catching up with the "Old," thanks to a growth rate that is roughly twice as high in Poland, Hungary, and the Czech Republic and three times as high in the Baltic states as in Western Europe. Moreover, Western Europe is also doing better than in recent years thanks above all to the painful purge to which German business has subjected itself in the last couple of years and that is now bearing fruit.

Yet both the "Old" and the "New" Europe are getting more and more anxious about what is politely called "energy security" and what in ordinary speech translates into "will the Russians blackmail us?"

Currently, about 40 percent of Europe's natural gas imports come from Russia. The two other main suppliers are Algeria and Norway. On present trends, their share will decline and Russia's will expand in the next five years, increasing Europe's dependence on a single seller who is not primarily motivated by market considerations, but by an obsessive craving for political status and influence. To date, Russian gas has been pumped westward through pipelines crossing the Ukraine or Poland. Their dependence on Russian gas is nearly total, but if they are blackmailed, they can retaliate by interfering with the flow of gas across their territory to the Western European markets. The equilibrium between Russia and the transit countries is precarious, but it is an equilibrium all the same.

This balance of unspoken mutual threat will be upset by the building of the big undersea pipeline from Russia to Germany that will bypass transit countries. Once at full capacity, it will increase potential Russian gas deliveries by a half. Projected to cost $10 billion, it will be between three and five times more expensive to lay than a land line through the Baltic countries and Poland. It is obvious, though, that Russia's main concern is not cost, but mastery over the flow of supplies. Evidence of this ambition was provided by the law voted in June 2006 by the Russian Duma, that transforms Gazprom's de facto sole right to export gas into a de jure monopoly—a sharp reply to the pious wish expressed by the European Union that Russian gas exports should be liberalized. Government-to-government agreements will now give Gazprom access to the German and Italian retail gas market in exchange for letting BASF and ENI take minority interests in certain Russian natural gas fields. Gazprom is also seeking to gain a share of the British retail gas market. Hinting that it would provide a counterweight to the domination of the European gas market (and the blackmailing potential it implies) by Gazprom, an instrument of the new Russian imperialism, it has been pointed out that in some Baltic areas the subsoil has a vast potential for gas storage and that for an outlay of 3 billion euros, 70 billion cubic meters of storage capacity could be constructed. The stored gas would cover more than one year's European consumption and offer insurance against blackmail.

Going ahead with such a project would be received very badly in the Kremlin. The mid-July G8 heads-of-government meeting in Saint Petersburg will resound with Russian protestations of reliability as a supplier and its readiness to enter into "energy cooperation" with Europe. The EU's energy commissioner Andris Piebalgis is confident that the meeting will ratify an "energy charter" securing the interests of both parties. He could hardly permit himself to say the contrary. Most seasoned observers would feel much safer if instead of Russian guarantees of good faith, they could rely on competitive market forces to ensure "energy security."

RUSSIA HOPPING ALONG ON CLAY FEET

The first half or so of Vladimir Putin's presidency started to look as if Russia were embarking on its history's third great attempt at becoming a "normal country" with a middle class filling the vacuum between her thin ruling elite (if "elite" is the fitting word) and her mostly miserable, passive masses, and with the benign consequences of such a structure for the country's stability, prosperity, and good-neighborly conduct. In 2004 one could still hope that after the liberation of the serfs in the 1860s and the Stolypin reforms of the 1900s, both of which ended in miscarriages that seem so typical of Russia, the Putin experiment might turn out to be the one that defies and lifts the old curse that sits on the country. Privatization of more than 60 percent of nonfarm production seemed to have passed the point of no return that would be followed by an irreversible loosening of the government's grip on the economy, on people's livelihoods, and hence also on their political obedience. It is now clear that this was a false hope.

Anatoly Chubais, the privatization tsar under Boris Yeltsin, held that it did not much matter who got hold of state assets and by what corrupt maneuvers. The important thing was to get the greatest possible volume of state property into private hands as fast as possible before the political climate changed and further privatization was stopped. He thought that there might be no time to arrange for a wide distribution of state property and for thus laying the foundations of a property-owning middle class of small shareholders and small entrepreneurs. The result was that many, probably a majority, of state enterprises were simply stolen by their previous "red directors" and wheeler-dealer insiders, creating some astronomical fortunes out of thin air. But unlike Schumpeter's "private fortresses" (the great business empires that acted as counterweights to the state), these concentrations of wealth depended to no small extent on the Kremlin's grace and favor,

First published by Liberty Fund, Inc., at www.econlib.org on January 8, 2007. Reprinted by permission.

if only because their illegitimate origin gave the authorities some hold over them. The fate of Mr. Khodorkovsky, now in an obscure Siberian prison, and his giant oil company Yukos, driven into bankruptcy by bizarre tax claims, was a shrill warning signal to the other "oligarchs" to very closely heed Mr. Putin's wishes. By all accounts, they now do. And are repaid with favors.

AMBITION AND SQUALOR

Mr. Putin rose from middle-level provincial KGB officer in occupied East Germany to all-powerful president, reputedly as part of a complex and secret deal between his secret service and military backers and the Yeltsin family. The deal has supposedly secured immunity for Mr. Yeltsin's daughter Tatiana for amassing a fortune by unorthodox means. His elevated role fitted President Putin like a glove. He soon perceived that the common Russian's and his wife's desire for normalcy, an end to queuing, more variety, less drabness, a modicum of free speech and foreign travel was really not their first priority. He did satisfy it to a limited extent, though in time-honored Potemkin for-show fashion the effect was mainly confined to central Moscow shop windows, with the provinces and in particular the villages getting little uplift from their Soviet-era squalor.

However, the real priority of the Russian people has proved to be the restoration of their pride in holy Russia, her greatness and virtue. They did not want it to be like "any normal country"; they wanted it to be unlike any other, once again a colossus feared by its adversaries and admired by the rest. The deep humiliation of the failed Soviet experiment, the bitter insult of the Baltic states, the Ukraine, Georgia, Azerbaijan, Kazakhstan, and some smaller fry all rushing to shake off Moscow's rule, the weakness of the Yeltsin years, the shame of the 1998 financial collapse, left deep wounds in Russian self-respect. The first priority of politics became to reassert Russian might. It is proving a stretch to do it with inadequate means.

In the service of this ambition, incipient democracy is now giving way to barely veiled dictatorship and covert renationalization of what they call "strategic" resources. Such liberal economists as Gref and Ilianorov, who had directed much of economic policy until recently, have little or no influence left and the winner of the 2008 presidential elections, reputedly already chosen by Mr. Putin, is likely to be an army marshal.

CLAY FEET SHOWING

The perception in the West is that Russia is advancing by leaps and bounds. To a critical eye, the advance is more like hopping along on clay feet. Admittedly, economic growth is proceeding fast at about 6 percent p.a. and has done so since 2000. However, some of this growth is clearly a catching-up after the shrinking during the 1990s. More sobering, though, is that once past the catching-up phase, little or no growth might have occurred if the oil price had stayed at its turn-of-the-century levels. Now, with $60 a barrel, oil money is pouring in and sloshing around the economy, forcing up prices and wages (the latter at a hardly sustainable rate of the order of 15 percent p.a. for industrial wages), sucking in imports, and making nonoil exports uncompetitive. Oil slipping back to $40 or less a barrel would be a nightmare scenario for Russia.

Another weakness, this time actual and not just potential, is the severely strained power generating capacity. Present capacity is 150 gigawatts, still below its Soviet-era peak. This is wholly inadequate. Many industrial companies are now rationed, and in Moscow no new consumer may be connected to the power grid, which has led to new housing being connected in exchange for fabulous bribes.

The root cause is not so much the typical Russian vice of careless, slothful maintenance, but rather the equally typical waste of power brought about by low state-controlled tariffs. The giant state-owned power utility UES, which controls 70 percent of all generating capacity, needs to install 23 gigawatts of new generating capacity by 2010 to meet demand and needs $83 billion to do it. It has neither the money nor the extra supply of natural gas to fuel the new power stations if it contrives to build them. Ironically, it is money and natural gas that Russia is supposed to have most of. The key reason is price control. Controlled prices in most provinces are either just below or just above break-even for "social reasons." Decontrol is promised, but comes slowly. In 2007, only an extra 5 percent of power consumption will be decontrolled.

Meanwhile, UES is seeking investment from abroad. In 2007, it plans to float between five and ten of its constituent companies on the admirably patient and tolerant London Stock Exchange, raising $10 billion. Even that much would not begin to ward off the looming power shortage.

A word needs also to be said about the clay feet of the much-feared giant Gazprom. It is alternating between assurances to Western Europe about how reliable it will be as its principal supplier of natural gas, and flexing its muscles and threatening to restrict supplies if it gets no direct access to the retail market that is more remunerative than bulk contracts. At home, however, it must sell gas at small fractions of export prices, starving itself of investment funds. Consumption at these controlled prices is appallingly wasteful and rising fast. Pipelines are decrepit, poorly maintained, and leaking badly (as do most of the oil pipelines). Gazprom has a monopoly of gas pipelines and exports from Russia, and is categorically refusing European demands to relax it.

Perhaps even more ominous than the rickety economic infrastructure is the biological future of the Russian people itself. Life expectancy, rising virtually everywhere else in the world, has fallen drastically in Russia. The population is already decreasing and a further and faster decline in the next two decades is written into the demographic statistics. Moreover, public health outside select spots is worthy of some poor third-world country.

In this as in so much else, Russia conceals what the now happily defunct Marxist language used to call “internal contradictions” behind a bold front of sham greatness.

THE FRENCH TRAGICOMEDY

The top slice of the French intellectual pyramid is hardly the Mont Blanc in the landscape of the mind. Its own estimation does not quite tally with its real height. But below the self-proclaimed peak, the ordinary Frenchman is surely among the very brightest of fellow Europeans and she no less so. He is quick-witted, sober in judgment, articulate, and both capable and ready to resort to his critical faculty. Yet while the individual Frenchman is mostly well up to the best European standard, the collective intelligence of political France works much like that of a mentally retarded child.

This strange discrepancy has many symptoms. Some of them spring to the foreground on the occasion of the current presidential election campaign. Despite their divergences the lead candidates have one common theme, namely that the indebtedness of the country at 64 percent of the national product is intolerable and must absolutely be reduced. Though above the 60 percent solemnly agreed to at Maastricht, this percentage is not catastrophic. It is its sharp upward trend that should worry families who have children. Despite its natural advantages, the French economy now looks wedded to slow growth—last year's 2 percent compares poorly with the European average of 2.9 and the OECD average of over 4—and it would take great future fiscal rigor to stop indebtedness as a proportion of national product from continuing to rise. Yet while all agree that this trend must be reversed, each candidate is merrily putting forward new spending proposals that would further worsen the deficit by 1.5 to 3 percent of GDP. By way of deficit reduction, they predictably undertake to eliminate "waste," while the lead candidate of the Left enigmatically plans "European solutions" for defense expenditure.

None of this bothers the electorate. The opinion polls testify that it responds favorably *both* to the vows of fiscal rectitude and the profusion of fresh spending proposals.

First published by Liberty Fund, Inc., at www.econlib.org on April 2, 2007. Reprinted by permission.

Of the two front runners, the candidate of the Left swears that she will not raise the share of taxes in GDP above the present 44 percent level. She will offset rebates to the poor by taxing "capital" (an entity that casts no votes). The candidate of the Right would actually try to reduce the share of taxes from 44 to 40 percent over two five-year terms. Both claim that they can pay for their programs by stimulating economic growth. The Right expects to achieve this by inciting everyone to work harder—which would make good sense if the economy were first reformed and the "social" burden weighing it down were at least partly lifted. Proposing that, alas, would be electoral suicide. Instead, fresh spending is the way to go.

The Left explains that by guaranteeing employment to the young, increasing the minimum wage to 1,500 euros ($1,960) a month, and raising the lowest pensions, they will increase consumption and more consumption will bring more growth. Do not we all know that growth can best be stimulated by piling on deadweight costs?

These absurdities, one must say, are not specifically French, but are part and parcel of any political system that lives by "one man, one vote" and has empowered itself to carry out almost any decision the majority will vote for. We call this democracy, and regard it as a good thing. Its capacity for harm is mitigated by the push and pull of rival groups, capital and labor, rich campaign contributors and poor health-care patients cancelling each other out.

However, the French reality is both more tragic and more comic than common garden-variety democracy. It is this tragicomic peculiarity that provides the ground for the present article.

For fourteen years under Mitterrand and twelve under Chirac, all governments leaned left in constructing, completing, and embellishing with bells and whistles the proud "French social model," reputedly the envy of other nations. It had two mainsprings. One was an almost laughably elaborate labor law, a code of over 2,600 pages which came close to giving the worker a *right* to his job. By making it very difficult to fire, it has spread a fear of hiring.

The other, and probably more destructive, mainspring of the "model" was a comprehensive system of insurance against sickness, old age, and unemployment, financed mainly by paying workers only about 55 percent of their earnings in cash and (by legal fiat and with union complicity) withholding the remaining 45 percent, calling it "employers' and employees' contributions" to social insurance. This was a paternalistic reversal to the old and discredited system of paying wages in kind instead of cash, not with a real intention of defrauding anybody, but to impose "social" values by forcing employees to accept insurance in lieu of cash. As a result, labor the worker would have done for 80 or 90 cost the employer 100, with predictable effects on the demand for labor. French unemployment in 2006 was still close to 10 percent. This is the tragic side of the French tragicomedy.

The comic side is the length to which the *rights* of the unemployed have been pushed. For instance, genuine or self-styled actors, actresses, and other show-business personnel are entitled to year-long unemployment pay if they can prove just a few days of paid employment—a proof that can be procured for a little love or money. It should surely cause no surprise that over the thirteen years of the scheme, the show-business population drawing benefits from it grew from 41,000 to 104,000 and its cost rose fivefold.

Unemployment pay presupposes previous employment that has been lost. However, people who have never had a job had also to be looked after, and the "social model" was accordingly widened. Jobless over-twenty-fives gained an entitlement to "insertion pay." Starting with 400,000, their number reached 1,100,000 in 2006, costing 5.9 billion euros—not a vast sum, but symptomatic of how a good intention can succeed a little too well.

Other countries whose "social model" was also mainly financed by compulsory payroll deductions, notably Sweden and Germany, have woken up to where it all led and have pushed through politically difficult reforms to good effect. In France, this was not done, in part because M. Chirac declared the "social model" sacrosanct, "Anglo-Saxon" liberalism as bad as communism, and always dreaded confronting the unions. A deeper reason, though, was the "retarded child" mentality of French collective opinion.

There is a subconscious belief in France that the state does not pay Paul by taking the money from Peter. It just *gives it* to Paul, and Peter is not made worse off. This is so because the money sits in an imaginary reservoir and the state can "unblock" it (*débloquér* is the French word used to describe this happy event). Consequently, when a group gets a costly favor, when "generosity" prevails toward the needy, and when 35,000 young people are hired to oversee schoolchildren and dissuade them from running riot, some gain and nobody loses. The money needed has been "unblocked" and that, surely, is what public money was for. There is always enough left in the reservoir, waiting to be *débloqué.*

This amazing failure to understand the realities of public finance—indeed, to understand reality—explains why in France the move of one pressure group to grab resources or "rights" is hardly ever countered by the resistance of other pressure groups that would have to bear the cost. Polls say that endlessly recurring rail strikes are approved by the majority of commuters who suffer great inconvenience from them. When tobacconists claim, and get, compensation for falling cigarette sales, everyone thinks that this is the least the state can do, and when imports make food too cheap, it is thought only fair to French farmers for the state to make it dear again. In the process, France, potentially so rich, is becoming a poor country "trying to travel first class on a second-class ticket" and feeling bewildered that the attempt does not quite work.

HOW THE FRENCH "SOCIAL MODEL" COULD SELF-DESTRUCT

Nearly everyone in France is proud of the "French social model," if only because it is so different from the hated and feared "ultraliberal Anglo-American" ways. For a people of high average intelligence, the French ignorance and credulity about the outside world is often staggering. Lurid tales about the misery of working people in Britain and the cruel lack of health care and poverty relief in America are avidly lapped up and much satisfaction is felt that such horrors are safely warded off by the pride of progressive France, the most caring and universal "social model" ever realized.

The principal achievement of this "model" is that it has maintained unemployment at about 10 percent since it was fully unfolded in the 1980s and looks like maintaining it around this level in the years to come. To this somewhat doctored figure should be added another 1–1.5 percent in make-believe employment funded with public subventions, and 1.2 million mostly young people not eligible for unemployment who receive a minimum income of about $400 a month. Regular visitors to France testify that they see more beggars on the streets than ever. However, French opinion from the presidential and ministerial level downward is convinced that unemployment and poverty are the result of "the Crisis" (there is always some undefined crisis going on in the outside world, and France is always its victim). The "social model" is not its cause; rather, it serves as the bulwark against it.

THE REVOLT OF THE IDLE

With the model at cruising speed, an average of a mere 80 parked vehicles a night are burnt by small street gangs in search of a kick. At

First published as "Urban Riots: How the French 'Social Model' Could Self-Destruct," by Liberty Fund, Inc., at www.econlib.org on January 9, 2006. Reprinted by permission.

30,000 vehicles per annum, the loss is hardly remarked. When last November the nightly burnings hit a peak of 1,400 vehicles, not to speak of the (partial) burning of 255 schools and kindergartens, 233 town halls and other public buildings, and even a church as the gangs competed with each other for reputation and television coverage, stoning firemen and battling the police, the "social model" was manifestly running in top gear. The police made 4,700 arrests, though they could secure only six hundred prison sentences from notoriously left-leaning magistrates who would "see no evil, hear no evil" and let the rest go for lack of evidence.

After the mutual exhaustion of rioters and the police brought things back to dismal normalcy, frenzied efforts got under way to explain, and explain away, what had happened. The intelligentsia of the Left Bank concluded that the riots were a very understandable protest against "social exclusion" in the high-rise ghettoes on the outskirts of Paris and other big cities where mostly second-generation descendants of Arab and black immigrants are cooped up, crushed by inequality and racial discrimination. The trigger of the broad revolt was allegedly pulled by the maverick minister of the interior, a suspected "ultraliberal," who unforgivably called some of the rampaging youths "riff-raff" and "scum."

This version of the story is mostly arrant nonsense, highfalutin rhetoric, and axe-grinding. The obvious reason for the flare-up is that a mass of closely packed young males living in almost total idleness, with their most likely prospect being continued idleness as far in the future as they can look, is as unstable as some kinds of high explosive. To be made to get up in the morning, wear clean clothes, do work involving reasonable physical exertion, forced to speak articulate French instead of the slurred *argot* they use to demarcate themselves, would liberate them from their deadly boredom and make them employable. However, putting them through such a cure would involve coercion, would "degrade and stigmatize them," and is politically unthinkable.

THE CURSE OF FUTILE EDUCATION

There is one sacred purpose, though, for which coercion is not only permissible, but an actual virtue, and that is compulsory education to the age of sixteen in what is arguably the world's most rigid, standardized, self-willed, exacting, yet ineffective system of public education. Dozens of books have been written about the decline and degradation of the once-glorious French state schools due to a mixture of political cowardice, egalitarian dreams, union tyranny, and silly dogmas. The single-minded aim of the French public school is to push 80 percent of final-year students through the *baccalauréat,* an examination in abstract subjects. Every graduate of the "bac" is entitled to a place at a university, and those who do not get some kind of diploma or degree are seen as failures or dropouts. Stooping to a blue-collar job is considered humiliating and a waste of precious education.

The net effect is a flood of unemployable psychologists, sociologists, law and arts graduates whose learning, such as it is, is of no use to anyone and most of whom are destined to live on unemployment benefits and in permanent boredom. Children of colored immigrants have even worse chances for reasons I will come to presently.

At the same time, there is all over the country a chronic shortage of plumbers, electricians, masons, carpenters, gardeners, repairmen, and handymen. Master artisans will not employ help because of the fear of paperwork and the fear of not being able to lay off the employee if need be.

The bane of an ambitious but deeply misguided education has been tragicomically illustrated after the November riots by what is not an apocryphal anecdote but a true story. Faced with 25 percent youth unemployment (reaching 50 percent in the "sensitive" suburbs that have rioted), and with a great shortage of blue-collar skills, the premier Mr. de Villepin announced that henceforth fourteen-year-olds would be allowed to become apprentices and not be forced to attend school until they turned sixteen. The teachers' unions produced the expected sound and fury about equality of opportunity and the socialist parties the expected condemnation of humiliation and leaving children to fend for themselves. What was shockingly unexpected was the reaction of the employers. One of their spokesmen apologetically explained that it is really quite important for apprentices to be able to read and write, and therefore it might be a little unwise to let them leave school at fourteen. A glowing tribute, this, to the results achieved by French state education that, incidentally, consumes one-quarter of the budget of central and local government and is perpetually and stridently asking for more as the number of school-age children is falling.

DO THE RIOTS PREDICT DECLINE OR BREAKDOWN?

The failure of "antielitist" universal education to teach pupils to read and write, let alone to spell and do sums—and above all to behave—is shared by many nations. The bias against blue-collar occupations shown by the educational establishment and the "culture" that surrounds it, and its overproduction of hopeless aspirants for white-collar careers that society cannot offer, is more particularly French and is an obvious source of bitterness and instability. Second-generation Arab and black youths are the worst affected by it. This looks like discrimination on grounds of race. The government rejects affirmative action as contrary to the precepts of equality. Instead, it is throwing money it has not got at "social housing" to thin out the ghettoes, it promises to double the teaching staff at the worst schools, and it will recruit for state jobs preferentially from the rebellious suburbs.

Some of the devices it is grasping at border on the pathetic. A prize example is the attempt to promote, and perhaps to make mandatory, the anonymous job application. The CV must not contain the name, age, sex, and address of the applicant to stop employers discriminating against Arabs, blacks, and also whites living in the suburbs that are politely called "sensitive." Employers are very unlikely to recruit anonymous applicants and would certainly find ways to get round such a measure, but the government can at least say that it is trying.

When unemployment is as high as the "social model" makes it, thanks to its top-heavy social insurance premiums which raise wage costs to the employer way above the take-home pay employees must get, many things start going awry in a society. One of them is discrimination: employers will recruit, if they recruit at all, among candidates about whom they know the most, who have credible sponsors and are within easy reach. Discrimination against Arabs and blacks will stop when unemployment decreases and the labor market reaches equilibrium—an outcome blocked by the elaborate barrier of the much-touted "French model."

The three weeks of mayhem in November 2005 had little or nothing to do with Islam, ethnicity, misery, and not much with the drug trade, except insofar as such things will thrive better when unemployment breeds hopelessness and boredom. The rebellion had no leaders, was spontaneous and chaotic.

It did damage France's reputation as a civilized tourist destination, but its direct material cost was a fleabite. It was, however, a warning signal that all is far from well with the French "social model." The chances are that the smallish explosion of November 2005 will not be followed by a much bigger breakdown within a few years. The most likely scenario is still that the country will continue to decline relatively smoothly. The remaining, smaller probability that the "model" will self-destruct, however, has become distinctly more visible since the riots.

A LITTLE BIT OF HISTORY REPEATING

Happy days are here again! Eager commentators hopefully speculate that, after a trial run last November confined to big-city outskirts, a nationwide replay of May 1968 is unfolding in France. You have to hand it to the young, to labor union officialdom, and to the left-leaning media: They are trying hard enough to make it happen.

The background story is quickly told. French unemployment has been rising for thirty years in uncanny lockstep with the building of the welfare state. At a shade under 10 percent—though that figure is doctored with a succession of state-assisted employment schemes—it is the second-highest rate in Europe. For people under twenty-five it is at 23 percent, Europe's highest rate. Net job creation in 2004 was zero and in 2005 between 50,000 and 145,000, depending on the method of computation. A healthy economy of France's size should generate over 300,000 net new jobs a year. But that is just a distant dream.

As rising unemployment menaced existing jobs, there was a rising clamor for ever tighter job protection. French society was unanimous in its belief that more "workers' rights" are always better than less, and after a spurt during the 1930s Popular Front and another after World War II, the legislative machine in the Mitterrand and Chirac years has again been churning out endless reams of job-protection laws. The French labor code is now 2,632 pages long and is an object of socialist pride. Public opinion—even right of center, let alone to the left of it—seems strangely unable to grasp what these 2,632 pages are really doing to French society.

Chronic unemployment in the euro-zone has two main causes, the "wedge" and job protection. The wedge is the excess cost of labor that the employer pays over to various social-insurance schemes, over the pretax pay he pays to his employee. This wedge, providing some security against "social" risks, acts as a payment in kind to the employee.

First published in the *Wall Street Journal Europe,* March 24–26, 2006. Reprinted by permission.

But payment in kind is typically valued less than payment in cash. In other words, the cash cost to the employer is always greater than its worth to the employee. This dead weight depresses employment.

Job protection acts differently but no less viciously. It accords ownership rights to the worker in his job, which the employer can only redeem or undo at a cost and by providing justification. The justification may or may not be accepted by the special labor courts (*prud'hommes*) where union representatives sit on the bench. Even if the grounds for laying off an employee are accepted, an expensive "social plan" may be imposed on the employer. Resolving the case may take many months of litigation by platoons of labor lawyers. As common sense could have predicted, the upshot is that prudent managers do not fill vacant jobs and do not stick their necks out to create new ones.

FIRST JOBS

It was to tear a rent in this straitjacket paralyzing the job market that French prime minister Dominique de Villepin proposed the "first-job contract." The contract would allow an employer to dismiss a worker who was under twenty-five and had never been employed at the time of his hiring, without providing grounds, during the first two years of the contract. The indignation was furious, the stamping of feet earsplitting, and the arguments against the new law simply wondrous. No one said that half a loaf might be better than no bread. Instead, it was hammered home that the government was taking away the bread that French youth deserved and offering them a precarious and paltry half loaf in exchange. Surely, most commentators argue with a serious face, an insecure two years is not much of a future for the young, and it is wicked to deny them the safe, permanent jobs they ought to be offered.

As I write this, French students, egged on by the main teachers' unions, are shrieking defiance and taking to the streets like ducks to water. Many university campuses are blockaded and some damaged. The two most radical general labor unions, CGT and FO, darkly mutter about a "general strike." Politicians on the left issue solemn warnings, while some on the right are clearly frightened and propose tame compromises. Knowingly or unwittingly, all are doing their bit to bring on May 1968 all over again.

The 2,632 pages of the French labor code suit admirably the 90 percent of the working population whose jobs are made supposedly safe by it, though no one can say how long those jobs will remain safe. There is a conspiracy theory that holds that the 90 percent of employed "insiders" cynically sacrifice the 10 percent of unemployed "outsiders" on the altar of their own job security, while loudly lamenting the sad and hopeless fate of the young. Plausible as this may sound, I believe it is false, as conspiracy theories usually are. Anecdotal evidence suggests that the "insiders" are just as incapable of grasping the elementary laws of economics as the youngest and greenest "outsiders." They really believe that if the government wants to, it can provide nice permanent jobs to the young instead of trashy temporary ones.

FRENCH FURY

There is a legend, dating from the Napoleonic Wars, about "French fury" that may have had a grain of truth in it. However, in time it has become political gospel on the right, and this is having grave consequences. President Jacques Chirac, in particular, is deeply convinced that in France violence must not be deterred and punished by violence, for that would bring the whole political house crashing down. Reform can only be attempted by dialogue, and if that does not work it must be deferred.

Having learned that the stamping of feet is soon enough met with capitulation, the French have become increasingly intractable, violent, and uncompromising. French fury is now a reality and could only be educated out of public mores with harsh and prolonged retaliation, for which nobody has the stomach. Other nations muddle on; the French shriek and gesticulate and end up staying in the same place.

THERE IS NO FRENCH EXCEPTION

For a country whose political elite is singularly impervious to economics, and much of whose public viscerally loathes capitalism and liberalism as "Anglo-Saxon" perversions, France has made uncharacteristic progress these past few years toward accepting the way the world works. But for all this progress, certain fundamentals remain intact. Intact above all is the compulsion to believe and assert that France is different, a brilliant exception.

Such convictions were evident in Prime Minister Lionel Jospin's address last week to the congress of world socialist leaders. Mr. Jospin distanced himself from his British and German colleagues who would dilute socialism by modernizing it. He conceded that the "market economy" is a superior instrument of wealth creation. But, he said, the market is mindless, blind, it lurches along without knowing where it is going. Politics must regulate it, give it a firm direction for the common good. Such ideas reflect the fallacy, so alluring to the economically semiliterate, that the production and distribution of wealth are separate and independent of each other.

FORTUITOUS TRENDS

Recent economic trends—growth along with a rapid expansion of the welfare state—are only reinforcing the belief in French exceptionalism. During the presidencies of Valéry Giscard d'Estaing and François Mitterrand, the headlong extension of the French welfare state went hand in hand with ever more sluggish economic growth. France moved near the head of the European unemployment and taxation leagues. Some socialist intellectuals even began openly to say that unemployment is the price the country had to pay for social justice, a price it mitigated by looking after its jobless. The "Anglo-Saxon," "neo" or "ultra" liberal

First published in the *Wall Street Journal Europe,* November 15, 1999. Reprinted by permission.

model, by contrast, buys higher growth and lower unemployment at the price of latent inequality and insecurity.

But coinciding with the advent of Lionel Jospin's coalition government of Socialists, Communists, and Greens, the tide started to turn in 1997. Though the share of national product preempted by public spending stayed at about one-half—one of the highest levels in the world—economic growth accelerated to about 2.5 percent per year from near zero, and the jobless rate, as measured in the official statistics, declined slightly to 11.2 percent from 12.6 percent. This took place while the welfare state was further extended by such measures as the guaranteed minimum income—in sharp contrast to the attempts of Britain, Germany, and Italy to curb the excesses in welfare provision that accumulated over the past three decades. Perhaps, it seemed, the *exception Française* would turn out to be more than just self-flattery.

Privately, even some left-leaning French experts recognize that a rising tide lifts every boat. But as the French economy rides a general upswing in Europe, the government is piling ever more ballast onto French enterprise. The heaviest ballast is undoubtedly the reduction of the workweek to 35 from 39 hours, tantamount to an increase of some 11 percent in wage costs. Though partly offset by side-agreements allowing more flexibility in the workplace, and partly financed by government assistance, this increase can only reduce employment below what it would otherwise be. Only in France can it seriously be argued that it would actually increase employment.

Perhaps less headline-catching than the 35-hour week is the rising pitch of anticapitalist discourse in both government circles and the media, excited by the spectacle of large stock-market gains and Anglo-American style takeover battles. The market can be suffered to create wealth, but only tamely, without the gainers gaining too much and without anyone being the loser. This schoolmasterly stance reaches beyond mere words into the regulation of the daily business of life, sometimes in grotesque forms.

Recently a large dairy farmers' cooperative in northern France applied for *permission* to lay off seventy-eight workers in one of its processing units. From the government inspector of labor relations, the matter went to the industrial court of Amiens, which refused permission on the ground that the layoffs were designed not just to safeguard competitiveness, but actually to enhance it—improving financial performance at the expense of employment. The judgment has been appealed, but whichever way the case eventually goes, it and similar judgments reflect the deeply ingrained French conviction that enterprises exist for their employees and letting enterprises make profits is at best a grudging concession to an ugly world that we must strive to change.

Firms are expected to hire but are not free to fire. Neighboring Spain realized a few years ago that if firing is made too difficult, firms will shy away from the risk of hiring, and even the Spanish labor unions supported the abolition of these controls—with gratifying results for all. France still seems to believe that the way to increase employment is to permit additions but prohibit subtractions, and that dividing the available amount of work among more people by having each work shorter hours is the mathematically surest recipe of all.

Yet France is being menaced by threats that look mundane, but against which there is ultimately no defense. They will, in due course, wrench the control of events from the Socialist leadership and prove that after all you cannot have it both ways.

One, simple and inexorable, is tax competition that is gradually depriving the government of means commensurate with its ambitions. At the present levels of taxation and regulation, there is already a serious drain of capital, brains, and enterprising spirit from France to other countries. Repeated French attempts to build a high-tax cartel by imposing tax harmonization within the European Union have so far largely failed, are likely to go on failing, and would not fully stop the flight of capital and talent from France even if they succeeded.

The other threat is posed by France's increasingly untenable public-pension system. Like every other Western country and Japan, the French are sitting on a demographic time bomb due to a changing balance between the active and the retired population. By 2005, the squeeze will start in earnest, as there are fewer working citizens to support a burgeoning population of retirees. But the French pension system, which like Social Security in the U.S. is a pay-as-you-go scheme, is headed for insolvency. Worse still, France has virtually no supplementary funded retirement schemes that accumulate capital in pension funds.

The radical remedy is an initially painful switch from pay-as-you-go to funded pensions, a switch that Chile performed with resounding success a decade ago. In France, however, such a switch is as good as unthinkable. Pay-as-you-go is a French Socialist ideal, the expression of solidarity between generations and a liberation of the old from the servitudes of saving and scraping to avert misery. The French labor unions, too, have an unshakable vested interest in it, for they run the system and obtain great powers of patronage from it. The government knows that the time bomb is ticking. The Charpin report, which it commissioned, recently confirmed this. Mr. Jospin met the dilemma by confidently declaring that it was not as grave as all that.

ADDING INSULT TO INJURY

Ironically, the French socialist government is not only losing control over its "model" because the country does not have and does not want private pension funds. It is also losing control because other countries do want and have them. Between a third and two-fifths of the hundred largest listed French enterprises are owned by nonresident investors, primarily American, British, and other foreign pension funds. This is adding insult to injury. Not only are these investors the hated pension funds, but they are also "Anglo-Saxon."

What's more, many of them are abandoning their traditional passivity and are now starting to exert an influence on the management of the French companies whose stock they hold. French managers who used to run to the Ministry of Finance and Industry for approval of some major corporate move now run to Wall Street and the City of London to solicit the favor of investment institutions. This is both a blow to French pride and a serious obstacle to running the country the Socialist way. Yet France cannot afford to buy back its blue-chip corporations, cannot chase off foreign investors, and cannot expropriate them without making itself into a pariah state.

The question thus arises: Will anyone think, in a few years' time, that the French can have it both ways?

THE HOBBLING OF PRIVATE FRANCE

In the lengthening list of French scandals involving money and influence-peddling—whose perpetrators tend to come to little harm—the case of Jacques Attali is among the least grave but the truest to form.

Mr. Attali was, and remains, a leading "ideas man" of the Socialist Party, having authored some thirty or so books about every imaginable subject, but mainly about what passes for philosophy and economics in Paris. He's also a most agile denizen of the corridors of power.

Fairly early in his career, he was found to have lifted large chunks from Ernst Juenger's *Hourglass* and deposited them into his own 1982 work, *History of Time,* without the benefit of quotation marks or attribution. Anywhere else, plagiarism of such audacity would have earned him derision and dishonor first, obscurity afterward. In France, people just shrugged. His publishers went on publishing him. A confidant and close aide of then president François Mitterrand, Attali continued to enjoy an ever-growing role and influence.

When he got too close to Mitterrand for the latter's comfort, he was kicked upstairs into one of the prize positions in the international bureaucracy. His alleged lavish spending of public money for private luxuries, serious questions about his expense account and about his reign in general, finally led to his resignation as head of the European Bank for Reconstruction and Development. Opinion outside France regarded him with outrage, within France with indulgent indifference. The scandals at the EBRD have done him no more harm than the earlier plagiarism. Though belonging to a Socialist Party clan that's not exactly at the center of power at the moment, he is still part of the political establishment. Most recently, he has been advising the government on how to reform the country's elite graduate schools.

First published in the *Wall Street Journal Europe,* April 4, 2000. Reprinted by permission.

COLLECTIVIST SUBMISSIVENESS

Mr. Attali's invulnerability to discredit and dishonor is not untypical of the way France, in contrast to most other civilized countries, treats its public men. No illusions are harbored about their devotion to the common good, no high standards are set for their probity. It is well understood that sitting on the seats of power confers privileges, and believed that honesty in a politician changes things only marginally if at all. There is in France an astonishing readiness to treat the arrogance and corruption of the ruling elites with indulgence and the exorbitant weight and authority of the state with acquiescence and indeed with positive approval. This collectivist submissiveness of a people that likes to think of itself as individualist is odd. Why does the private France so willingly put up with the public one?

For private France is bright, has better than average skills, taste, and manners, and a civilized life style. It is sober, thrifty, and hard-working. Despite its limited understanding of the outside world, it is doing remarkably well in international competition. Labor relations are as good in the private sector as they are ghastly in the public one. The private France carries on its back a largely parasitic political authority that maintains its power by extensive redistribution, siphoning off and spending half of what the private France produces. Costly social provisions bring forth the national shame of chronic double-digit unemployment. The unemployed, living on the dole, swell the battalions of public France, securing a built-in majority for ever more social provision. All this private France must bear.

There are deep historical roots of the enduring relation between a burden-bearing and yet vital private, and a parasitic public, France. Power in France has been gravitating from the provinces to the center, from subject to king, at least since the thirteenth century. Cardinal Duprat, the Duke de Sully, Cardinal Richelieu, and Jean-Baptiste Colbert are but the outstanding names in an unbroken line of strong centralizing ministers. When the country was bled white and impoverished by the wars of Louis XIV, a potential turning point and a revolutionary situation was reached. State power under Louis XV and XVI began to weaken. It was at this point that the wrong turn was taken. While the English revolution of 1688 and the American one of 1775 shifted power from the king to the individual, the French Revolution of 1789, whether by accident or by "historical necessity," did the exact opposite. With great violence, the revolution forced society back into the great and age-old centralizing, collectivist mold of the Valois and the previous Bourbons. There have since been no independent structures of countervailing private power in France; the monopoly of state power is undisputed.

History dealt one further blow to the chances of a freer society emerging in France. From the late seventeenth century to its final defeat at Waterloo in 1815, France fought a second Hundred Years' War for supremacy in Europe (which at that time meant world supremacy). This autocratic design, pursued by a great administration and great armies, was cruelly frustrated by the ships and the money of prosaic England, the incipient liberal free-trader.

Craving greatness and admiration, the French have never forgiven the English and perhaps never will. For some obvious and some less obvious reasons, this resentment was soon extended to America. The need to rely on English and American help in two world wars has not helped matters either. Much of the antipathy against the "Anglo-Saxons" is reflexive, visceral, and hardly conscious. Its effect, however, is that "Anglo-Saxon" ways are automatically opposed as a matter of patriotic self-assertion, and "liberalism" has become a near-obscenity.

FOISTING FREE TRADE

With a straight face, Maurice Allais, the only French Nobel Prize–winning economist, has asserted in a recent series of articles that the cause of unemployment is the trade liberalization that he says has been foisted upon France since 1975. With an equally straight face, others (though, to give them credit, not all economists) assert that the compulsory shortening of the workweek will reduce unemployment. Liberal arguments and policy proposals are seldom understood, let alone accepted, in this environment.

The effect of having a huge, monopolistic state hovering above civil society, feeding on it, yet being accepted by it, is manifold and often veiled. Some aspects, though, stand out clearly enough. There is, as Marxists like to put it, an "internal contradiction" between the private and the public personality of the country. The private one would like to get on with its life, prosper as modern countries with reasonably free economies generally do, keep what it earns, be rid of the intellectual terrorism of political correctness, and send its children to decent schools of its own choice.

This same private France clings however to obsolete beliefs about the indispensable role of the state in protecting national independence from the evil forces of global caplitalism and wants the state to see to it that the weak are not "trampled under" by the strong. This mission is concocted from second-rate theories, but the first-rate ones do not go down well in France. Once the mission is entrusted to the state, up springs the public France, subjecting all to the priorities of *dirigisme* and its attempts at redistribution.

Swept along by the present worldwide upswing, France for the time being manages to eat its cake and have it too. It makes some inglorious U-turns but comes to no major grief. No law of nature tells us that this talented country cannot go on muddling through, "internal contradictions" notwithstanding. It is a fair conjecture, however, that anything better than muddling through can emerge only from a passage through the purgatory of failure, humiliation, and disgust. It was this type of experience that led to the rejection of dysfunctional political regimes in Britain in 1979, the United States in 1980, and the Soviet ex-satellites in 1989. Does one always have to put one's hope on despair and calamity?

PART 4

The Capitalism They Hate

THE CAPITALISM THEY HATE

THE INEQUALITY MACHINE

Freedom of contract is inexorably followed by streams of voluntary exchanges and a widening division of labor. Individual ownership of the goods exchanged and of the factors that produce them completes the necessary conditions of the capitalist system. It is easy to grasp that this system must ceaselessly generate unequal distributions of income and wealth and also that these distributions will not settle down to any particular durable pattern.

Unequal distributions spring from two sources. One is inequality of endowments, inherited or acquired. Talent, force of character, strength of will, industry, and thrift may be genetically implanted or learned; knowledge, a "network" of friends, acquaintances, and patrons, and command over capital and credit may be inherited or acquired. Some of these differential endowments can in principle be destroyed or leveled out by forcible collective action. Capital, for one, may be confiscated and held in "social ownership" or redistributed equally. Knowledge may be more equally spread by setting up a universal and "anti-elitist" educational apparatus. Most endowments, however, cannot be eliminated or equalized and will inevitably produce unequal incomes and possessions. However, even if in some utopia all individual endowments could, by clever legal, fiscal, educational, and technical devices, be flattened out, there would still remain one generator of inequality, probably the most powerful of all, namely luck. It is by definition random; it rides roughshod over government policies as well as over personal merit and desert. If nothing else made for inequality, luck alone would suffice to keep the great Inequality Machine of capitalism churning out a kaleidoscopic pattern of incomes and wealth, in which any advantage gained would provide means for further advantage, helping the rich to become richer.

First published as part 1, "The Inequality Machine," and part 2, "Indecent Earnings," of "The Capitalism They Hate," by Liberty Fund, Inc., at www.econlib.org on February 5, 2007, and March 5, 2007. Reprinted by permission.

Dislike of inequality may have many motives. Some ascribe it to the genetic heritage of humanoids and preagriculture humans, for whom equal sharing may have been a good survival strategy for one's genes—though it has become an obsolete and inferior strategy since man has learned to grow and store food for himself and his family. Others, plausibly enough, trace the roots of egalitarianism to plain envy. Be that as it may, the expectation of gain from the flattening out of the distribution would always serve as an egalitarian incentive for all with below-the-mean income or wealth. However, none of these motives is really avowable; none sounds unselfish or noble enough.

Charitably screening any such naked opportunism from open view, educated opinion has put up the moral imperative of "social justice," whose runaway success in academic and other intellectual circles in the last half century is a sad illustration of how easily gaseous concepts and pompous jargon overcome straightforward logic. Instead of saying that many desire equality for a variety of more or less respectable reasons, we must now say that inequality is unjust—a very different proposition.

(A little thought reveals an awkward feature of "social justice theory." If, by some miracle, complete equality were once brought about, social justice would still not be satisfied, for it can never be. It would at that point require the creation of new income inequalities in order to achieve equality of some other welfare criterion, e.g., utility levels. However, since nobody knows or can ever discover anybody's utility level, to affirm that they are now equal is no more valid than to affirm that further income inequalities are required to make them equal. Any distribution could be found unjust on some ground and such a finding would be no less valid than any other. This insight highlights one of the pathetic infirmities of social justice, namely that it has no rules by which a socially just state of affairs could ever be identified. Trying vainly to capture it, the foolish carousel can keep going round and round forever.)

At all events, thanks to social justice "theory," capitalism as the great Inequality Machine, stands guilty of spreading injustice all over the social landscape. From 1917 to 1989, the social and economic disaster that was the Soviet empire served as the great excuse that made most sober-minded people forgive capitalism's sins. Capitalism delivered the goods, and socialism did not. This was very nearly a knockdown argument. Attempts at building social-democratic halfway houses in which one can have it both ways have had indifferent success. As the dynamics of the welfare state are coming to be better understood, these attempts carry less and less conviction. Yet, as the hopelessness of "real existing" socialism fades from immediate memory, and as it is being taken quite blithely for granted that no matter what, capitalism will always deliver the goods whether we prize or blame it, opinion toward it is becoming less forgiving.

"Globalization," or rather its great acceleration in recent decades, has made forgiveness harder to grant. If the world economy were made up of many well-insulated compartments, the Inequality Machine would soon neutralize itself by starting to work in two opposing ways. Once capitalism took hold and the rate of capital accumulation exceeded the rate of growth of the active population, the rich would no longer become richer as the poor became poorer. Instead, with the supply of labor expanding less fast than the demand for it, both the rich and the poor would become richer, but the poor would become richer a bit faster, offsetting some of the extra inequality resulting from the rich having more capital working for them. The net effect would depend on the actual numbers and on the pace of technological change, but it is a fair conjecture that no Marxian "iron law" would rule the scene.

When, however, the compartments open up, this equilibrating effect may be much retarded. Goods are generally distant from where they are most wanted (or effectively employed), namely distant in time and in space. The distance in time may be overcome by borrowing from the future, and the cost of doing so is shown in the spectrum of interest rates augmented by some risk premium attaching to the borrowing. Today's moderate interest rates and more particularly the unusually low risk premiums reduce the cost of overcoming distance in time, and make the economy more open to a wider range of choices. Distance in space is overcome by incurring transport costs and the communications costs of sending instructions and making payments.

To judge by the persistent widening of the range of tradable goods and of long-distance trade, the development of transport technology and communications may have been faster than the technology of production, and this development seems recently to have accelerated. The shrinking of time and space probably accounts for the greater part of "globalization," dwarfing the effect of lower tariffs and weaker nontariff barriers to trade.

Quickening globalization in recent decades has impacted inequality in the developed economies of the Western world in two ways. The return on capital has increased and so has the share of capital in national income. Concurrently, the rate of increase in the real wages of the semiskilled and the unskilled has slowed down or, in some areas, stopped altogether. The joint effect accounts for the widely voiced impression that the rich are getting richer and the poor poorer, though the latter part of the diagnosis is not really correct. The impression is in any case strong enough to condemn severely the Inequality Machine for sacrificing the middle and lower working classes on the altar of free trade, and to lend urgency to demands for protection of all kinds.

Some defenders of globalization argue that it is not the opening up of economic compartments that causes the unskilled and semiskilled to be left behind, but labor-saving technological progress. Even admitting that technological change is nearly always labor-saving and hardly ever capital-saving, its supposed effect on the supply-demand balance in the labor market is conjectural. It can lead to the conjecture that a run of labor-saving innovations could push the level of wages crashing down unless generous unemployment pay is offered to those who will not work for lower wages. However, recent economic history suggests that chronic unemployment is more typical of welfare states obsessed with social justice than of countries where labor-saving information technology has made the fastest progress.

The most plausible explanation of stagnating or slowly rising wages in the Western world is that globalization is indeed the culprit. The elasticity of supply of labor in Western economies has been drastically increased by the addition to their labor force of hundreds of millions of Chinese, Indian, and Indonesian workers who have for practical purposes become part of the Western labor market due to the vastly reduced cost of bringing their output to Western product markets. There is, as yet, no matching increase in the supply of capital, even though its accumulation has accelerated somewhat. Elementary reasoning leads one to expect that income distribution in the West will tilt in favor of capital. The facts bear out this expectation. The Inequality Machine of capitalism is guilty as charged.

What this judgment conveniently fails to notice is that globalization is global. Income distribution is changing not only in Western Europe and North America in the wake of shrinking transport and communications costs, but also in China, India, and Indonesia. Third-world employment is expanding rapidly, labor is migrating from the subsistence to the market economy, and its wages, starting from an abysmal level, are catching up with first-world levels at a double-digit annual rate. The factor price equalization theorem is hard at work thanks to the fusion of insulated compartments into an open world economy. Here, the Inequality Machine is producing more equality on a colossal scale by lifting the Eastern very poor to near the level of the Western poor. Nothing else, no development program, no "war on poverty," no humanitarian campaign is in sight that would be remotely capable of doing the job. The envious and the morally indignant may hate capitalism for making the rich richer, but would they rather have the very poor remain very poor?

INDECENT EARNINGS

At the end of 2006, a year of which the financial services industry had little reason to complain, the head of Wall Street's most prominent investment bank was rewarded with a bonus of $40 million. Some less prominent houses gave their heads bonuses ranging from $20 to $50 million. Very successful security or commodity traders were given twice or thrice the bonus of their own chief executives.

Promoter-managers of what are, in most cases quite misleadingly, called "hedge funds" (for few of them really hedge anything) who take 1 percent off the bottom year in, year out and 20 percent of gains off the top had no reason to complain either. Their investors ran greater-than-average risks, but most of them were fairly well rewarded by the 80 percent of the gains going to them. The managers took no risk and their 20 percent share made some of them a very large fortune in a single year.

Some top corporate executives, in fact employees of the shareholders, received compensations in the low to middle eight figures for loss of office, in addition to their pensions, when asked to make room for someone else. Golden handshakes were 24-karat, often awarded by board committees whose members were acting by the Kantian rule: Do as you would be done by.

Promoters of private equity funds, unlike directors of publicly held corporations, have great freedom to operate with borrowed capital and are indeed encouraged by their investors to run high risks by using high leverage. By good judgment and good luck, they usually succeed in making astronomical fortunes for themselves while their investors are adequately but not indecently rewarded for carrying most of the risk.

Part of the public in the United States, and a tiny handful in Europe, contemplates these spectacular earnings with admiring awe. Everyone else considers them indecent. They provoke the most virulent kind of hatred for capitalism.

The reason is not so much the vastness of the sums involved and the glaring inequalities they create, as the great ease with which they seem to come and the perversity of the value system they are supposed to reflect (though there is no reason to suppose that they reflect anything like a value system). Glaring inequalities are as old as history, and though they were occasionally rebelled against, they were not really perceived as indecent, esthetically disgusting, and morally reprehensible. All ancient empires were extremely inegalitarian. The states of ancient Greece appear to have been fairly egalitarian with the king perhaps ten times richer than the shepherd or the fisherman, but in ancient Rome the wealth and income of a rich senator must have been thousands of times greater than that of the proletarian *plebs,* let alone his outdoor slaves. Many of these differences were a matter of hierarchical status and were part of the tacitly accepted established order of things. There is no compelling reason why some of capitalism's inherent inequalities should not in the fullness of time also be so accepted or (more probably) grudgingly acquiesced in, though the reasoning spirit of enlightenment will want to understand why the established capitalist order deserves at least tacit acceptance.

The same forbearance would be much harder to obtain for the inequalities due to "indecent" earnings. One obstacle in the way of their social acceptance is that they accrue to upstarts, fast-talking, fast-moving smoothies who have had too easy a ride to the top. They are too unlike the Dick Whittingtons and the legendary shoeshine boys who overcame adversity and rose by hard work and harder thrift.

But a possibly deeper reason is that there is little or nothing in the "indecent" multimillionaires that strikes the observer as truly entrepreneurial. They do not invent and do not make things that the market might either accept with pleasure or reject with indifference. They take few or no risks, but are parasitic on the risks taken by their investors and clients. Many of them are pure intermediaries, a function whose contribution to the economy is seldom appreciated by the wider public. Others, typically executive board members of large corporations, appear to be abusing the principal-agent relation, and though they do serve their principals, the shareholders, with moderate zeal, they serve first and above all themselves. Paying them with stock options is designed to attenuate the principal-agent problem (and it does resolve it to some extent), but is on the contrary suspected of being a corrupt practice fixed up by crony directors who expect to be similarly fixed up in return.

Most of us react to the decency or otherwise of large incomes and quickly made fortunes by moral reflexes that evolved under the capitalism of a generation or two ago. They have not yet been adjusted to the changes capitalism has since undergone. One such change is the flood tide of pension funds in the Anglo-American type of capitalism which, after all, sets the mode of operation the rest of the world is beginning to imitate. The needs of pension funds and the competition between their managers sets the maximization of asset values as the primary goal, and the more classic goal of profit maximization by corporate enterprise tends to become a mere instrument of the primary goal. Socialists whose rejection of the "system" is visceral rather than intellectual call this "casino capitalism," run by and for "speculators."

An even more far-reaching change is the great increase of financial relative to nonfinancial capital in private ownership. This is no doubt due to ever greater intermediation, which in turn is a by-product of the splitting up of risks and the distribution of different types of risk-bearing instruments among those most willing to carry each particular type. One result is the availability of immense pools of financial capital demanding what by historical standards looks little in the way of risk premium.

How all this leads to "indecent earnings" is clear enough. Corporate assets are now very mobile. They are readily hived off or reassembled. Whole corporations merged with others at the drop of a hat with or without the intervention of private equity firms, often spurred on by advisers eager for commissions. On the whole, this is probably a good thing, as it makes it much easier to redeploy assets from less to more productive uses than was the case only a couple of decades ago. Today, a $2–3 billion merger or acquisition hardly makes the financial columns of the press, and a deal must exceed $20 billion to make real news. Consider a $20 billion deal. The principals on either side are probably prepared to pay some fraction of the deal's value to make doubly and trebly sure that there is no hitch, that nothing has been overlooked, that regulatory problems have been duly considered, and there is no flaw in the documentation. One percent of this deal would be $200 million. In fact, the teams of bankers and the batteries of lawyers will between them probably share a 0.5 percent fee—an absurdly high sum that is absurdly low relative to what an avoidable mistake or a derailed transaction would cost. Competition should keep the fees down, but the need for the advisers to have prestigious names will keep them up.

The outrage roused in the public by such sums being thrown around may stir politicians to action against "indecent" earnings. Capitalism would presumably be less hated, and more assured of survival under majoritarian voting, if such earnings could be outlawed or otherwise wished away. On mature reflection, however, any legislative or regulatory remedy is likely to prove worse than the disease, ultimately leading to evasion, corruption, immobility, and an ever-lengthening series of further measures to correct the perverse effects of their predecessors. The experience made with the Sarbanes-Oxley legislation in a somewhat different domain should serve as a lesson before it is decided to let politics deal with indecent earnings.

The least bad remedy is still to leave it well alone. It is a remedy that, for all its homeopathic modesty, has a shining virtue. Experience shows that people who have made indecently large incomes sooner or later seek to earn the esteem of their fellow men by making correspondingly vast donations to good causes. If anyone is ill tempered and ill informed enough to think that Warren Buffett's gains are indecent, he should be told that the gentleman in question has recently donated $35 billion to charity. All big earners are not like him, but even the most unpleasant characters tend to end up doing the right thing in their testaments, if not sooner. Society has ways of exerting gentle but persistent pressure on the new rich to do good after they have done well and yet leaves them with the satisfaction and good conscience that voluntary benefaction affords them. It is surely best to leave things at that and not wreck the chances of the world's poor by trying to make the very rich less rich.

STRIVING TO GET RICHER AND POORER

Among the "apple pie and motherhood" words, "democracy" shares pride of place with a small and select group of terms signifying uncontested value that nobody in his right senses would call into doubt. Democracy, however, is far more complex in its consequences than most other "value words." It is a mark of poor judgment to accord it instant approval. Democracy has in particular many mutually contradictory consequences in the economic sphere, and it is incumbent on the economist to be at least aware of them.

"Government by the people for the people" is as apt to make them richer as it is liable to make them poorer. That its effects go both ways is not the fault of the government alone, but also of the people who, as the putative masters in this peculiar master-and-servant relation, send perverse signals and instructions to their putative servant. In obeying the people, the government does them much disservice. But it is in the nature of democracy that it has little choice in the matter if it wants to remain in office.

Normally constituted individuals do not deliberately seek to get poorer. The vast majority strive to get richer. For the economist and perhaps for the moralist, too, one undying virtue of democracy is that it lets them strive without brute prohibition, even if, like the beekeeper who lets his bees gather the honey, though it does not let them eat it all, it does interfere with the free disposition of the fruits of human striving. Dictatorships often try, sometimes successfully, to force people to give up striving for prosperity and devote all their efforts to some more or less insane goal they fix for them. Democracy is at least innocent of this sin.

Most economists ascribe further virtues to democracy that positively help people get richer. Such virtues are credited with giving society the rule of law, education, health, and (other) public goods. Each of these boons is contestable and needs a closer look.

First published by Liberty Fund, Inc., at www.econlib.org on June 5, 2006. Reprinted by permission.

To regard the rule of law, surely one of the most crucial positive externalities an economy can possibly enjoy, as a by-product of democracy is simply erroneous and is belied by history. The rule of law has prevailed in England from the end of the seventeenth century onward. It dominated some aspects of civil and even public life in France under the absolute monarchy of the Bourbons. It established itself in Prussia in the eighteenth and in Austria-Hungary in the nineteenth century. None of these countries waited for democracy before submitting to the rule of law. Democracy may produce a favorable climate for the rule of law to take root. However, it does not always do so, as witness some Latin American countries that adopted universal suffrage and majority voting as their means of choosing governments in the second half of the twentieth century. Saying that they are not really democracies because they do not have the rule of law would be to turn the relation of the two into an empty tautology.

DEMOCRATIC EDUCATION

Compulsory instruction of every child in the three R's has strong arguments in its favor, apart from the obvious advantage literacy confers on the individual and the positive externality it represents for society. Compulsion may be excused by the fact that children cannot be asked to choose voluntarily, while voluntary choice by negligent parents may be detrimental to dependent children. Democracy, however, cannot stop at the three R's. Electoral majorities soon come to find it iniquitous that some children's education stops at twelve while others go on till sixteen, eighteen, or, at university level, to their midtwenties. The school-leaving age is thus ratcheted up, the socially very valuable institution of apprenticeship is stifled and often violently condemned by the teachers' unions, and (at least in most of continental Europe) universities are thrown open to all comers with most or all of the cost of tuition being a charge on the community. Selective admission is resented as undemocratic, elitist, and inegalitarian. The result is a serious decline in the quality of higher education, an often unhappy and rebellious student body, a chronic shortage of skilled young entrants to blue-collar trades, and a hopeless surplus of graduates in "soft" subjects where even the unfit are allowed to scrape through and given a useless degree. This involves massive waste of time and resources, but much recent experience suggests that democratic political systems do not tolerate attempts to stop, let alone reverse, these trends. It is as if society were striving to impoverish itself by self-inflicted educational excess.

Nor is universal compulsory health insurance, a typical democratic objective now widely achieved in most European countries, immune from perverse effects. These act at the two ends of the demographic spectrum. Widely accessible health care, including the publicly financed benefits of advancing medical technology, is a major cause of the spectacular lengthening of life expectancy we are witnessing. It would probably not have happened without the spread of majority rule, and we should no doubt regard it as a welcome by-product of democracy. However, so are legalized and widespread abortion and the easy availability of the Pill. Democracy and some social trends that accompany it are at least partly responsible for the falling birthrate that casts a baleful shadow over the future, notably of the German and Italian peoples.

The obvious result is the "ticking time bomb" of increasing numbers of those who are retired and nonworking overwhelming the falling numbers of those who are still of working age. No creative national accounting can undo the fact that one way or another average incomes must fall. This effect can be mitigated by more immigration and a lengthening of the retirement age. However, neither measure is likely to help reelect an aspiring politician.

The provision by government of public goods in a democracy is likely to be more extensive and more costly than under political systems that depend less directly, or not at all, on majority support. The reason is, broadly speaking, that while everybody has a free-rider incentive to throw the cost of public goods on the community as a whole, it is only under majority voting that the free-rider can enforce his wish to ride free by voting for more public goods. The government cannot avoid bowing to this wish even if it leads to disproportionate spending. (Deficits, as we know, are a charge on future generations who do not vote at the next election.) The upshot is a "mix" of the national product between public and private goods that is apt to leave most people discontented, yet unable to resist the free-rider temptation that is the root cause of the "wrong" public-private balance.

WRECKING THE RESOURCE ALLOCATION

Voters do themselves probably the worst possible service when they try to use the mechanisms of democracy to obtain by politics what the economy is denying them. Car owners hurt by high gasoline prices will then demand an "energy policy," sugar-beet farmers want an import tariff on cane sugar (euphemistically called a "trade policy"), assorted business interests tired of sundry taxes call for a "positive fiscal policy," farmers blockade roads with their tractors to defend "national self-sufficiency in food," small shopkeepers demand that supermarkets be refused building permits in the name of a "policy of proximity," the labor unions threaten to strike if there is no "meaningful policy of employment," regions ill served with roads urge a "balanced transport policy," and all who have pet schemes in mind call for a "policy of purposeful public investment." As some of these demands are met, the unmet ones are urged with ever greater stridency.

It would be starry-eyed classical liberal purism to claim that in the absence of politics, the allocation of resources in the economy would necessarily be optimal. We are not even sure whether "optimal allocation" really has a meaning except perhaps that it is the outcome of untrammelled voluntary exchanges. It is safe to say, though, that each "policy" will only make the allocation worse, more contorted, further removed from the position that free individuals would bring about by the matching of their marginal benefits and costs. "Policy" will block, upset, or reverse equilibrating forces. It will redistribute income, punish those who best succeed to satisfy the wants of their fellow humans, and reward those who fail to do so. Success is not always admirable and failure not always the fault of those who fail. But to make it a policy systematically to do justice in these controversial matters can only have the direst economic consequences.

It is thus that the striving of some to get richer (or less poor) by using the leverage democratic politics offers them looks very much as if they were striving to get poorer, though it takes an outsider to see how pitifully they defeat their own purpose.

"BREAD AND CIRCUSES" IN THE MODERN WELFARE STATE

From about the third century A.D. onward, between a fifth and a quarter of the population of Rome, some 200,000 people, regularly received free distributions of bread and cooking oil from the emperor. The emperor, in turn, received the bread and the cooking oil one way or another from the producers of these goods. The welfare state had duly started to churn. We all know how the churning ended, in slow and messy agony, three centuries later. One quibble one could raise against Gibbon's monumental *History of the Decline and Fall of the Roman Empire* is that he does not really answer the obvious question of why the agony lasted as long as it did.

As vital as the bread and the oil for keeping the people happy were the numerous and frequent circuses scattered all over the city, where gladiators fought wild beasts and each other. This free entertainment, too, was provided by the emperor. In the modern welfare state, the equivalent of the gladiators are professional football players and athletes, and the equivalent of the circuses are mainly provided by the television networks out of the advertising revenue they attract. Like in ancient Rome, so in our modern civilization, it is ultimately the final producers of all goods who provide both the bread and the circuses. They do so both for themselves and for those who do not produce.

As then and so too today, there is a variety of reasons for producing nothing, or at least less than one could with a reasonable effort. Laziness and shirking are probably not the chief culprits. The dominant causes are more complex. Some are bad and cannot be defended, but others can honestly be argued both for and against.

First published as "'Bread and Circuses' in the Modern Welfare State: Is the Worm Finally Turning?" by Liberty Fund, Inc., at www.econ.lib.org on August 2, 2004. Reprinted by premission.

UNEMPLOYMENT: WHOSE FAULT?

Unemployment over and above the rate consistent with normal between-jobs mobility, about 3 to 5 percent of the labor force, cannot be defended. Rates much above this can perhaps be excused at the trough of a business cycle, but high rates that have become endemic in good times as well as in bad are unforgivable. At present, South Korea can boast the lowest unemployment at 3.4 percent, the Netherlands at 4.5, Britain 5, Japan 5.3, and the USA just below 6 percent. At the other end of the scale, Poland (for special and presumably transitory reasons) is at nearly 20 percent, Spain shows a notoriously overstated figure of 11.3, while France is stuck at just under 10, Germany at 8.7, and Italy 8.4 percent.

Some of this unemployment is widely suspected to be voluntary, in that some people prefer to live on the dole rather than go for jobs that look to them too lowly or too low-paid. Thus, the French construction industry is short of 300,000 workers, while Germany has just relaxed its immigration laws to let in people who would fill jobs for which no German is supposed to be available. The remedy against voluntary unemployment is well known. It consists mainly in reducing the period over which unemployment pay is available, and gradually cutting the link between the last salary and the unemployment compensation. The Netherlands, Britain, and Denmark have successfully done this, Germany is preparing to do it to a cautious extent. Elsewhere, it is still rejected as antisocial. Here one might rightly say that it is the political system that maintains voluntary unemployment.

The same is largely true of involuntary unemployment. It suffices to think of the array of labor laws and regulations that "protect workers' rights" and make the laying off of workers so difficult that creating jobs and hiring workers whom you may have to keep paying till they retire (whether or not you have work for them to do) has become a reckless act few dare undertake. In fact, virtually all "social" measures have ultimately to be paid for in reduced employment, a truth European public opinion has until recently furiously denied.

WORK, LEISURE, BOREDOM

The other major cause of nonproduction is the way people prefer to divide their time between hours worked and hours off the job. To choose what one prefers is hardly inconsistent with rational conduct, so that it is difficult to quarrel with the length of time people arrange to spend on and off the job if time on, time off, and pay are freely negotiated. In language that now sounds a little unfashionable, economics used to teach that individuals seek to balance the marginal "utility" of wage income against the marginal "disutility" of work. The former falls as you earn more, the latter rises as you work more, and your preferred use of your time is where the two just match. Like other valid theorems, this is a truism, but it is not useless, for it helps in organizing the argument.

The average gainfully employed American works about 1,950 hours in the year. This corresponds to forty-nine standard 40-hour weeks, leaving three weeks for sick leave and paid holidays. Average annual hours worked in Britain are much the same. In sharp contrast, the average German and French working year is about forty-three standard 35-hour weeks. It takes an effort to believe that the balance between more income and less work is so vastly different for the English and the Americans on one side, and the Germans and the French on the other. In addition, these statistics tell us nothing about the intensity of effort the average worker in these countries devotes to his work. Per capita income in Germany and France is in fact a little higher than the low number of hours worked would predict.

Moreover, weekly hours are often not freely negotiated. For the last four years, France has had a monstrous law fixing the "legal" workweek at a maximum of 35 hours—a paternalistic impertinence that passes for a great "social advance." Part of the present center-right majority would like to dilute or repeal this law, but President Chirac has vetoed attempts to do so. In Germany, there is no "legal" working week; but labor union hierarchies have done their utmost to whip their members into demanding shorter hours until it became the politically correct thing to prefer this "social advance" to higher wages (though it was preferable still to demand both).

Finally, with the gradual disappearance of heavy manual labor as well as of deadly monotonous assembly-line work, it is no longer evident that work necessarily involves "disutility." Some people actually enjoy doing what they are paid for. Many more may not enjoy the work itself, but they enjoy the amenities and atmosphere of the workplace and the company they find there—often in pleasant contrast to the solitude and boredom of their evenings and weekends. Bread they can earn, and no doubt they would continue to get some, in the modern welfare state, even if they failed to work for it; but by way of circuses, most of them are reduced to watching television. If labor laws, institutional arrangements, and the motives of union officials were different, many workers might well settle for longer hours and higher incomes. They might also settle for longer hours rather than see their jobs disappear, if that was the choice that faced them and their government and their union permitted them freely to take it.

THE WORM THAT TURNED

Precisely such was the choice that recently faced two thousand employees of two Siemens plants in northwest Germany. The company could no longer make the production of mobile phones pay with a 35-hour week. It proposed to its employees to work 40 hours for the same pay, or else it would move the whole operation to Hungary, where willing and good quality labor was available at a fraction of the cost. The two thousand German workers massively accepted the 40-hour week.

One swallow does not a summer make, but a few more are now seen to be fluttering. Daimler Benz and Bosch have already followed Siemens. Over a hundred similar moves on hours or paid vacations are said to be in preparation. The political weather may be changing in Germany. A few months ago Chancellor Schroeder scolded German entrepreneurs who talked about moving their business to the former Soviet satellite countries to the east. Early in July, in what seemed a wildly improbable about-turn, the chairman of the ruling Social Democrat Party warned the labor unions against "selfishness."

The significant thing is not that some groups of workers now dare ignore their unions or that politicians take the electoral risk of showing some understanding of economics. It is, rather, that business leaders, for long years cowed into timidly suffering "codetermination" and the exactions of both the tax collector and the labor hierarchy, have finally regained some courage and started boldly "telling it like it is." The worm seems to have turned.

WHO MINDS THE GAP?

At the Lisbon summit of European Union heads of government in 2000, there was much talk of how the blessings enjoyed by Europe—a civilization of the highest order, a well-educated population, good communications, an internal market of close on 400 million, peace, and the rule of law—fail to be translated into economic performance. In the debates and outside the conference room, the conservatives and Blairite "socioliberals" levelled some unspoken accusations against the German and French socialists for clinging to policies, notably in the matter of what was politely referred to as "labor market rigidity," that greatly hindered the adaptation of the economy to worldwide free trade and fast technological progress. Though the words "labor market flexibility" made the socialists fume with silent indignation, a set of pious resolutions were adopted, amounting to what came to be known as the Lisbon Program that was supposed to transform Europe into "the world's most competitive economy" by 2010.

At the March 2004 summit in Brussels, progress was cursorily reviewed, though other items on the agendas have left little time and interest for the economy. Each government awarded itself good marks for its wise and decisive policies. In fact, with the exception of Spain, Portugal, and the Netherlands (Britain was already ahead of the rest thanks to the radical Thatcher reforms of the 1980s that Labour has preserved and built upon), progress by most of the others consisted of two steps forward and two steps back. In France, "progress" has consisted rather of three steps back. Romano Prodi, the outgoing president of the European Commission, told them to their face that he wished they would stop pretending that they are even trying to implement the Lisbon Program.

First published as part 2 of "Economic Theories and Social Justice," by Liberty Fund, Inc., at www.econlib.org on June 7, 2004. Reprinted by permission.

1. MIND THE GAP!

Users of the London Underground are familiar with the sonorous warning of the loudspeaker at certain stations to "mind the gap!" between the carriage and the platform edge when getting on or off. The message of the Lisbon Program can be compressed into the same warning shout to "mind the gap," though here both the gap and the danger it holds are metaphorical, but no less serious for all that.

The gap, of course, is that between the sadly wilting economic performance of the core states of Europe and the vigorous growth of China, South Korea, India, and—more painfully and embarrassingly—of the United States. For it must be recognized that while most Europeans think that fast development in Asia is rather a good thing, they find being outperformed by America in the last two decades quite hard to take.

In fact, one cannot really grasp the contradictions of European opinion in matters of political economy without constantly bearing in mind the mostly subconscious, visceral hostility to America felt by so many Europeans (the "intellectuals" and the politically articulate and active more than most) that Americans find so mystifying. Because America is growing faster, "we," as the aforementioned Europeans argue, must speed up and at worst stop the gap from widening, at best close it. But because America is brazenly capitalist and knows no social justice, "we," they argue further, reject capitalism (except as a last resort the well-regulated, tame sort) and insist on widening and deepening the sway of social justice.

The gap is deplored and there is a genuine desire to reduce it if that is feasible without sacrificing what goes by the name of "the European social model." They wish this, but only in part because more growth is still widely regarded as good in itself despite ecological objections. In great part, however, reducing the gap is a matter of pride, a virility symbol that would sweep away any suggestion of superior American prowess.

To mitigate shame about the gap, a good deal is made of statistics that cast doubt on its very existence. Relatively recent growth rates of national product favor the U.S., but statistics going back fifty years or a century do not. Moreover, faster American growth since the 1970s was accompanied by a swelling of the current account deficit, i.e., by heavy capital imports from countries poorer than America, an apparent anomaly that tarnishes the U.S. record. In a sense, it was "too easy" for America to grow faster by hogging the savings of the rest of the world, even if the rest of the world had willingly lent itself to this aberrant relation.

Another line of European defense rests on productivity comparisons. It is accepted that American productivity per man-year in manufacturing is higher, and in services much higher, than the European one. But this is wholly accounted for by the much longer American workweek—an average of 42 hours against 34 in Western Europe (ex. Britain)—and the much shorter American vacation. Productivity per hour worked in the euro-zone is fully as high as, and in some areas higher than, it is in America.

(It is worth noting, though, that the high European productivity per hour is in part due to the age composition of the workforce. Many under-twenty-fives linger on in real or pretended higher education, and many over-fifty-fives go or are eased into early retirement. The twenty-three-to-fifty-five age group, which is somewhat more productive than the younger and the older ones, is thus overrepresented in Europe. Heavier unemployment among the young and the old acts in the same direction.)

Where the gap is more threatening, and where it ought really to be minded, is not in the comparative levels of productivity, but in their growth rates. Statistics can be made to say many things, but most things they say about productivity amount to a gap of about 1 percentage point between the U.S. and European growth rates of the various productivity measures in America's favor. This would be no great matter if it were a passing phase. But if it is destined to persist for a generation—which on the present showing looks far from impossible—the gap could become abysmal and the effect truly shattering for European self-respect. Europeans might come to look upon America with the same sense of failure and despair as Arabs now look at Europeans.

2. THE FAVORITE MODEL

While large segments of European opinion—the self-employed and much of the political right—do "mind the gap," the majority of opinion-makers and behind them the political center and left, hold a more ambiguous and self-contradictory position. For public consumption, they mostly refuse to see the gap or explain it away by citing transitory causes. When speaking more frankly, they acknowledge it as part and parcel of a "European model" that is less moneygrubbing, milder, gentler, and above all socially more just than the American one. Some diehards still insist, carrying on the Soviet tradition despite the catastrophic results it had brought, that with proper planning an egalitarian, socially just society is not only capable of creating wealth just as fast as the capitalist "free-for-all," but can in fact show it a clean pair of heels.[1] The great majority, however, reluctantly admit that this model is intrinsically slow and could only run faster if the parts they most cherish were drastically modified.

The long and short of it is that increases in material wealth and social justice are regarded by the dominant strand of European opinion as two rival goods. If the economy is driven to deliver more of one, it will inevitably deliver less of the other. The social and political mix incorporated in the American model will make it deliver more wealth and less social justice; the European model will make it do the opposite.

This is very broad-brush economic theorizing and it is easy to bring it down to earth with some hardheaded scrutiny. However, it has the great strength of meshing remarkably well with the ideological defense of social justice. For if material wealth and its equal distribution are two rival goods that can be "produced" in variable proportions—more of one entailing less of the other—asking which is "better" is a silly question. There shall be no dispute about tastes; it is for the consumer to decide what dose of each good he prefers. The American appar-

1. As the Italian economist and statesman Antonio Martino once put it, this is now a minority opinion voiced by few outside Pyongyang and Cambridge, Massachusetts.

ently wants to tilt the "product mix" more toward riches, the European favors a mix with more equality even if that means somewhat less wealth.

But how do we know this? The center-left and socialist answer is that we have it from the horse's mouth: European voters time and again vote for the "European model," punishing governments that flirt with liberal economic policies, dismantle subsidies, embrace free trade a little too heartily, tamper with the legal privileges of labor unions, refuse to finance an ever-growing share of health care from general taxation, try to reform pay-as-you-go pensions, and give public education an "elitist" twist. Governments do make small and cautious steps toward such goals simply in order to keep the system from seizing up. But they have to pay a heavy price and are lucky to last out a legislature if they deviate perceptibly from the pursuit of "social justice." The electorate apparently knows very well which model is its favorite.

3. WHEN RATS START FIGHTING ONE ANOTHER

Something, however, must be wrong with the confident claim that the "European model" of superimposing on the economy a far-reaching redistributive mechanism is in fact a straightforward case of revealed preference: the electorate gets the advancing welfare state because that is exactly what it wants. How does one square this idyllic picture of consent and contentment with the infighting, the sourness, and the strife that are becoming the mark of everyday life in most of these societies?

A parallel suggests itself that is crude and disrespectful but—alas—fairly accurate. When population and the food supply are in equilibrium, a rat colony is internally peaceful, but when the balance tilts the wrong way, its members begin to quarrel and fight each other. Likewise, when the development of the welfare state takes place on the back of a vigorously expanding economy, creating a new welfare entitlement for one group—say, old-age pensioners, single mothers, aspiring college students—does not prevent the claims of other groups to be satisfied the following year. Health-care coverage improves, unemployment benefits increase or are prolonged, the unsaleable works of would-be artists are bought by the local government and warehoused (as was till recently the case in the Netherlands), and so forth. At a rhythm dictated by the electoral calendar, bits of additional social justice can be handed down all the time. Each claimant group gets its turn and there is enough, or nearly so, to go round.

These good times were enjoyed in "never had it so good" Britain in the 1950s and '60s and in much of continental Europe in the 1970s and '80s. In both areas, the trade-off between wealth and social justice eventually shifted much too far, and welfare started to stifle the economy. In Britain, the absurdity of the result became so apparent in the strike-bound '70s that finally the Thatcher reforms became politically possible. On the Continent of Europe, rival interest groups are still mostly deadlocked, the economy is broadly speaking still stagnant, and unemployment is bumping against the 10 percent ceiling. Reform in Germany and Scandinavia is creeping on timidly, but is stuck fast in Italy and especially in France. Every interest group is defending its "social rights" with tooth and claw and is trying to gain additional ones to preempt similar attempts by the other groups. Outside the strict welfare sphere, the same preemptive infighting is going on in the public services and the industries where the employer is the government, so that in these sectors of the economy labor's unbeatable bargaining lever is its voting strength.

Arguably, all this must first get worse before it can get better—as one day it probably will. Meanwhile, this desolate and strife-torn scene offers admirable scope for studying how the economics of social justice really works.

FLOAT OR SINK?
THE MILLSTONE OF THE "SOCIAL MARKET" IN GERMANY

It has long been observed that instinct, the product of selective evolution, tells man to choose behavior that is most conducive to his and his genes' survival. It has long been overlooked, however, that at some crucial junctures instinct tells man to choose behavior that does the exact opposite. When he falls in deep water, the nonswimmer should lie flat on his back, let his head submerge, and keep only his nose and mouth above the surface. If he does this, he may survive. Instead, he will instinctively try and straighten up to keep his head and neck out of the water, thrash about, swallow water, sink, and drown.

Behavior supposed to defend against some danger, but in fact making the danger more threatening and the defense ineffective, is worryingly frequent among groups that decide their conduct collectively, for example by majority vote. Job protection is a classic case. It is not hard to get a majority to vote for "workers' rights," including a worker's right to his job that he should only lose under the most compelling circumstances. In Germany, it is left to the courts to say whether there are really compelling reasons for allowing this, and cases can drag on and on. Only firms with fewer than five employees have a relatively free hand (which provides a good reason for not expanding beyond that size). Comparable "job protection" measures have cropped up in other European countries over the last quarter century, and have mostly been tightened up as unemployment started to become endemic.

German businessmen now say that if you hire at all, you must know that you hire for the very long term and as long as an employee chooses to stay with you, you must pay him, rain or shine. The employer carries the risk that it will rain and not shine, and to cover this risk among

First published by Liberty Fund, Inc., at www.econlib.org on May 15, 2003. Reprinted by permission.

many others, he must mentally add a risk premium to the wage he must pay. It is hardly surprising that the effect of "job protection" is to reduce the number of jobs that should be protected. Like the man trying to keep his head above the water, the German job market has been sinking at an accelerating rate; the latest unemployment figure is 10.6 percent, and the latest growth forecast is 0.1 percent per quarter for the current year (the only-just-positive number showing a naive faith in the precision of statistical output and income measurement).

Needless to say, job protection is not the only, nor even the main cause of the appalling performance of the once-mighty German economic machine. "Be assured, my young friend," as Adam Smith famously remarked, "that there is a great deal of ruin in a nation," and it took more than just a few manifestly counterproductive measures to bring about stagnation. The ever heavier millstone of the world's most elaborate welfare state was carried with growing difficulty as Germany progressively emerged from the fiercely energetic and productive era of postwar reconstruction and settled into bourgeois comfort. The loss of buoyancy finally got the best of the "social market economy" that left-of-center world opinion used to applaud as the living proof of the "European social model," the Third Way, social and market all rolled into one!

Like in other European countries where Left and Right outdo each other in being "social," many horror stories circulate in Germany about how much it really costs to employ the average worker. Some employers claim that it costs them 300 euros in all the various statutory deductions, health, disability, unemployment and pension contributions, to give their employee a pretax take-home pay of 100. Aggregate national income statistics tell a less lurid, but still fairly preoccupying story. A pretax take-home pay of 58 must be topped up by employers' and employees' various social insurance contributions of 48, raising the total cost to the employer to over 100. To this must be added about 20, representing the contributions of the general taxpayer to the various social services. All in all, the total cost of a worker to the German economy is a little more than twice his take-home pay.

Many economists now believe that German labor has become too expensive and this is the root cause of high unemployment. The labor unions, whose power in Germany is still great because of the monopoly role labor legislation reserves for them in wage bargaining, furiously refute this. German wages are in fact too low, they argue, for if they were not, the country would not have a visible trade surplus year in, year out. Once again, here is proof that a little economics is worse than none, for the trade balance depends on many other things, and depends on them more strongly, than on domestic wages. Nevertheless, like the argument of the illiterate that if jobs are menaced, the lawmaker must protect them, the trade balance argument is widely believed to show that wages are not too high and the unions are responsible corporate bodies, exercising statesmanlike restraint in wage bargaining.

Cornered and finally persuaded that "something must be done," Germany's social democratic government is now proposing to turn against its own parliamentary supporters and introduce a long overdue reform of the "social market economy." It has a majority of only eight seats in the lower house, and two-thirds of its legislators are union officials or union members. To pass reform legislation, it needs some support from the opposition, much of which is just as "socially" minded and, if only for sound electoral reasons, may refuse to curtail "workers' rights." As a result, the proposed reform package is decidedly timid. Some say it is just a bandage on a wooden leg, though others think that the very fact of a socialist government at last repenting is good news in itself.

A few items in the reform are significant. Entitlement to full unemployment pay is reduced from thirty-two to twelve months, a fixed tariff is proposed for severance pay, and the obligation to engage in industrywide wage bargaining is somewhat relaxed. If they pass, these would be useful measures. Much of the rest is little more than cosmetic. All in all, however, they are far too weak and far too anxious not to hurt, to restore the natural buoyancy of the economy.

Any but the boldest and widest-ranging reform is up against a force greater than itself, the dynamics of the advanced welfare state that acts as a giant automatic destabilizer. The incipient welfare state begins with social services absorbing under 20 percent of GDP. With the economy growing fairly briskly, more can be afforded, and bidding for votes ensures that "social" spending rises to the neighborhood of 25 percent. In fact, by 1990 the fifteen-country European average was 25.4 percent and Germany's spending was exactly the same as the average. This level seemed sustainable though, from the point of view of productivity growth, probably not desirable. Some items of expenditure grow autonomously whatever you do; health service and pay-as-you-go state pensions are of this kind. Others grow when the economy starts doing less well; unemployment pay does this. The upshot is that the slower is economic growth, the more of GDP is absorbed in social spending.

By 1996, German social expenditure as a share of GDP passed the 30 percent mark, beaten only by a short head by France and the Scandinavian countries. After a slight easing in 1999–2000, the percentage continued its trend rise, and as we write it probably exceeds 32 percent.

Believers in socialist or communitarian doctrines will take it that this chunk of expenditure on all that is "social" rather than "market," apart from its morally attractive aspect, is really a stabilizer. If things go awry on the market side, they are rescued by the rocklike solidity of social spending that, in addition, makes people feel safer and more willing to spend. I will not try and answer the claim of moral worth except to wonder about the moral worth of forcing workers to spend half or more of their gross wages on compulsory social insurance. Extortion is extortion even if it is "in your best interest." However, let that pass.

Regarding the effect of a high and rising social service overhead on the course of the economy, to contend that it acts as a stabilizer is tantamount to saying that fewer incentives produce more jobs and more growth. Though such beliefs cannot be categorically disproved, they are very, very unlikely to be true. The commonsense view is that poor economic performance augments the relative share of social spending, and a higher share of social spending leads in turn to poorer economic performance—and so we go on until something totally unforeseen breaks this circle. Until then, thrashing about without quite sinking is probably the best the "social market economy" could hope for.

HOW GERMANY AND FRANCE, THE SICK MEN OF EUROPE, TORTURE THEMSELVES

What used to be called the "welfare state" has lately been renamed the "European model." This clever linguistic maneuver is meant to stress that it is the polar opposite of the "Anglo-Saxon" or, worse still, the "American model." Therefore good Europeans ought to like it as much as they dislike the English and the Americans.

It is an absurd claim that this is a model that all, or even most, of Europe follows. It is essentially Franco-German. This is not the first time, though, that a French interest, idea, or claim is made less provocative by pretending that it is all-European. The "model" has origins in orthodox French socialism, in its Gaullist version, in German social democracy and trade unionism, and in a Christian socialist tradition that, though stronger in Germany, is also alive in France. Ideologically, it is eclectic and somewhat confused, as one would expect in view of its diverse origins.

It has two very basic and constant features, one old, the other relatively new. The old feature is a belief that the distribution of the national income is the government's business as well as its natural prerogative, and that whatever it happens to be, the government must use its powers to make it tilt a little more, and a little more again, in favor of the lower income groups. It is very important, though, that such repeated redistribution should mainly take the form of "social" benefits *in natura,* rather than simply cash transfers.

The main ambition of the "model" is to develop an ever-wider system of "social" insurance against sickness, unemployment, and old age, as well as ever longer paid vacations and ever shorter "legal" working hours. This is supposed to be a more proper kind of government solici-

First published as "Socio-Masochism: How Germany and France, the Sick Men of Europe, Torture Themselves," by Liberty Fund, Inc., at www.econlib.org on June 6, 2005. Reprinted by permission.

tude than to help the unions to press for higher money wages. In the deeply paternalistic spirit of its various authors, it is also supposed to be more valuable to working people than giving them the same money in cash rather than in kind. Herein lies the "model's" most fatal defect.

The cost of all this "social" insurance, except a minor part which is financed from general taxation, is raised by payroll taxes. They are partly employers', partly employees' contributions; but this is just an accounting fiction, for in fact both contributions come out of the gross wage the employer pays but the worker does not take home. In Germany and France, taking the gross wage cost as 100, an average of 50–55 goes to social insurance contributions and 45–50 is pretax take-home pay. The two together, however, are not worth 100 to the worker, but always a little less, perhaps 80 or 90, for cash can buy anything (including insurance), but insurance cannot. There is a permanent gap between the subjective value to the worker of what he gets and what it costs the employer to give it to him.

The upshot of this gap—the excess of the cost of labor to the employer over the value of the wage the worker gets—is that the market for labor cannot clear. No matter how desperately governments try to create jobs by fancy make-work schemes, unemployment becomes chronic. In the thirty years since the "social model" has become a political "must," unemployment has crept up from an average of 4 percent to over 10 percent in France and over 12 percent in Germany.

Unsurprisingly, these sickly economies are incapable of growing at the same rate as their neighbors Spain, Great Britain, Holland, and the Scandinavian countries, let alone the new east-central European members of the Union who benefit from catching-up phenomena. France is lucky to be growing at just over 2 percent p.a. at present, and Germany at half that rate. Neither country's government seems willing to tell its public the stark truth (as Margaret Thatcher told the British after 1979) that without scrapping much of the "model," things cannot get better. France's political leaders, in particular, will do almost anything to appease any sectional interest that shouts "boo!" at them. It is now an open secret that both Germany and France are in decline. They are very much the Two Sick Men of Europe.

Hereby hangs the second, and more novel, feature of their much touted "model." Any society that is failing and feels its own decline badly needs to reassure itself. Like the Arab societies that have so signally failed and now swear by Islamic values while hating and denigrating the Western civilizations by whose standards they have failed, Germany and France are beginning to talk of their different value system and are showing a violent antipathy to the liberal, Anglo-American civilization that is leaving them behind. "Liberalism" (in the classical sense as it is used outside the U.S.) is now a hate word, almost an obscenity in France, and not much better in Germany. The more Germany and France feel that liberalism and America function while they do not, the more convinced they are that the "European model" is far superior.

Opponents of the new European "constitution" oppose it because it fails to order, by force of law, a "really social" Europe. They would like it to impose stricter labor laws and more generous welfare provisions all over the Union so as to protect the Franco-German center from "social dumping."

Bitter political adversaries in the two Sick Men countries are equally eager to preserve the "European social model" from the largely imaginary liberal menace, seemingly quite oblivious to the total failure of the "model" to produce the blessings it is supposed to bring. The detached observer must rub his eyes to believe what he sees. Medieval friars and nuns who wore hair shirts knew what they were doing; they were making a down payment on a place in heaven and the torture was worth it. But the hair shirt of the "European social model" tortures the societies that were naive enough to fall for it, without the torture buying them anything beyond false pride. It is a case of sociomasochism where, however, the masochist is not even drawing much perverse enjoyment from the pain it inflicts on himself.

Worse still, the pain hurts most of all the very working class whose well-being the model is meant to promote. Near-stagnant economies with chronic unemployment in the 10 percent range not only demoralize the unemployed themselves. They also undermine the bargaining power of those still employed, and desperately clinging to their jobs. In private industry, management now has the upper hand and can in some cases even impose longer hours, changed work methods, and wage freezes that would have been unthinkable when unemployment was at only 5–6 percent.

It is only in the public sector that labor can still make demands and use the strike weapon. In Germany, where union membership is about 22 percent of the employed labor force, the unions still have some influence in the private sector. In France, with union membership at 7–8 percent, almost entirely in the public sector, the only union presence in the private sector is the paid union official, maintained there by the grace of the labor code and generous government support. It is hard to believe but perfectly true that unions in France no longer ask for higher wages in the private sector by going to the management. They go to the government instead, asking it to tell "big business" to increase wages.

Both governments try to please labor by "job protection" measures of Byzantine complexity. They make dismissal very difficult and expensive, hence hiring new employees very risky. The logical consequence is that net job creation has come to a complete halt. Without "job protection," one could expect to gain around 300,000 net new jobs annually in Germany and 200,000 in France. Losing this is like putting an extra wrinkle in the hair shirt. Sociomasochism is made more intense. However, smoothing out the wrinkle in the hair shirt by dismantling the more absurd aspects of "job protection" would be a surrender to "liberal heartlessness."

Sociomasochism is more complicated than common or garden-variety masochism. A sociomasochist society refuses to admit that it is being tortured, and fails to see that the pain is of its own doing. Rather than recognizing its own foolishness, it convinces itself that if it took off the hair shirt, it would feel the cold on its naked torso. Perhaps we may hope that once the air is clear of inane debates about a no less inane new "constitution," Germany and France can be reminded that the hair shirt is not the only kind of shirt one can wear.

SHALL WE BORROW FROM THE CHILDREN?

"Tax and spend" is the usual charge levied against democratic governments seeking popular support by dipping into the pork barrel. "Spend and tax" would be more accurate. The typical pattern is for expenditure on worthy and less worthy programs to rise first, with revenue seldom if ever catching up. The money never runs out, for unlike households, the government can always borrow whatever it needs to cover the deficit, almost regardless of how large it is. It owns a sort of widow's curse whose magic lies in the state's power to raise the taxes in the future that it has no stomach to raise in the present. The day of reckoning need never come, for old borrowing is always refinanced from new borrowing. The debt-to-income ratio must not get out of hand, but in actual fact the markets tolerate high ratios for unsecured government borrowing, whilst they would demand individual debtors to put up some security.

In the nineteenth century, with Victorian probity permeating both ethics and economics, public deficits were felt to be perilous, and running them systematically a short route to ruin. Modern public-finance theory has reduced these fears to the status of a superstition, knocking down one barrier to the steady rise in the share of the national income absorbed by state spending. Perhaps enlightenment is not always the unmixed blessing that we unthinkingly take it to be.

However, there subsists in the public mind a faint unease about budget deficits. While no longer believing that a state that gets ever deeper into debt will finish by going bankrupt, many sensible people are worried about the propriety of the government doing something on behalf of its citizens that it would be imprudent if not downright wrong for the citizens to do for themselves. It is worth looking more closely at the mainsprings of this unease.

For believers in the freedom of contract, there is no objection in

First published by Liberty Fund, Inc., at www.econlib.org on November 3, 2003. Reprinted by permission.

principle to willing borrowers selling bonds to willing lenders; any transaction between consenting adults deserves the presumption of being an improvement in well-being. Good reasons must be advanced to show that this is not the case.

What effectively shatters this presumption is that public borrowing that is never repaid, but is constantly rolled over and keeps swelling in volume, is not a transaction between consenting adults. With only a mild recourse to metaphor, we could represent it as a transaction in which consenting adults borrow from their children and their children's children who do not consent and could not do so, especially if they are not yet born.

While this undoubtedly deprives deficit financing of liberal credentials, there is no need for moral alarm bells to ring too shrilly about it. It is not the only, nor the gravest, instance of the present generation mortgaging the interests of their descendants. In this particular instance, though, it is doing so not out of sheer selfishness or carelessness, but as the somewhat incoherent, self-contradictory act of a split personality. Its public persona is doing one thing, its private one the opposite.

The great majority of private individuals achieve some positive saving over their lifetime, the ratio of saving to personal income averaging from 2–3 percent to near 20 percent from country to country and year to year. The ratio is highest for individuals near the peak of their earning power and declines in old age, but it seems to be a near-universal aspiration, not confined to people who have children, to leave more at the end of one's life than one was given at its start. Dissaving via cumulative budget deficits runs counter to this objective. It consumes resources now which would otherwise have been available for future consumption. To add insult to injury, this preemptive move is not costless. Its cost, the debt interest which reflects the present generation's time preference, will be paid mostly by our descendants through the indefinite future.

Governments buy support by spending money, not by siphoning it away in taxes. Spending now and deferring the matching taxes to an indefinite future is dictated by the most elementary political know-how, and it should not surprise or shock anyone to see it happen again and again, especially when elections approach and politicians start getting desperate. They are not wicked, they are just playing by the democratic rules. That the electorate is quite content with these rules, or at least does not try to alter them, is perhaps more difficult to explain.[1] It may be that the bulk of the electorate just does not see the connection and cannot be bothered to think about it. Public choice theory has several other, less simple explanations for the contrast between collective and private behavior. Whatever the reason, they are mutually contradictory and the economic and social consequences are fairly weighty.

The deficit-and-public-debt problem shows up to varying degrees in the USA and most European countries, and very acutely in Japan. The U.S. has tried to stem it by placing a ceiling on the federal debt, a measure whose only effect is to oblige the Congress to raise the debt ceiling every time the rising debt catches up with it. Japan has so far not done anything systematic to control the debt. In Europe, fiscal histories and outlooks differ widely between countries. The twelve states that have adopted the euro have understood that a common currency combined with widely divergent fiscal regimes could give rise to dangerous and unfair free-riding. To forestall this, in the Maastricht treaty founding the currency union they accepted the obligation to keep the national debt under 60 percent and the budget deficit under 3 percent of national income (GNP).

As was obvious from the outset, the treaty obligation is proving unenforceable. France showed no embarrassment in declaring, almost in so many words, that it will reduce its deficit to the Maastricht limit when it finds it convenient to do so. Less arrogantly, Germany is following much the same course. Only poor little Portugal is scrambling to obey the treaty, for what will not be enforced against big states may be enforced against small ones.

However, it is instructive to see what would happen if euro-zone countries were strictly to stick to the 3 percent limit year in, year out, not deviating from it in either direction. Let us suppose, counterfactu-

1. A well-known theory (Robert J. Barro, "Are Government Bonds Net Wealth?" *Journal of Political Economy* 82 (1974): 1095–1117) asserts that households knowingly compensate for a rise in government debt by increased saving, because they anticipate a rise in future taxes they (or their descendants) will have to meet. The theory would seem to reconcile the apparent contradiction between public borrowing and private saving.

ally, that they all start with a national debt at 60 percent of GNP. (This limit is in the treaty but carries no sanction.)

What happens under this hypothesis as we move over time depends primarily on the average rate of growth of GNP. Assuming that the zone as a whole achieves growth at 2 percent a year looks optimistic from the perspective of the dismal present, but should be feasible with only reasonable luck. Consider a ten-year time span—not a long time for a currency union. At the end of Year 1, GNP rises from 100 to 102 and the national debt from 60 to 63. At the end of Year 10, GNP is at 122. The national debt rises to 93, which amounts to 76.4 percent of GNP. The longer the period considered, the more glaring becomes the effect of the growth of the debt being faster than the growth of national income.

It would seem, then, that unless economic growth were much faster than we can realistically expect in a zone of welfare states, even durable obedience to some such self-denying ordinance as the Maastricht treaty cannot guarantee long-run equilibrium. Regardless of questions of morality, economic realities alone tell us that "borrowing from the children" had better not become a steady habit.

LOW PAY

The tail end of the twentieth century and the beginning of the twenty-first have been exceptionally kind to both capital and labor, but kinder to capital than to labor. Overall economic growth, apart from some sluggishness in continental Europe and Japan and violent but brief upsets in Southeast Asia and Russia in 1998, went on more briskly and for longer than at any other time in known history. While the rise from poverty was the most spectacular in China and India, even such hitherto unpromising areas as black Africa and much of Latin America began to share in the benefits of freer trade, relative peace, and the rudiments of the rule of law.

FREER TRADE

Within an expanding world income, profits rose markedly faster than wages, so that the relative share of labor declined fairly continuously. This shift in relative shares concerned labor as a whole, and must not be confused with the quite different shift within total labor income in favor of those with higher skills. In fact, separately from the faster rise of profits than of wages, there was a widening of wage differentials, most pronouncedly favoring managerial, accounting, and legal work and computing skills. Unskilled labor and labor using old, established technologies lagged behind. The net effect for labor incomes was a relative loss compared to the income accruing to capital. The era is widely perceived to be one of high profits, low pay.

There was and still is much aggrieved feeling about this by the blue-collar, the casual, and the part-time workers in the Western world, which is understandable enough, and much righteous indignation by socialists of all hues, which is only to be expected. The more muddle-headed blame the IMF, the World Trade Organization, "unbridled"

First published by Liberty Fund, Inc., at www.econlib.org on July 2, 2007. Reprinted by permission.

liberalism, greedy multinationals, and the "dictatorship of the market." It is fruitless to argue with them; if you do, they win by talking faster and louder. More reasoned inquiry about the cause of low pay in the midst of unparalleled prosperity focuses on two major trends, one in trade, the other in technology. The present paper sets equal store by a third. That trend is less widely understood than the first two, but worth close attention for that very reason. It is the rising ideology and the attendant legal machinery of job protection.

The diagnosis that freer trade favors capital more than it does labor runs roughly thus. In a more or less closed economy, capital formation raises the marginal product of labor and leads to higher demand for it. Since the labor force is limited, the wage rate will quickly catch up with the marginal product. As employment approaches the over-full level, labor's marginal product may indeed fall, for lower-quality workers are employed, labor discipline slackens, and shirking and dawdling involve less risk of sanction. The share of wages in total factor income reaches a maximum. As it now pays to substitute cheap capital for dear labor, the marginal product of capital recovers and capital formation is stimulated. The relative shares of the two factors of production swing back in favor of capital, until capital reaches a maximum and the pendulum starts to swing back toward labor. For decades at a time, the relative shares of capital and labor may change only a few percentage points either way, for the pendulum need swing only a little in favor of one factor of production before it is quickly pulled back in favor of the other. A more or less fixed, inelastic supply of labor is the great stabilizer of this distributive machine.

When such an economy is opened up to the wide world, what happens depends on what the world is like, notably in terms of its factor endowments. Its stock of capital and its supply of labor are the decisive determinants of how freer trade affects income distribution.

In our age, Europe and North America have opened up, first and foremost, to two very large areas in China and India with a huge rural population with no opportunity to deploy its productive potential but eager to do so, and a low stock of capital. As obstacles to trade were partly dismantled and transport costs shrank, the demand for labor of Western capital met, not the limited supply of labor hitherto available to it in the Western world, but the seemingly unlimited supply of Chinese and Indian peasants flocking from rural misery to slightly less miserable urban work. They did not physically move to Europe and North America; the garments, plastic toys, components, electronic subassemblies and gadgetry (and no doubt soon complex, highly sophisticated equipment, too) incorporating Asian labor did all the moving from East to West that was necessary to simulate the conditions of an almost infinitely elastic labor supply in the West. Delocalization of production from West to East, painful to its direct victims and politically poisonous, created more protectionist emotion than its tangible effects might have warranted, but it certainly added to the general sentiment that blue-collar workers in advanced countries were getting a raw deal at the hands of ruthless, greedy bosses trying to please ruthless, greedy financiers. Some of the measures proposed in all seriousness to stop delocalization and curb greedy finance could match Bastiat's famed virtual railway for silliness.

Under these conditions, as capital accumulation proceeds vigorously in response to the marginal product of capital staying high or rising, the demand for labor increases but the price paid for labor—the price of T-shirts, jeans, plastic articles, consumer electronics—does not increase. In the Western world, the pendulum is not swinging back in favor of labor. Wages in "old" industries lag behind overall income growth and even more so behind profits, even as wages in China and India rise fast as they catch up with the sharply increased productivity of urban compared with rural work. The process leads to convergence of factor prices between West and East, though their actual equalization is no doubt very far off. Meanwhile, in the West "globalization" is blamed, reasonably enough, for low pay.

ADVANCING TECHNOLOGY

Economists worth their salt have a more than merely intellectual commitment to free trade, and regard protectionist arguments with no more sympathy than Vatican prelates regard liberation theology. It is in part their subconscious disgust for findings capable of being turned against free trade (such as those detecting some ill effects from "globalization") that induces many economists to reject the thesis of "globalization" being the root cause of low pay. They are only too ready to ascribe it to technological change instead (and are supported in this stand by recent studies done at the OECD that minimize the role of Asian exports produced by cheap Asian labor and stress the effect of information technology).

When we hear the words "technological progress," we almost automatically couple them with the words "labor-saving." Indeed, if technological change is progressive, we should expect it to enable a given output to be produced with less labor, or more output produced with no more labor. We have the mental picture of a little man pushing a wheelbarrow filled with earth and next to it a great yellow earthmoving monster driven by another little man doing what it would take a hundred wheelbarrow-pushers to do.

If it is the case that technological progress is intrinsically labor-saving, then one should expect it to be reflected in a lower marginal product of labor (not to be confused with "labor productivity," which is total output divided by the number of workers engaged in producing it, and includes the contribution to output of capital as well as of labor) or a higher marginal product of capital. It would explain why the share of capital in total income increases more than the share of labor.

But it is quite wrong to suppose that technological progress is typically, or even predominantly, labor-saving. Those who tacitly assume that it is typically labor-saving nowadays have information technology in mind. However, if you reflect that a few decades ago a mainframe computer would fill a good-sized room and cost many times its handy-sized contemporary equivalent, it will dawn on you that even information technology can be capital-saving. In fact, changes in production equipment can go either way and indeed both ways at the same time, though labor-saving may be more characteristic of it.

Apart from fixed equipment, though, much of the rest of capital employed in the production process is more likely to be hospitable to capital-saving than to labor-saving technology. Two kinds of capital are involved: work-in-progress and goods in transit.

Work-in-progress tied up in producing a given volume of output can be reduced by using statistical probability to estimate the need for various inputs at various times, and by more precise and reliable delivery schedules of materials and parts thanks to advances in logistics. The "just-in-time" methods made famous by Japanese car manufacturers are but a prominent example of a much wider phenomenon that has vastly reduced the amount of capital absorbed in work-in-progress.

Probably more important by a great deal is the effect of advancing transport technology on the volume of both raw materials and finished goods in transit. Depending on the geographical structure of commerce, all goods travel a greater or lesser distance between final seller (the farmer, miner, lumberman, or manufacturer) and final buyer (the consumer). If the average good spends three months in transit on road, rail, and sea and in warehouses and depots, the transit function absorbs a volume of capital equal to 25 percent of physical (goods only) GDP. If advances in transport technology cut average transit time to one month, the capital requirement shrinks from 25 to 8 percent of physical GDP.

These figures, of course, have not the remotest pretension to accuracy, yet may be near enough to reality to illustrate the vast effect that technology is liable to exert in a capital-saving direction. If the numbers are anywhere near reality, the belief that technological progress is intrinsically labor-saving must be at least suspended. As a consequence, it can hardly serve as the most important and most probable explanation of low pay, for capital-saving would, if anything, raise wages.

JOB PROTECTION

Neoclassical economics teaches that in large-number interactions where many agents deal with one another, and all or most act so as to maximize some entity that can be represented by "the measuring rod of money," capital and labor will each earn their marginal product. It will be only just worthwhile to employ the last unit of capital at the going rate of interest and the last unit of labor at the going wage rate.

There are two standard objections to this theorem. One is that it works only under diminishing or constant returns to scale, but breaks down under conditions of increasing returns, where paying capital and labor the values of their marginal products would require more than the total product available. The other, close to socialist doctrine, is that it is impossible to identify the marginal product of a particular unit of capital or labor, for all product is social and must be imputed to society as a whole. Therefore society alone is entitled to decide how capital and labor are remunerated. I shall pass by these two objections. A third seems to me more interesting.

Let us admit that in a static economy, which reproduces itself without any change from one day to the next, a firm can both ascertain the marginal product of its labor force and know that tomorrow and the next day it will be the same as today. In that case it will hire labor if its marginal product is higher than the wage rate, and fire it if it is lower.

In a dynamic setting that keeps changing in all kinds of ways, the firm cannot rationally rely on current experience alone. It needs to form expectations about what the marginal product of its staff will be at future dates. These expectations, though obviously unreliable, are still the best guide the firm has as to whether it should hire, fire, or do nothing. They form a probability distribution, some values of it lying above the going wage rate, others lying below it. Basic decision theory suggests that if the mathematical expectation ("certainty equivalent") is lower than the wage rate, the firm should "restructure," "outsource," "delocalize," or otherwise contrive to fire some of its workers, lifting the marginal product of the remaining staff.

However, in an economy with freedom of contract, this decision "model" rests on false premises. Suppose that as the future rolls on, times turn out good and the firm's best expectations prove to have been right. The marginal product is comfortably above the wage rate. It would have been right to hire more labor. Suppose, however, that the firm did not do so, because it was frightened off by the unfavorable half of its expectations, which pulled the "certainty equivalent" down to, or below, the actual wage rate. Now this would have been a rather foolish way to act, for if the firm *had* hired more labor *and* found that this did not in fact pay, for times turned out to be bad, it could have without much ado fired those it had hired and suffer little loss; while if it never hired the extra labor and times have in fact turned out to be good, it would suffer an opportunity loss. To rectify its mistake, it could at best belatedly scramble and hire the labor left over by its less timid competitors, while at worst it would miss the chance the good times have offered. Therefore the right decision would have been to hire the extra labor to start with.

The logic of this argument tells us clearly enough that under complete contractual freedom where labor can be hired or fired subject only to the agreed terms of the employment contract, and the length of notice is freely negotiated between employer and employee, there will be a distinct "speculative" incentive for firms to expand. Evidently, if enough firms respond to this biased incentive, it will prove to be a self-fulfilling prophecy. The expansion of many will justify the expansion of each. Subject only to the proverbial slip between cup and lip, expectations held with *some,* albeit limited probability that times will be good could succeed to bring about full employment and good times.

It needs no great analytical acumen to see that when freedom of contract is suppressed and job protection of some stringency is put in its place, the above argument is turned on its head. If firing workers is made excessively costly, requiring a long-drawn juridical process, or becomes impossible unless justified by manifest problems of the employer's solvency, the unfavorable half of the probability distribution of future marginal products becomes menacingly relevant, for once it hires them, the firm has to carry its workers almost indefinitely, whether or not it pays to do so. The "speculative" incentive is not to hire, perhaps even not to replace staff lost by natural attrition. A powerful bias toward unemployment is created, and reinforces itself in the manner of self-fulfilling expectations.

As the inexorable force of politics by majority rule continues to strengthen job protection by both labor legislation and the pressure of public opinion, the firm must come to regard its wage bill as becoming dangerously like a fixed cost which it is only prudent to keep lower than would be profitable if it were a truly variable cost. Unemployment, the bias that job protection imparts to the firm's expectations of probable future outcomes, and the loss of labor's bargaining power, all combine to keep wages low. Job protection is certainly not the only or even probably the most important reason for the least well-off getting the worst deal in the present era of burgeoning growth and economic serenity. But it is a cause that was meant to have exactly the opposite effect and that it would be fully within political society's power to remove if only its perversity were more widely understood.

FREEDOM TO STRIKE OR RIGHT TO STRIKE?

Keep using the same word for two different meanings, and after a while the effect on public attitudes can become momentous.

The freedom to strike and the right to strike mean two different things, just as freedom and right mean two different things. Failure to distinguish between them generates a confused understanding of what is at stake. The confusion facilitates public acquiesence in practices that have two deep vices. They clearly violate the freedoms and rights of the passive victims of these practices, and they can lead to costly and painful breakdowns in the functioning of entire societies unless one party to some pending negotiation bows to the will of the other.

The more advanced and complex a civilization, the more vulnerable it becomes to certain, often very small, groups that are thought to be exercising their "rights" when they interfere with the liberties of others in order to get their way. The current strike of truck drivers in France, the second in two years to involve the blockade of crossroads, fuel and other merchandise depots, and cross-border goods traffic by road, is a case in point. The last one is estimated to have cost 0.4 percent of gross national product. Whatever the present one will cost is too much for France, whose chronic unemployment problem renders it more vulnerable than most to such blows. Yet French public opinion accepts that what the lorry drivers are doing is the exercise of the right to strike.

The dividing line between a freedom and a right is crystal clear and there is little excuse for the sloppy usage that confounds the two. A person is free to perform an act, and therefore to engage in a practice involving such acts, if no other person has a sufficiently strong cause to object to it. To reduce the scope for subjective argument about what is a sufficient cause, society has evolved conventions. These are widely accepted, and in some cases have been formalized and elaborated into laws. A free act, then, is one that no one else has a right to stop.

First published in the *Wall Street Journal Europe,* November 4, 1997. Reprinted by permission.

A right, in sharp contrast, enables one person to require another to perform some act, or to stop performing some other act. I am free to enter or leave my house as I please. However, if I have rented it, the tenant can require me to let him have the keys and stop me from entering it except as authorized in the rental agreement. He has rights and I have obligations which I must fulfill if he chooses to exercise his rights.

The freedom to strike means that there is no sufficient cause for one person, or indeed for society as a whole or its supposed representative, the government, to stop another person (or group) from withholding its labor. When there is a sufficient cause—the maintenance of certain public services and valid employment contracts may count as sufficient—there is no freedom to strike. Otherwise, however, it is generally taken as incompatible with our civilization to force someone to work or punish him if he will not.

The right to strike goes further than the freedom to strike. But how much further? It involves some degree of legitimate power over what others must, or may not, do. The problem is precisely the degree of this power, and it is a very slippery slope. The right to station pickets at factory gates, who should be able peacefully to explain to would-be strikebreakers that it is wrong to be a blackleg, is a small degree of power. How could one object to it on the grounds that it requires the strikebreaker to listen to the strikers? From here, however, very small steps lead to increasingly more robust forms of exercising the "right" to strike. From moral suasion to covert intimidation, overt threats, and secondary picketing of employers not party to a dispute, the slippery slope eventually leads to violent interference with the free conduct of the daily life of ordinary citizens and to blackmailing the government to give the strikers what they cannot get by the mere threat of withholding their labor.

The tragedy is that society usually will not meet such violence with violence because public opinion, especially its literate and idealistic half, would think it wrong to do so. It considers the right to strike as almost sacred because it confuses it with the freedom to strike, and it interprets that right as obliging innocent third parties obediently to submit to whatever the strikers need to make their strike successful.

PART 5

Creating Unemployment

STAMP YOUR FEET AND DEMAND A FAIR DEAL

Last November's riots in the outskirts of Paris and other major cities have not yet been forgotten, but the French are at it again. The country is living up to its sorry reputation of lawlessness and violence as the accepted means for any interest group to defend itself against the facts of life. When truckers find that freight rates do not pay, they block the highways and blockade the refineries. When fruit and vegetables are too cheap, growers overturn supermarket shelves and spill cargoes of Spanish fruit into the ditch. Imports of Italian bulk wine are treated with no greater respect. When the tobacco tax goes up faster than usual and cigarette sales dwindle, tobacconists threaten the government with revenge, and receive compensation. Schoolchildren respond to poor marks or words of blame with beating up the teacher; real little revolutionaries stab her. Hardly a week passes without a futile demonstration or factory occupation where layoffs menace. Such resorts to violence are routine and pass almost unnoticed.

Many observers, including President Chirac, are convinced that the French are ferocious by temperament and must be treated with kid gloves, for if their violence is met by violence, mayhem and civil war will break out and blood will flow in the gutters. France has one of the world's largest, and very efficient, riot police, the CRS that, however, is hardly ever used in politically sensitive conflicts for fear that worse might ensue. In his eleven years as president, Mr. Chirac has never faced down street crowds and has been especially quick to capitulate when all too necessary school and university reforms were met, as they always were, with protests by students and their teachers.

The obvious result is that street crowds have in fact become ferocious and the young self-willed and intractable because they have never been resisted or punished. Every interest group has learned the lesson that it always pays to stamp their feet and shout "boo!" for the government to cut and run.

First published by Liberty Fund, Inc., at www.econlib.org on April 3, 2006. Reprinted by permission.

Currently, the young are at it again, with over fifty out of eighty-four universities paralyzed by small groups of militants who shut out the bulk of the student body. High schools are joining in the fun. Eager commentators are promising that it will be the May 1968 youth "revolt" all over again.

French unemployment for the under-twenty-five age group is 23 percent compared with an average of under 10 percent. French labor law is among the most elaborate in the world. As I write this, it is 2,632 pages long and is growing longer almost by the hour. It is aimed at ever tighter job protection. Laying off employees has become very difficult. It can be prohibitively expensive and may involve batteries of labor lawyers litigating endlessly while the employees in question draw their salaries. The obvious result is that business fears the risk of getting caught with labor it no longer wants. Firms are reluctant to hire anyone, let alone the untried and untrained young. To get round this, the government has just amended the labor law, which permits employers to dismiss under-twenty-five-year-old workers (who have not been previously employed) without specific justification during a two-year period, though with normal notice and fairly generous compensation. Not unreasonably, the government argues that even if the young employee is not retained beyond two years, she will have gained work experience, learned the habit of getting up in the morning, and become more employable. In any event, two years in an insecure job is better than the mortal boredom of idleness. It is against this relaxation of the labor code that French youth is now stamping their feet and shouting "boo!"

As the Latin dictum has it, *poeta non fit sed nascitur*—"One is not made, but born a poet." We owe another version of this truth to Milton Friedman. When he was asked whether the study of economics was a good thing, he allegedly replied: Yes, it can be useful, but you have to be an economist to start with.

Some nations have economics in their basic culture and indeed in the way their mind works. They instinctively understand opportunity cost, scarcity, they know that you cannot have it both ways, that you do not create more jobs by making labor more expensive, that the state can give to Peter only what it takes away from Paul, and that there is no free lunch. English-speaking nations, the Scandinavians, the Dutch, and to some extent the Germans are economists in this instinctive way. It has just been proved that 68 percent of the French are, at no little cost to themselves, not economists. The proof lies in a recent nationwide poll, which showed that 68 percent of the French wish the new legislation for promoting youth employment to be revoked without further ado.

It stands to reason why. You only have to ask the right questions. They might go something like this:

Are secure, permanent jobs not better than insecure temporary ones? (Yes, they are much better.)

Is it fair to allow an employer to give his employee notice without sufficient grounds? (No, it is grossly unfair.)

Does a business need two years to decide whether a young worker is worth being made permanent? (Of course it does not, a month or two should do it.)

Can you expect the young to respect the law and behave responsibly when it is treated without due respect? (No, it is only normal that the young cut up a little rough and one cannot blame them.) And so forth. Small wonder that 68 percent agree with answers of this kind.

Public choice, a study that combines economics and politics, teaches that what is happening in France is perfectly rational and intelligent. Ninety percent of the working population is in more or less safe jobs, and within that vast majority there are public service employees (notably in the state railways and in Électricité de France) and union officials who are doubly safe and enjoy privileges. They fight tooth and nail for the most restrictive labor laws and "worker rights" in an ever more elaborate welfare state, cynically sacrificing the 10 percent unemployed and the 23 percent young unemployed whom these policies condemn to joblessness. The privileged keep up a hypocritical rhetoric lamenting the fate of the jobless and the hopeless young, but this is only a fake alibi.

It would be almost comforting to believe that public choice has got it right, for rational calculation, however selfish and cynical, is not quite so frightening as sheer stupidity. Looking around him, however, this writer strongly feels that what has brought France to her present pass and what is stirring up the current minirevolt of the young is not rational calculation, but, well, the other thing.

PATERNALISM AND EMPLOYMENT

Reading "Stamp Your Feet and Demand a Fair Deal," the Nobel laureate economist Milton Friedman remarked in a letter to the author that he was not surprised that 10 percent of the French labor force and 23 percent of the young had no jobs, but wondered how 90 percent did have one.

Why do they? It is a good question and we do not really know the answer. In moments of despair and disgust, as one surveys all that has been done in this rich and talented country to pervert the normal functioning of the economy, combat reality, foster illusions, and make water flow uphill, one is tempted to say that the worst has become plausible and anything better is a surprise. Perhaps we should not think it absurd that all jobs should just disappear. In any case, the question now is to explain *any* level of employment between 0 and 100 percent, rather than minor shortfalls from the 100 percent norm.

In a centrally planned and commanded economy, the state in practice owns the workers and employs such proportion of them as it wishes. It pays them with what they manage to produce. Even if all are employed, they cannot produce much, the system is hardly workable, and too many of the potential workers have to be employed as policemen of one kind or another to keep down the rest. This "model" is now confined to the museum, though some intellectuals still hanker after it and would dust it off if they had their way.

Employment in competitive economies based on individual ownership and freedom of contract is explained in terms of equilibria in which producers and consumers are each doing the best that is feasible for themselves, provided that all or most others do the best that is feasible for themselves as well. The neoclassical model of explanation runs in terms of such equalities as the one between the marginal product of labor and the wage, between the (risk-adjusted) return on capital and the rate of interest, between the quantity of money divided

First published by Liberty Fund, Inc., at www.econlib.org on May 1, 2006. Reprinted by permission.

by the price level and the demand for real money balances, and between consumption and abstinence rewarded by the rate of interest. Under not too implausible conditions, excess demand or excess supply is corrected, the necessary equalities are satisfied, and the standard solution in general equilibrium is 100 percent employment subject only to frictional losses.

The "Austrian model" runs mostly in different terms (though the difference is often only one of semantics) and makes less use of the concept of equilibrium, but it produces a solution that resembles the neoclassical one. In a normally functioning free economy, employment will tend to be full. In the Keynesian scheme, full employment is a special case that may or may not be achieved according to certain variables. Two of these, the level of wages and the minimum achievable rate of interest (caught in the "liquidity trap") are inflexible and this permits equilibrium to be maintained at some low level of activity and employment. Each of these explanatory models can be, and has been, refined almost out of recognition by generations of economists as they climbed the ladders of academic preferment, but the main outlines subsist.

Enter the modern welfare state in the particular version that it took on in the main countries of continental Europe, notably in Germany, France, and Italy. With the welfare state enters a paternalistic economy that operates to shred, grind, and send down the drain some of the value it creates. A kind of paternalistic economic model might help to explain how it works and why it destroys jobs.

The ancestry of the value-grinding machine goes back to the custom in the English weaving and metalworking trades of the seventeenth century to pay workers not in cash, but in kind, usually in the very product—e.g., cloth or nails—they were making. Despite repeated Truck Acts prohibiting the practice, it survived into the mid-nineteenth century. In America, it persisted into the twentieth century in the form of the company store where workers had to spend the vouchers they were given in lieu of wages. Even if the worker was not cheated on the rate at which his nominal wage was converted into cloth, nails, or groceries, the payment of his wage in kind instead of cash deprived him of the choice of spending the wage as he saw fit, hence reducing its value to him.

The modern version of the ancient truck system, practiced on a gigantic scale, is compulsory social insurance which the worker is legally obliged to accept in lieu of part of his wage.

A schematic illustration will make it clear what is going on. If in Germany or France the cost to the employer of employing a worker for a given length of time is $100, the employer pays $20 of that sum into publicly administered health, unemployment, disability, and pension schemes on behalf of the worker. This is misleadingly called the "employer's contribution" though it is in fact part of the employee's wage compulsorily deducted rather than paid out to him. Of the remainder, a further $20 is deducted and paid into the same insurance schemes on behalf of the worker. This is called the employee's contribution. Though the fact is masked by a fraudulent vocabulary, the employee in reality contributes not $20 but $40, for both contributions come out of his wages. However, what he receives in cash is only $60.

The worker is told that his wage is $80, of which $60 is in cash and $20 is in kind, namely insurance against various contingencies. He is pleased to know that on top of this, his employer is also paying $20 to make his insurance cover fuller. However, basic value theory tells us that cash of $100 is worth more to the recipient than a basket of goods—including a basket of insurance policies—that would cost him $100 to buy and that he has not himself chosen but that was chosen for him. Between the $100 cost of the insurance basket that he is compulsorily made to accept and the worth of the basket to him, the recipient loses value as it is shredded and ground to dust in the coercive social insurance machine. The lost value is subjective and cannot be readily measured, but it is a loss all the same.

The effect on employment is easy to diagnose. The demand price of labor is $100. The supply price is also $100 because the employer cannot hire labor that would cost him less, given the compulsory insurance premium included in the wage cost. However, if the whole wage were paid in cash, the supply price would lie somewhere at or above $80 but below $100 (though we cannot say precisely by how much below). At this reduced supply price, the demand for labor would expand until demand price and supply price reached equality again above $80 and below $100. It is this potential increase in employment that the compulsory conversion of part of wages from cash into kind (i.e., into "social" insurance) prevents. Putting it the other way round, moving from payment in cash to payment in kind destroys jobs by forcing up the supply price of labor.

The paternalist takes the view that social insurance must be compulsory, for workers would otherwise not insure themselves. This is a vast topic that offers no simple answers except possibly the moral one that it is wrong to deprive workers of the freedom to spend their wages as they choose. It is highly likely that while some would insure themselves, others would not, and to this extent the paternalists are right. In the longer run, however, they would be less and less right, for bitter experience would gradually ingrain the insurance habit and buying some cover suited to personal circumstances would become part of standard behavior.

In the meantime, compulsory social insurance keeps the cash cost of labor way above the supply price of labor that would obtain if the wage were paid in cash rather than kind. In the gap between the two, value disappears and chronic unemployment becomes the equilibrium in which the economy of welfare states maintains itself. It is a copper-bottomed bet that neither the paternalists nor the workers they treat as children realize the reason why this is so.

THE THINGS LABOR UNIONS ARE UP TO

"Unions protect the worker on the shop floor." "Unions foment strikes." "Unions are the indispensable channel of communication between management and labor." "Unions promote the interests of a blue-collar elite at the expense of nonunion workers and the really poor." "Unions make for orderly industrial relations." "Unions conspire with big business to rip off the consumer." "Unions are an outdated relic of the smokestack era." "Unions carry the workers' cause from the bargaining table to the political arena."

None of this is wholly false, but none reveals much of the chain that links effects to their causes. The difference unions can make to a society is one of the most complex and emotionally tainted byways in political economy.

At the level of the single firm, organizing the employees in a stand-alone union not affiliated to a larger body has effects on wages and nonwage relations. Prior to being organized, employees get the "rate for the job" according to local custom. The ultimate origin of custom lies in acts of individual bargaining that establish the area or band of ready acceptability. To change this, the union must be strong enough to discipline its own members so they will only work at the rate negotiated by it on their collective behalf, as well as to discourage nonmembers from free-riding on the union's efforts. The bluntest way of achieving this is the closed shop.

Where the closed shop runs into strong opposition in the community because it violates the freedom to work, the union can still achieve its objectives if it can browbeat nonunionized employees into not undercutting it and to support strike action if need be.

For collective bargaining to have a real point, it must achieve wage rates and nonwage conditions more favorable to the employees than the customary rate. It is difficult to verify whether it is really achieving

First published by Liberty Fund, Inc., at www.econlib.org on February 12, 2004. Reprinted by permission.

this. Attempts can be made to compare the union rate with rates in nonunionized shops, but for these comparisons to be convincing, all other things must be equal, and of course they seldom are. All in all, however, it is reasonable to hold that unions can raise the wages of unionized labor. They also make wage rates more uniform and less flexible. This would tend to make the wage contract less efficient, equating the firm's demand for labor to its (local) supply at a lower level than would be the case under less uniform and more flexible wages.

Higher average wages reduce the firm's profit, lower its output, and raise its prices. How much of each depends on the nature of competition. A special case is conceivable where the firm continues to sell the same output at the same price under perfect competition, but what Alfred Marshall called its quasi-rent gets transferred to its workers. It is this case, in the form of a subconscious dream, that inspires much of prounion sentiment.

Everything becomes more complex and harder to disentangle when labor organization becomes industrywide, let alone nationwide. If wages are pushed up across a whole industry, prices may well follow suit all the way, since there is little or no competition to hold them back. Consequently, profits may be largely maintained. Most or all of the impact falls on the nonunionized sector, which operates under competitive conditions and cannot raise its prices. Therefore its terms of trade will worsen and its profits and employment levels shrink. The pressure will be mitigated and dispersed if capital is mobile and migrates, taking jobs from the unionized to the nonunionized sector, as it did in the United States when it migrated from the Northeast to the Southeast and Southwest, and as it is doing in Europe when it is "exporting jobs" to China, Thailand, and India.

Unionization also shifts the terms of trade in favor of (some) producers at the expense of (all) consumers. This is a common symptom found in all corporatist social organization, guilds in the Middle Ages, chambers of industry in Fascist Italy and Nazi Germany, and labor unions in Western democracies.

Looking at how matters may evolve over time, it seems that in the short run profits and employment in the economy as a whole may suffer but union wages may increase. Unions, then, will have acted to good purpose from their members' point of view. However, since a far higher proportion of profits than of wages is saved, capital accumulation, productivity, and growth should all be reduced. The long-run damping effect on wages should eventually swamp the short-run boost unionization can give them. Yet like all elected officials, union leaders cannot afford to worry about the long run.

Analyzing the manner, purpose, and effects of union action in largely economic terms is a good enough approximation to American conditions. American political culture accepts capitalism as the best of possible worlds. It finds it normal to think of wages as the price of labor and of labor as one of the several factors of production. In most of Europe, this is either not understood, or if understood, it is rejected. For several generations, the political classes and the teaching professions have taught the people that labor was not an economic, but a "social" category, deserving of higher consideration and a different treatment from the mere economic.

It is something of a philosophical puzzle to decipher what is meant by the word "social," though it is used confidently enough to suggest that it has a clear meaning. One key to understanding policy and politics in most European countries is to take it that "social" indicates that the matter in hand imperatively demands a political decision to override any market solution that would otherwise emerge.

It should be no surprise, then, that European labor unions are really political organizations, straddling the economic and the "social," closely allied to left-wing movements, and permanently camping in the "corridors of power" of all governments whether left or right. Their interest is as much to "change society" as to negotiate good wages and conditions for their members.

An exception to most of this is Britain, where the Thatcher reforms of the 1980s have transformed the union landscape. "Official" strikes now require vote by secret ballot, picketing has been curbed, the most glaring legal immunities of the unions have been removed and the rule of law enforced. After the chaotic disruption of the 1970s, Britain has since these commonsense reforms enjoyed unprecedented industrial peace and a clear lead in prosperity over most of continental Europe, where governments of all shades sought to appease and share power with the unions.

Like in most of the industrialized world, union membership in Europe has been declining for decades. But it is not numbers that make for union strength. Union membership as a share of the labor force is over 80 percent in Scandinavia, in the mid-20s in Britain, Germany, Italy, and Spain, and only 8 percent in France, with virtually zero in the private sector. Yet if you guessed that it is in France that the unions have the tightest armlock on the government, you would not be far wrong.

Of the four largest French unions, the largest is the CGT; it is orthodox Communist. The third and fourth largest are the FO and SUD, both of Trotskyist persuasion. Only the second-largest, CFDT, is moderate. The CGT has a mere 670,000 members. However, they are concentrated in the state-owned railways, the Treasury, and the public schools. The CGT can stop all the trains, disrupt tax collection and government payments, and shut the schools. While the latter might not unduly upset the government, the former two fill it with visceral dread.

Led by the CGT, the unions keep on refusing a spate of long-overdue reforms of all kinds, condemning them as "neoliberal." The government either keeps postponing them, or withdraws them altogether if the unions cry "boo." Having a comfortable majority in the legislature is no use; it is the unions' consent the government thinks it needs.

Unions are supposed to live on members' dues. In France, they cover perhaps a quarter of the budget of the only union, the CFDT, that is honest enough to publish any accounts. It is common knowledge that the bulk of union expenditure, including the cost of keeping their bureaucracies in the comfort they feel entitled to, comes from the government, some avowed, some disguised in more or less ingenious ways.

The system began in 1968 and kept growing in the fond belief that one could buy the cooperation of the unions by bribing them outright. This has never worked, but the bribes have proved habit-forming and curtailing them would drive the union hierarchies to paroxysms of fury.

Yet union strength depends on their members' obedience, and the members follow the leaders almost entirely because the government treats them as if they were supremely powerful. There is no one to say loud and clear that they are not, that it would suffice to face them down once and for all to realize that the emperor has no clothes.

However, this is not the first nor the last time that governments fail to do what is good for them and their peoples. If failing to do the sensible thing were not their habit, this column would soon be reduced to writing about apple pie and motherhood.

THE INSTABILITY OF THE WELFARE STATE

Stability is a property—most of the time rightly regarded as a desirable, virtuous one—of economic variables, such as price, output, demand, or indeed an entire economic system. When dislodged from its position (in statics) or from its path (in dynamics), resistances are generated that will eventually return the variable to its original position or path. The resistances that achieve this act as automatic stabilizers.

Throughout economic history, the demand for money balances—what was later called "liquidity preference"—acted as such a stabilizer. In sharp cyclical downturns, commodity prices fell, often drastically so. The real value of money balances in the hands of consumers and merchants rose accordingly, exceeding the proportion of their wealth they would normally wish to hold in cash form. Consequently, when they no longer expected prices to fall much further, they started to spend money to reduce their cash balances. The total quantity of coin and liquid paper money being broadly given, they could not reduce its nominal amount, but its value in real terms was reduced as the higher spending led to higher commodity prices as well as to greater income and wealth, until the real value of money balances again became equal to the real amount demanded.

The last time this old-fashioned stabilizer had any noticeable effect was exit from the Great Depression from about 1934 onward, though of course the recovery had other causes as well. Since World War II, economists have been, quite rightly, dismissing the stabilizing potential of the price level, since they found that average prices, like average wages, can in the modern world hardly ever move downward and that the money supply will in practice always accommodate a rising price level.

First published by Liberty Fund, Inc., at www.econlib.org on August 1, 2005. Reprinted by permission.

GOVERNMENT—THE PASSIVE BALLAST

Instead of the value of money, economics, in assimilating the Keynesian schema of analysis, discovered another stabilizer, the public sector. In a downturn, sales taxes fell promptly and in proportion to the drop in sales, while income taxes fell with a lag, but more than proportionately. Government expenditure, much of it fixed well in advance by legislative or contractual commitments, was maintained. As a result, the public sector pumped a maintained stream of income into the private sector but pumped a reduced tax charge out of it. The sharper was the downturn, the stronger was this effect, and the greater was the share of central and local government expenditure in the national income, the more resistant became the latter to cyclical fluctuations. The beauty of this effect was that all the government had to do was to remain passive as a heap of ballast at the ship's bottom; no policy response was required from it, hence it could not get it wrong.

Then came, first slowly, but accelerating rapidly, the rise of the welfare state with successive Labour governments in Britain, with the social democracy of Giscard in France and Helmut Schmidt in Germany, and of course LBJ's Great Society in the U.S. Under these governments, two things happened to the public sector. It expanded in a seemingly inexorable way as a proportion of national income, and as welfare entitlements took a growing share of it and welfare entitlements moved inversely with economic activity, government spending actually rose when the economy turned down. The automatic stabilizer became, so to speak, a supercharged turbo engine.

In the last three decades, the amplitude of economic fluctuations has in fact been relatively moderate by historical standards, though of course a large public sector was only one of the likely reasons. That initially, at least, it did have a smoothing-out role is hard to deny, even if we believe that its other, less easily discernible effects did greater long-term damage than the good stabilization may have brought us. In recent years, however, the public sector, and more particularly its welfare component, has very likely become a powerful factor of instability, pushing the system ever farther away from equilibrium once it has been dislodged from it.

"MERIT GOODS"

Goods that the political elite thinks ought to be consumed in greater quantity than they would be if left to unaided matching of supply and demand are flatteringly called "merit goods"—they are said to merit a better sort than the market would mete out to them. "Culture" is the classic merit good, and in its name concert halls and theaters are built, museums, operas, and libraries subsidized, artists kept afloat with public money. The class of merit goods can be stretched almost at will to include anything of which people might consume too little for their own good if left to themselves. Cod liver oil is a merit good, and so is saving for a rainy day and for retirement.

What the welfare state—more precisely, the version of it practiced above all in Germany and France that calls itself the "European model"—has gradually done was to replace a large chunk of everyone's wages by merit goods. Instead of earning, say, $1,300 a week in cash, they earned $800 in cash and $500 in the form of mandatory deductions (employees' and employers' contributions) to pay for the foremost merit goods: unemployment insurance, health care, and pensions.

Paternalism, the inseparable satellite of the welfare state, firmly holds that if wage-earners had the extra $500 paid out to them, they would buy little or no unemployment insurance and would save too little for medical care and retirement. This may or may not be the case. What is certain, though, is that if they were paid the $500, they could spend it on these merit goods, but also on anything else they wished, so that having the $500 would never be worth less to them than the merit goods they received in its place, and might be worth appreciably more depending on individual preference and judgment. Cash of $800 plus merit goods provided by the welfare state at a cost of $500 would be worth less than $1,300 to the average worker but would cost $1,300 to his employer.

A MACHINE TO GRIND JOBS

The real cost of labor to the employer and the real remuneration to the worker are normally equal. Welfare, given in merit goods, opens up a gap between the two: the cost of the part-cash, part-welfare package to the employer rises above the real value the workers subjectively place on the package.

Real cost to the employer and real value to the employee are two jaws of a machine that grinds and destroys jobs. Unemployment that should hover around 5–6 percent gradually moves to double digits. It is now 11.9 percent in Germany, 10.2 percent in France, and 9.6 percent in Italy. These are official statistics that need some interpretation. In France, for instance, the unemployment figures do not include about 1.2 million people who do not qualify for unemployment insurance but are paid a minimum income by the state. In every country run on the "European social model," the public sector is stuffed with make-work jobs whose sole real purpose is to keep some hopeless young people off the streets. These jobs, too, escape the unemployment statistics.

If due to some shock unemployment rises from 5 to 10 percent, but the welfare state maintains the income of the newly unemployed, there is a temporary rise in the budget deficit. However, maintaining aggregate income eventually restores employment and rebalances the budget.

Under the new dispensation of the modern welfare state, with the big job-grinder going round and round, this does not happen. The gap between the real cost of labor and what labor really receives remains rigidly in place. A double lock is, in fact, put on it because dismissing labor is now very expensive and may involve legal procedures lasting many months and sometimes years, and the employers will not hire if they won't be able to fire. The same total income and the aggregate demand consistent with 5 percent unemployment are now consistent with 10 percent unemployment. The budget deficit, too, becomes chronic and steadily rises above the diminutive growth of the economy. In the short run, there is stability of a miserable situation, but in the longer run there is a seemingly inexorable decline that is cumulative, self-reinforcing.

Serious reform will not take place before the apparent short-term stability is widely enough recognized as creeping instability. Such recognition seems now to be dawning.

SOME BAD NEWS COULD BE GOOD NEWS

The bad news is that despite the harsh experience of the last decade or more that should have brought home the damage done by socialist tinkering, there is still no electoral majority for a more liberal economy in "core" Europe. Crucial elections in Germany last September were supposed to sweep away the social-democratic government and install in its place the alliance of conservatives and liberals whose program openly aimed at cutting the overblown welfare state down to size and at tackling unemployment by doing away with the more absurd features of the prevailing "job protection" laws. Instead of winning the comfortable majority predicted by the polls, the center-right alliance failed to gain control of the legislature. The social democrats, the "greens," and the hard left, though by no means united, could and assuredly would defeat any radical reform proposal. Mathematically, the only issue was a coalition government of the center-right with the center-left, capable only of uneasy compromises and half measures, and bound to preserve the essentials of the "social protection" that the electorate insisted on maintaining.

All this had a profound knock-on effect in France. The French left is leaderless, has no program, and is in disarray. The right has the majority by a wide margin. However, the right is internally divided into a mainstream and a radical reformist part. The mainstream wants to continue the postwar tradition of an anti–"Anglo-Saxon" ideology and of "social" appeasement at almost any cost. It is led by a second-term president who, contrary to his high-profile postures in foreign policy, in domestic policy never faced down a strike and never failed to give way to noisy street demonstrations. Interest groups have duly learned the lesson and have become more intransigent and menacing than their intrinsic strength would normally permit. Despite the overt and covert government subsidies meant both to strengthen and to buy them off,

First published by Liberty Fund, Inc., at www.econlib.org on November 7, 2005. Reprinted by permission.

French labor unions are intrinsically feeble, with a total membership of less than 8 percent of the labor force, but behave as if they held all real power in the land.

Until recently, the reformist wing of the French Right looked highly likely to defeat the mainstream at the next presidential and parliamentary elections in April 2007. The result of the German elections caused all calculations to be remade and all positions to be shifted leftward. "A liberal economic program is the surest way to lose the election" has become the received wisdom.

If this wisdom is in fact true, it has a drastically simple explanation. The "average" voter, frightened by the chronic 10–11 percent unemployment rate, is desperately clinging to the system of "social protection" that prevails in Germany and France. He stubbornly refuses to see that it is the very system of "social protection" that is the main cause of unemployment.

The good news lurking behind these bad ones is that it is never possible altogether to outlaw and smother the adjustment process by which an economy pushed off balance by shocks and extraeconomic constraints, seeks to right itself. If cowardly politics shuts down one corrective mechanism, another will start up. The result will not always be as smooth or efficient as if the first, most obvious, mechanism had been allowed to work, but adjustment will still take place, albeit in roundabout and costlier ways. The Soviet Union had banned profit-and-loss and frozen the price system. In their place, much of the work of resource allocation shifted to queues, black and gray markets, and the sort of corruption that spreads when direct ownership interest is suppressed or overlaid by principal-agent relations.

With all adjustment mechanisms intact, unemployment depresses wages, which in turn stimulates rehiring. As capital's appetite for hiring labor increases, investment using standard technology to create workplaces expands. Expansion continues till the demand for labor lifts wages sufficiently to arrest the process. Throughout, there is a sort of pendulum movement between the share of profits and the share of wages in national income. More appetite on the part of capital to hire labor boosts the share of wages and reduces the share of capital—as used to be the case in the 1960s and '70s when employment was still near to full.

What happens instead in the Franco-German welfare state "model" of today? Companies do not hire, because under "job protection" laws they may not be able to fire should it become advisable to shed labor. It is extremely difficult to reduce wages or tighten working conditions; indeed, there is pressure from the government and the media to do the opposite. Everybody would like to cut costs by shedding labor when this is feasible. German companies now manage to do it, but the cost is fearful; Daimler Benz is providing 960 million euros to fund the cost of letting go 8,500 workers from its plants in Baden-Württemberg. In France, even high severance payments may not permit payrolls to be cut. Hewlett Packard intended to reduce its work force in Grenoble by 1,250 persons, mostly by natural wastage over two years. Because the company was profitable in its worldwide operations, there was outrage at this manifestation of ruthless and shameless greed. President Chirac called upon the European Union to intervene, there was a barrage of accusations against the management, and Hewlett Packard eventually back-pedalled some of the way. The example can only encourage other companies to shed labor when they can get away with it at an affordable cost, and in any case not to create new jobs.

However, there are exceptions and they also tell a tale. Toyota did create several thousand new jobs in northeast France. Its president is reported to have said that he chose this location in preference to England because English workers do not fear for their jobs and will "talk back," while French ones are so intimidated by the surrounding unemployment that they are easier to handle. Unions are highly aggressive in the public sector but hardly ever strike in private industry.

Despite such exceptions, the overall tendency is to refrain from hiring and fire (or "delocate" to eastern Europe, India, or China) when one can get away with it. Manufacturing employment is now 22.5 percent of the total in Germany and 15 percent in France, still way above the American and British figure of 10 percent, but falling. Investment has a strong labor-saving bias as companies are reaching out for new technologies. Instead of "widening" it, the stock of equipment is being "deepened." As the nineteenth-century Austrian economist Böhm-Bawerk would have put it, the "period of production" is lengthening (without necessarily taking more time).

The irony is that to relieve unemployment, it is precisely "widening" and not "deepening" that would be needed. It is "widening" that the normal corrective mechanism of falling wages and the ensuing demand for labor would have produced.

What the roundabout adjustment mechanism permitted by the counterproductive policies of the Franco-German "social model" is bringing about is bad for employment and bad for wages in the short term. In the long term, however, it may prove to have been a great leap forward. Sooner and faster than would have been normal, it forced the "core" European economies to adopt technologies appropriate for tomorrow's economies that are short of labor—an unexpected achievement for countries suffering from double-digit unemployment. It greatly accelerated their exit from traditional manufacturing industries and their transformation into service economies along much-maligned Anglo-American lines—another unexpected by-product of the European "social model." Whether lagging growth, unemployment, and rising national indebtedness are prices worth paying for this result is of course an open question, but at least these prices are not being paid only to keep up the futile illusion of "social protection."

BUILT-IN UNEMPLOYMENT
SOCIAL PROTECTION COSTS MORE THAN IT IS WORTH

A generation ago, unemployment was understood to be a cyclical phenomenon, not quite as regular as the four seasons of the year but rather like periods of wet and cold following periods of balmy sun. However, unlike the weather we could not change, we have found ways that promised to give us control over unemployment. We were taught that the awful years of the 1930s need never return. We could largely smooth out fluctuations in activity by commonsense methods of demand management. Fiscal and monetary policies, with an occasional nudge from exchange rate manipulation, were powerful enough to prevent major swings, while the human cost of the minor ones that could not be avoided was alleviated by social insurance, a small burden society could easily bear and broadly approved.

Those confident times are gone—it would seem irrevocably so. By the mid-'70s, "smoothing out" ceased to function as the books said it should. Unemployment became significant again, and its social cost began to be felt. By the '90s, both economic and political alarm bells started to keep up a shrill music, social safety nets were spread in haste, shedding labor was made ever more difficult in order to keep the employed at work, but blocking the exit discouraged the entry and the unemployed numbers went on rising. Today in Germany and the other core countries of the euro-zone, for every ten or eleven members of the active population, one is out of work. Though some of those are suspected of not trying very hard to get harnessed, there is little doubt that the bulk is involuntarily idle. For a little green man just landed from outer space, this situation must be wholly incomprehensible. For us, it is a matter for shame, a proof that we have ruined a mechanism of

Reprinted from *L'Homme libre: Mélanges en l'honneur de Pascal Salin,* ed. Mathieu Laine and Guido Hülsmann (Paris: Les Belles Lettres, 2006), 324–28. Reproduced by permission.

economic adjustment by trying to fix it. Unemployment looks to have become endemic, stable. What makes it so grave is that no realistic observer expects it to be reversed in the foreseeable future. Something must have gone very wrong.

Let us shift the perspective for a moment. Between the fifteenth and seventeenth centuries, when wage labor in industry was in its infancy in England and the money economy was displacing payment in goods, the payment of wages in kind was fairly widely practiced and just as widely detested. In handloom weaving, framework knitting, the making of nails and other hardware, though nominally there was a customary wage fixed in shillings and pence, many masters paid their men in kind, choosing goods they could procure cheaply, goods that were a little shoddy, or indeed some of their own products. Two griefs were felt by the workers against this "truck" system. The basket of goods they got instead of the money might be counted by the master at more than it cost him—he made a profit out of imposing payment *in natura*. But even if he gave full value, the basket of goods was worth less to the worker, because he lost the freedom to buy exactly what he wanted in the exact quantities that most suited him. He was deprived of the advantages of a money economy and the value of consumer choice.

Parliament tried to outlaw this practice by Truck Acts in 1604, 1621, 1703, and 1831. Ordinary market forces helped more than legislation to do away with truck, for the best workers could only be hired for cash wages. Nevertheless, as late as 1871 a royal commission into truck still found cause to condemn the "outright compulsion" involved in the deprivation of consumer choice. A lesser degree of compulsion subsisted in the United States into the 1930s, especially in the mining industry, where some wages were paid in "company scrip" the miner could only spend in the company store. By and large, however, truck as a substitute for money wages has withered away before World War II . . .

. . . Only to be reborn, a thousandfold bigger, in our day.

And, as the saying goes, this explains that.

A German worker earning, say, 3,500 euros a month is paid about 2,100 euros in cash before income tax. The remaining 1,400 is paid directly by him or indirectly on his behalf by his employer in premiums into various social insurance schemes, notably against sickness, accident, disability, old age, and unemployment. Generally, the greater part of the premium is called an "employer's contribution," the smaller his own contribution, but it has all been earned by his work. Though purely formal, this distinction between the two contributions has some psychological significance—it tacitly suggests that the employer gives the employee some kind of extra bonus on top of the wage. In reality, all social insurance premiums represent money that is the counterpart of the employee's work but that he does not get to take home and spend as he and his wife would choose.

Instead of the money, he gets the various kinds of insurance against most of life's risks that may or may not materialize (including the "risk" that he does not die before age, fatigue, or the rules in his branch of industry induce him to stop working).

Whatever else this is and whatever it may be called in our day, this is a system of payment of wages in kind, once known as "truck," and it is done on a gigantic scale. It may well be a marvel of universal, wise, and caring social protection. It is nonetheless a case of "outright compulsion," to cite the pithy judgment of honest nineteenth-century English liberals, for the worker is forced to accept a large part of his earnings in kind (i.e., in social insurance) unless he is prepared to dive down into the illegal "black" economy where he gets all-cash wages. Compulsion is applied to both him and his employer. The latter pays in kind not because he profits from it, but because the law says that he must. The law, in fact, is a sort of Truck Act turned upside down.

Since the scheme works on an all-encompassing, gigantic scale, it would be surprising if its effects were not comparably vast. Yet the strange fact is that economists and sociologists seem to pay little attention to what the massive shift from the cash nexus to the truck system may have done to the "European social model." There is lively debate about the virtues and vices of the welfare state, about rewarding failure and punishing success, about forcing the strong to help the weak, about the economic effects of redistribution in general. None of this debate takes into account the likely effect of forcibly moving two-fifths of all wage incomes from the money economy into the economy-in-kind where one good or service is exchanged directly against another and where the range of available goods is limited to one or two. What would be disposable income in the former takes the form of "social" insurance cover in the latter.

It is perhaps worth reflecting a little on what the most basic economic theory can tell us about the implications for unemployment.

For two nights in a row, an economist had a nightmare. The first night, he dreamt that a mad dictator had ordered all employers to pay him a payroll tax of 40 percent and had ordered all the money so collected to be paid out to the wage-earners as a supplement to their wages. The economist then woke up abruptly, rubbed his eyes, and found that if he had continued his dream to its conclusion, the employers would have started paying only 60 percent of the original wage, but the workers would still be getting 100 with the state supplement, so that nobody would end up either worse- or better-off. Things maintained their old equilibrium.

The next night, his nightmare took a different turning. The mad dictator again collected the 40 percent paytoll tax, but did not pay out the money to the wage-earners. Instead, he gave them insurance cover against sickness, disability, old age, and unemployment. The cover cost just 40 percent of the previous payroll to provide. The provider was the dictator's own insurance company that was no more inefficient than most private insurance companies and did not make any profit. Waking up again abruptly, the economist worked out how the dream would have ended. The employers again tried to reduce wages by 40 percent, arguing that 60 in wages and 40 in payroll tax made 100, the wage cost level at which it just paid them to keep employment at the previous level. However, the wage-earners could not accept this, for they were doubtful about how much the insurance cover was worth to them. Some said it was a useful thing to have and worth buying for 40. Most, however, said that if they had their initial 100, they could always buy the full insurance cover for 40, or a part of it for 25, or not buy it from the dictator's insurance company, or not buy any insurance at all and spend the money on a great variety of other things. If they were really forced to accept the cover provided by the dictator, they would not give up 40 of the wage for it. Maybe a deduction of 30 would be acceptable, leaving a money wage of 70.

This second nightmare would thus end with the employers' wage costs per employee rising from 100 to 110 in order to give the marginal employee the same total wage (cash plus insurance cover) as before, i.e., the equivalent of 100 in cash. The economist would conclude that wage costs in reality would settle somewhere midway between 100 and 110 and employment would fall below its previous equilibrium level. Unemployment would result, and it would be "built in," perfectly stable as long as social insurance remained universal and compulsory.

He would find this prognosis confirmed by the facts he found, even though they had not come about by the same process as in his dream. The fundamental cause would be the same in both dream and reality: providing universal and mandatory social protection costs more than it is subjectively worth to the beneficiaries. The difference is a net loss, a deadweight burden on the economy.

Beyond the loss of economic welfare, which we cannot objectively measure because much of it is a matter of the subjective value individuals place on the basket of goods available to them both when they can freely choose its content and when they cannot, and both when they are employed and when they live on unemployment relief, there lurks another intangible yet real loss.

Replacing a part of the cash wage with social protection also has an ethical dimension. It is just as important to clarify it as the economic one, and we can hardly get much clarity if we do not simplify it just as brutally as we did the economic aspects.

The ethical problem has two main components. One is the curtailment of free disposal of incomes, which is prima facie objectionable. However, even in modern libertarian doctrine, compulsory social protection is not unanimously condemned. Hayek, for example, thinks it is a lesser evil, and as such he accepts it. The reason is the threat of a particularly noxious form of "moral hazard." Moral hazard infects all kinds of insurance, for if you are compensated in case of a loss (e.g., the loss of your job), you try less hard to avoid the loss. Apart from this more or less "normal" moral hazard, voluntary social insurance throws up a different, nastier version. If you are not forced to insure yourself, you may quite cynically and coldly leave yourself uninsured in the safe knowledge that if worst comes to worst, the state will not allow you to suffer too much misery but will rush to your rescue at the taxpayers' expense.

Since this is very likely to be the case, only two choices are left. One is to resign ourselves to living with the stifling machinery of universal protection and bear its severe and degrading economic consequences. The other is not to rush to the rescue of the irresponsible and the cynical when, lacking insurance, they get into trouble, but *pour encourager les autres,* let them suffer and scramble for private charity. This could be politically very difficult to do. But if it were done for a period, lessons would be learned and the problem would progressively diminish.

The second hard-to-digest lump in the ethical problem has to do with the question: "Do people know what is good for them?" If allowed freely to spend their money as they choose, won't many of them bitterly regret their choice a month, a year, or half a lifetime later? It is quite likely that many in fact do regret having spent some of their income on life's little luxuries rather than on more generous health insurance or a private pension. Orthodox theory considers, reasonably enough, that each person strikes a balance between present and future goods according to his time preference, and nobody has any business striking the balance for him. But is today's young buyer of the shiny motorcycle or the designer dress really the same person as tomorrow's sick patient or pensioner? And if these young buyers somehow become different persons with the passage of time, what is the moral status of the decision of the young that affects not only their own well-being but also that of their future alter ego?

Each of these questions can spawn dozens of more subtle ones. The literature of modern utilitarianism is overflowing with them, and each is more sophisticated than the one before it. A clear view over the entire complex seems more and more unattainable. Some clarity can nevertheless be had if instead of trying to assess "utilities" arising from free and unfree consumer choices, we pursue a simpler question: "Who is entitled to decide for another?"

Forcing someone to do something for his own good is immensely widespread, and its tradition is as old as humanity. Fathers and mothers have been doing it to their children ever since fathers, mothers, and children have existed. Nothing can seem more natural, more in tune with our sense of the right order of things.

When we do it to grown-ups, we still call it "paternalism," though we cannot claim paternity. The word nevertheless lends our action an air of benevolent wisdom, of knowing better and "tough love." However, while we may have the force to force those whose happiness we try to further, we simply do not have the innate authority for it that parents have traditionally had over their children.

LET'S THROW THIS MODEL AWAY

One of the reasons Continental governments resist letting go of the "European model" is that some intellectuals keep telling them that it's economically viable. A school of thought maintains, for example, that the existing intricate network of social protection not only is morally good because it levels off sharp inequalities, but can be efficient too. This is an important argument to hang on to when the rest of the world seems to be going in the opposite direction. With free trade and a single European currency making protectionism and competitive devaluations more difficult, the "European model" is coming under threat. What better salve than to tell yourself that it's good economics?

An example of this type of intellectual succor for the European model came recently from the influential National Bureau of Economic Research. Richard Freeman has argued that the "European model" has nothing much to fear, for the effect of social protection on economic efficiency is, broadly speaking, neutral. If this is a correct view, it is vastly important. If it is not correct, it is important to say so and to find the source of the error. Let's explore the issue.

Mr. Freeman's main claim is that productivity growth is on the whole no higher in countries with flexible labor markets than in those with regulations that gum up the system. His explanation is ingenious and goes to the heart of our social system. I also believe that it is seriously wrong.

"OWNING" ONE'S JOB

Invoking a famous theorem enunciated by the British Nobel laureate economist Ronald Coase, Mr. Freeman reminds us that, with freedom of contract and low transaction costs, an asset will end up in its most productive use regardless of who happens to own it initially. Now, a job

First published in the *Wall Street Journal Europe*, May 11, 2000. Reprinted by permission.

protected by administrative controls over hiring and firing, by a closed shop or other union restrictions, or by "lifetime employment" traditions can with some exaggeration be regarded as "owned" by the employee. A job unprotected by such "workers' rights" devices is "owned" by the employer. He can freely dismiss his employee, close down the job, or fill it with someone else.

Suppose the employer wants to "close down" one job because, by reorganizing the shop or the office, he can get the work done by one fewer employee. If he "owns" the job, the marginal employee is fired and the employer pockets the productivity gain. If the worker "owns" his job, he cannot be dismissed.

However, in Mr. Freeman's scenario, the employee will agree to be "bought out," for he will not value his lifetime job any more than the sum the employer can save by getting rid of him. Consequently, he will go, the productivity gain will take place, and it is the departing worker who will pocket it in the form of a lump-sum severance payment. Under this version of the script, the distribution of income will be tipped in favor of the employee but the progress of productivity will be exactly the same. The economy benefits equally.

Except that is is hard to see why a worker should never value the chance of preserving his job more highly than the productivity gain his employer could obtain by firing him. If he does not give up "his" job, the script will not play well. Numbers of unproductive workers are liable to stay in their jobs. Productivity gains will be forgone due to the "ownership" of jobs being vested in the workers. This is labor market inflexibility.

Yet this is not even the major source of error in the thesis that the "European model" is neutral in its effect upon economic efficiency. Let's say that the unproductive employee does always agree to depart, taking with him a capital sum representing the present value of some or all of the productivity gain his departure generates. Let us suspend judgment about what such a shift might do to efficiency, not to speak of entrepreneurial incentive. We're still left with the irreducible hard core of the error in the whole neutrality argument.

If every employee has two prospects—keeping his job until he retires, or leaving it early with full compensation—this means that everyone starts their jobs with an insurance policy providing either an annuity or a capital sum. The policy is paid up by the enterprise. It makes no difference to the outcome whether the premiums are paid to the government body, a private insurer, or if they're accounted for as a reserve on the enterprise's own balance sheet. They are payable whether productivity gains are forthcoming or not. They are obviously a cost that can be avoided by not hiring labor.

Offering job-loss insurance as part of a worker's compensation is no different from offering any of the other guarantees that make up the arsenal of social protection under the welfare state, guarantees that today in Europe are not freely negotiated between labor and capital in employment contracts but are imposed upon them by law. Job security is but one part of the far wider and more general range of protective measures that make up what interested parties like to call the "European model."

WHO PAYS THE INSURANCE?

Who "really" pays the premium on the various kinds of social insurance that the welfare state has decreed to be an obligation to provide as part of a worker's entitlement? Ostensibly, in addition to his cash wage, his employer pays the insurance. But could the employee demand instead to have the cash rather than see it paid over as premium on voluntary social insurance policies? If he had the option to take the cash instead but did not, the employee would in effect be a consenting, voluntary buyer of social protection, willingly paying its cost.

Clearly, however, the employee is given no choice in the matter. The cost the employer incurs is of some benefit to the worker. But if the worker must be denied the option of giving up the insurance, something is surely getting lost somewhere. The employer provides social protection at a cost he can't escape, but the worker who would rather take the money can't—legislators have wished on him a benefit that is worth less to him than it cost his employer to provide.

Though there are some minor differences, in its sheer wastefulness and value-destroying capacity, this is nothing but the old "truck" system of forcing workers to accept wages in kind rather than cash. Truck was repeatedly outlawed as oppressive to workers, while social protection is on the contrary imposed by politicians who say they want the best for the workers.

This deadweight of social overhead, owing to the cost of protection being higher than it is worth to the intended beneficiaries, is hard to assess. A fair guess would put it somewhere between "significant" and "colossal."

There is no call to be upset about the sacrifice of some efficiency for the sake of something more worthwhile. But when the main fruit of the sacrifice is chronic unemployment with all its corrupting consequences, it is urgent to reconsider the merits of the "European model." At all events, the illusion that it is neutral and innocent must not be indulged.

HOW TO STIFLE EMPLOYMENT BY "SOCIAL PROTECTION"

In 1998, nearly one European in eight is involuntarily out of work, due largely to the state-sanctioned (indeed forced) return of labor-market practices that were rightly decried as unfair when practiced by private industry in the not-so-distant past.

In 1871, a royal commission in England reported on the "outright compulsion" exerted on workers by "truck," the payment of wages in kind. The customary (and later, the collectively bargained) wage rate was set in money, but in some trades the less scrupulous masters converted it to a basket of goods of their own choosing and gave that to the laborer. Room was thus made for abuse, cheating, the passing off of shoddy goods, and so forth. But even if the truck was a fair exchange, employees would invariably rather have the money to do with as they chose.

The practice of truck went back a long way. It was widespread in handloom weaving, and there were legislative attempts to ban it between the fifteenth and seventeenth centuries. Truck was likewise entrenched in framework knitting, as well as in the handmade-nail trade that employed sixty thousand nailers in northwest England in the early nineteenth century. Less uniformly, it was resorted to in other hardware trades in the British Midlands. Employers practicing it were generally badly regarded and tended to lose the best employees, who gravitated to employers paying proper money wages. In this way, the labor market started to correct some of the ill effects of the truck system.

"OUTRIGHT COMPULSION"

Nevertheless, there were repeated legislative attempts to do away with it altogether, with Truck Acts in 1604, 1621, 1703, and, particularly,

First published in the *Wall Street Journal Europe,* March 20–21, 1998. Reprinted by permission.

1831. All were largely ineffective. Though truck survived in isolated coal mines for a few more years, as a system it was practically extinguished in Britain by the end of the nineteenth century—not by regulation, but by the ordinary interplay of supply and demand. In the United States, in mines and mill towns isolated by geography or language, the practice was preserved somewhat longer. As late as the New Deal era, the National Recovery Administration was impelled to turn its attention to employers paying in company scrip to be spent in the company store, an attenuated form of the "outright compulsion" involved in pure truck.

What is the point of turning over these old leaves today? Is it relevant to modern industrial society how Staffordshire nailmakers, Montana miners, or estate laborers in East Prussia, Poland, and Hungary were paid generations ago? Before proposing an answer, two things should be noted. First, as a matter of historical fact, employees hated truck, often reselling the goods in question for far less than their nominal worth. Second, there is a strong potential defense of truck: The goods a worker gets in exchange may go to feed and clothe the worker and his family, while if he gets money, he may improvidently blow it on payday and leave wife and children in misery for the rest of the week. This is the classic paternalist argument for gentle constraint, if not for "outright coercion" of the working classes for their own good. For all its plausibility, it was little used to defend wages in kind. Tellingly, it is not used at all to justify the massive reintroduction of the truck system into the modern welfare state. In fact, the mere suggestion that the manifold aspects of social protection are perfect products of (and difficult to justify without frank recourse to) paternalist doctrine makes the left blush with embarrassment or explode in fury.

For the truck system is back with a vengeance, more uniformly and inescapably than ever, and instead of trying to liberate them from it, state power now turns "outright compulsion" on workers and their employers and forces them to live with it.

It is readily accepted by public opinion that everyone needs some security against the common hazards of illness, unemployment, or incapacity to work. Plainly, some people will voluntarily buy insurance to protect themselves and their families, but some others won't or can't. The incipient welfare state will insure the latter in a fairly minimal way.

The notional "premiums" are either borne by general taxation or—politically less unpopular and administratively easier—are charged to payrolls, with the employer seemingly paying all or most of it. Once the system takes hold, there usually develops a strong democratic constituency in favor of extending these policies to cover ever more risks, ever more generously. With social insurance, it is obscure who pays what for whom. As a result, health benefits become progressively more comprehensive, unemployment pay longer-lasting and less conditional, and pensioners get younger as time goes by. The incipient welfare state is transformed into a mature one. Willy-nilly, it conducts itself like the lady who could not say "no"—indeed, to stay in office, modern democratic government must say "yes" even before being asked. (Take France's new 35-hour workweek.)

More benefits paid out on policies of social protection mean that more premiums must be collected. Whoever pays them in the first place, ultimately they fall upon capital and labor. How much is really borne by employers and how much by employees may matter a good deal to present well-being and future growth, but it is not germane to understanding how truck, the provision of social protection as part of the wage, may generate endemic unemployment.

How this comes about is inherent in the compulsory nature of social protection. It is a benefit in kind. Its money equivalent to all wage-earners cannot be more than its total cost; to most individual workers, it is substantially less. They like the insurance, but if they could, they would rather have what it cost, or even a good deal less, and spend the money as they see fit. Whether they would be wise to prefer the money is immaterial if, in fact, they do. For if they do, they will subjectively undervalue social protection, and its cost will thus be higher than its worth to those it seeks to protect.

VICIOUS CIRCLE

However, this is tantamount to saying that the cost of labor—the money wage plus the premiums employers and employees must pay to produce all the social protection on offer—will nearly always be higher, perhaps much higher, than the effective wage—take-home pay plus the money value the worker puts on his prospective social insurance benefits. To offer any given effective wage, employers must incur higher costs under this social truck system than they would otherwise have to do. Consequently, they will "restructure" and eliminate jobs. The resulting unemployment will be endemic, in the sense that it will resist both cyclical upswings and fiscal or monetary stimuli. As long as the cost of labor is generally higher than the value such cost buys for the employee, employment will remain stifled.

The dynamics of this mechanism are intimidating. With more unemployment, more insurance benefits are paid out and more premiums must be charged, which should normally increase the gap between total labor cost and effective wages; enhancing the gap increases unemployment some more, and so on in a vicious circle. It is once this circle gets going (which may be a matter of passing some threshold) that the problem becomes nearly intractable, as it seems to have done in much of the European Union. For it is of little practical use to say that the one real cure of unemployment is to abolish the insurance against it at the very time when this could only be done over the dead bodies of the jobless and the justifiably scared.

WORKABLE ALTERNATIVES

Just a few weeks ago, German or French workers accepting to work longer hours for the same pay, forgoing pay rises already agreed to, and conceding flexible work practices would have been but a delirious vision. All the news flow went the other way, and has been going the other way for decades. Shorter hours, higher pay, more "codetermination," more workers' "rights," and fewer prerogatives for management seemed an inexorable trend. It demarcated the "European social model" from such deviations as the Thatcher reforms, the Dutch sobering-up, or the Swedish attenuation of their welfare state. The "model" entailed chronically high unemployment, which governments and unions took as a good reason for imposing still shorter hours to share the available work—and so the merry-go-round kept going round.

All of a sudden, the business scene is swarming with deals, concluded under negotiation or tentatively floated at board level, in which labor makes concessions in exchange for management forgoing job cuts or—the ultimate threat—moving operations and leaving the employees behind. Everyone in Paris, plus a vocal minority in Berlin, now indignantly cries "blackmail." Is it?

OCCASIONS OF BLACKMAIL

Strictly speaking, a threat meant to extort a concession from someone is blackmail only if the threatened act is a tort. Making employees redundant or moving production from Baden-Württemberg to South Africa is not a tort. Nor is it, until further notice, unlawful. Any attempt to make it so would entail an ever-lengthening string of other controls to shore it up, leading to massive evasion, a speeding up of the eurozone's economic decline, or both.

However, while deals in which labor won all the concessions used to pass muster with public opinion, the deals management has recently

First published in the *Wall Street Journal Europe,* October 6, 2004. Reprinted by permission.

been winning seem to create concerns for justice. For in a loose, colloquial sense there is indeed an element of blackmail in these novel agreements. They have the ring of blackmail because they have posed such drastic choices. It is as well to say, though, that anything less drastic would have failed to reverse the long-established trend of less work for the same pay.

The sophisticated case for the blackmail argument is that our choices are free when we have no or only a slight preference for one alternative over the next-worse one, but that the choice becomes progressively less free as the next-worse alternative gets worse and worse. With full employment, saying no to the boss and looking for other work is hardly worse than accepting his terms. With grim job prospects and unemployment at the French or German level, however, the next-worse alternative to accepting the bosses' terms is bad indeed. The workers, as the saying goes, have "no alternative." They are being blackmailed.

One might well ask: And whose fault is that? Who caused the loss of French and German economic vigor since the mid-1970s and its concomitant unemployment? Who dreamed up the "European social model," who built it up by relentless tinkering, who is "struggling" for job creation, and who is resisting any timid attempt to let loose the normal forces of normal job creation?

Government apologists who boast of a relatively high level of inward foreign investment as proof that their economies are not as unhealthy and unattractive as all that, should look instead at the dismal trends in business investment from domestic sources. Across all industries, returns on capital in the Franco-German "core" of Europe are mediocre. Where the average is mediocre, too many individual branches and firms have sunk or fear soon to sink below the break-even point. The threat to relocate unless more work comes forth for no greater pay is an obvious enough escape route. Once a few bold spirits have shown the way by braving the political signposts that signalled "no entry," "no through road," the rush to cut costs by putting drastic choices before labor has quickened and broadened.

What of the near-term future? "Blackmail" is widely resented but will not be easily resisted. Despite its obligatory "social" overtones, German discourse still regards the employer-employee relation as a matter of contract and not the reserved domain of public law. Moreover, after several decades of asking water to flow upward, it is recognized that its natural inclination is to flow downward. Most Germans have some respect for economic realities, and major new legislative attempts to suspend them are on balance not very likely.

FRENCH HOSTAGES

The French case could hardly be more different: President Jacques Chirac has resolutely vetoed attempts to repeal the thirty-five-hour workweek, which he deems a "social right," and calls tampering with it a "slippery slope." His premier, Jean-Pierre Raffarin, has condemned the use of unequal bargaining power and declared that he will "not accept blackmail" of labor. On June 28 the official government spokesman promised measures in 2005 to "control the relocation of enterprise," with a preliminary "social dialogue" to start next September. If this is what a government that calls itself center-right proposes to do, how would a government that called itself Socialist go about it? Some would answer that in France you could not tell the difference.

In any event, it is hard to see how the French, or any other, government can in practice "not accept" the purported blackmail of wage-earners. It can hardly make firing them any more difficult than it already is. It could, as a last resort, try and stop employers from escaping their own hard-to-fire employees by relocating abroad. Pushed to its logical limit, the remedy would be to take existing enterprises hostage within the national jurisdiction—never mind that there would thereafter hardly be any new ones. The suggestion is cloud-cuckoo silly. No logic, except possibly the renowned Cartesian one, could seriously advance it.

A TALE OF TWO MODELS

French president Jacques Chirac has a knack (as he famously put it in 2003 with respect to Poles, Balts, and other "lackeys" of America) for "missing good occasions to stay silent."

Campaigning last month in Barcelona for the new European constitution, he praised it as a fair compromise "between the European and the liberal model" (in American English, he meant classical liberal). Which is to say, he as good as laid it down that a liberal "model" could not be European. It very nearly follows that the European one must be socialist. With this in mind, we may enjoy watching the Battle of the Models.

In the liberal model, profits accrue to the providers of capital and enterprise, wages to the providers of work of all kinds. When profits run ahead of wages, it pays to expand employment, and wages catch up. When profits run dry, the opposite tends to happen. A natural pendulum movement keeps the share of wages and the share of profits in national income swinging back and forth over the economic cycle.

The European model will have none of this. Under it, the shares of profits and wages are first determined by ordinary economic forces. Society is watching the result as it emerges, and keeps adjusting it in a great variety of ways if it does not think it just (or, more prosaically, if the balance of democratic forces pushes for the adjustment).

In practice, for at least three decades now, the net adjustment has invariably been one way—in favor of labor. This is how the intricate system of entitlements of European welfare states has gradually been built up. Translated into moral terms, "social justice" was being done. No one thought of asking whether social justice can cut both ways and, if it could, why it always cuts only one way.

As was to be expected, reality in due course caught up with the European model, causing it increasingly to backfire in the face of the

First published in the *Wall Street Journal Europe,* March 2, 2005. Reprinted by permission.

politicians who still pretended to steer it. Above all else, the model radically stifles the demand for labor, generating a seemingly incurable, endemic unemployment that for years has stuck at around 10 percent in the major euro-zone economies that still believe in the model, while it is only 4 to 5 percent in Britain and other European users of the rival "liberal" model.

This is a fact even French politicians recognize, although they refuse to accept responsibility for it. It does not, in itself, warrant an article in the *Wall Street Journal.* But it has intriguing implications that perhaps do, for they have not so far been openly discussed.

CAUSES OF UNEMPLOYMENT

Built-in unemployment around 10 percent is caused by two features of the European model. One is the weight of vast schemes of social insurance financed via payroll taxes, whose cost is greater than their value to the insured wage-earner. Hence the cost of wages exceeds their value and the demand for labor stays chronically deficient.

The other, perhaps less powerful, cause is job protection. Labor laws, meaning well, make the shedding of labor so difficult and expensive that employers are afraid of taking the risk of hiring. They either resort to short fixed-term jobs or just make do with the staff they have. Both these features of the European model—social insurance and job protection—are, of course, meant to favor labor over capital. But in practice, they do the exact opposite.

They make the economy function less well, but within a sluggish, sickly environment, they favor capital. They bring about a wholly unintended hiring strike by employers (who would never ever consciously organize one). Labor finds its economic bargaining power reduced to impotence. Companies learn to get by with stagnant or reduced payrolls, productivity rises, profits increase, and wages stay flat. Ironically, the European model does better by the corporate sector than the liberal one, and less well for its own supposed clients—the workers.

Even educated opinion seems to be unaware that this is going on at all, much less the reasons it is going on. Like the secret about the emperor's clothes, it is still a secret, though it can hardly stay so for much longer.

Recently, the French oil major Total declared a 2004 net profit of €9 billion. Coming amid a rush of other brilliant earnings reports, €9 billion has proved too much. Within two days, the knee-jerk reaction duly came. French premier Raffarin issued a statement warning French corporations that "if they wish to continue making profits," they must see to it that their employees share in them. The note of menace, though meant mainly to cheer up public opinion, which remains viscerally left-leaning, was audible.

THE ULTIMATE OWNERS

Needless to say (though you would not know from listening to the French chattering classes), the €9 billion did not go in the pocket of a Mr. Total. They were shared by hundreds of thousands of shareholders, the majority being present and future pensioners. Nevertheless, shared they must be again. Oddly, the European model and its conception of "social justice" nowhere provides that when the corporate sector is doing miserably and many companies are bleeding their net worth, there should be sharing too, but in the opposite direction.

Such "sharing" has been known to happen, notably in recent years in the U.S. airline industry, where labor made major wage concessions. But this happened within the liberal model through bargains that followed the normal two-way swings of the profit-wage pendulum. In the European model, there is no pendulum. Labor has been stripped of its natural powers, and all it has left to lean on is a solicitous government that is unwittingly keeping it poorer than it need be.

A VICIOUS CIRCLE OF SOCIAL KINDNESS

Unemployment in the industrialized West is now clearly endemic and not cyclical as in the past. No reversal appears in prospect. At best the next few years will bring a minor rise in employment, at worst a further fall.

In the search for an explanation and cure, many old—but unsatisfactory—chestnuts are trotted out: a deep technological transformation is taking place (it always is); world trade has become too free and not fair enough (but freer trade, surely, brings greater riches?); or labor markets are too rigid and training inadequate (but did not the same apply twenty years ago?).

There may, however, be a different explanation for high unemployment in modern, redistributive democracies.

This is best illustrated with a simplified example. Imagine an economy where income comes from only two sources—profits and wages. Rents are negligible, and there is full employment. If the government wished to redistribute income in favor of wage earners, it would tax employers' profits and add the money raised to wages.

The natural response would be for employers to cut the wages they offer—and for employees to demand less. Consequently, the impact in terms of redistribution would be negligible and harmless: there would be no unemployment created and after-tax, after-subsidy incomes would remain unchanged.

But imagine that instead of transferring money, the government offered employees a basket of "social protection"—insurance against illness, unemployment, or destitution in old age. If we make the (large) assumption that collecting the tax and distributing it in the form of social protection are costless, the effect on the demand and supply of labor would depend on the difference between the cost of the package and the value attached to it by recipients.

At first sight, it would appear that employees would attach great

First published in *Financial Times,* April 29, 1994. Reprinted by permission.

value to social protection: reaction to proposals for curtailing benefits is usually virulent. But that is because most wage-earners are under the illusion that the greater part of the "insurance premium" is being paid by someone other than themselves.

If wage-earners understood that, ultimately, the cost had to be borne out of their own wages, would they prefer to have the "social protection" on offer—or would they rather buy some private insurance, save some, and spend the rest?

There is a strong paternalistic argument for saying that wage-earners should not be given such a choice—improvidence would make many take the money and "blow it." But the important point is that "social protection" costs more than it is worth to at least some of those that it protects.

The result is that, at the margin, employment is taxed more than the subsidy is worth to workers. The two no longer cancel out and there is a net extra burden on the economy. Enterprises have to "restructure" and unemployment is born of "social protection."

Worse, a vicious circle comes into operation. The initial unemployment created by the tax-subsidy inequality increases the amount of "social protection" that has to be handed out.

That extra cost results in a further increase in the tax on employment, widening the gap between the nonwage costs of labor and the value of the benefits in kind. Demand for labor is further depressed relative to its supply, more unemployment is created, and the cycle is repeated.

Under an optimistic scenario, noncyclical unemployment would stabilize, at some point, at a level that society would have to support indefinitely. But under a pessimistic scenario the rise in unemployment would prove inexorable.

There is empirical evidence to lend weight to such a theory. Comparisons across countries show a high correlation between cyclically corrected unemployment and "social protection" expressed as a share of national income. Unemployment in Europe, where the welfare system is more costly per head, is twice as high as in the U.S. and many times higher than in East Asia.

Within post-Maastricht Europe, unemployment is worse in the center than on its periphery, and the more "social" the country, the more it is plagued.

Democracies, we are told, cannot relax social protection. Are they, then, condemned to smother the young and the long-term unemployed with their caring kindness?

PART 6

The Future of Europe

THE ECONOMIC CONSEQUENCES OF A UNITED STATES OF EUROPE

The grandfathers and the fathers of the current generation of Europeans helped bring about two catastrophic wars in the last century. Even the two decades of peace in between (1919–1939) were not idyllic, graced as they were with the rise to power of Nazism (1933–1945) and the "real existing" socialism of the Soviet Union (1917–1990). The sons were forever marked by these dark memories. The sins of the fathers were being visited upon them, and they were determined not to commit the same sins, which, in their turn, would be visited upon their sons. "Never that again!" Much of what is happening in today's Europe is driven by the subconscious dread of "that" and the will to make sure it does not happen again. It is in wanting to make sure of this that the sons risk committing new kinds of sins.

When in the 1990s the debate was raging in Germany about the adoption of a common European currency "like the dollar," there was a steady majority against it of just short of two-thirds. The political parties, academia, and the press unleashed a barrage of arguments about the economic benefits of such a move, but the polls remained unpersuaded. The old recipe used to be that when the people do not agree with the government, change the people. Lately, the recipe has been "if they don't agree, don't ask them," and this is what the German government has finally done, adopting the euro with the full complicity of the people's elected representatives.

The real motive of the political classes was not the putative stimulus to economic growth which a common currency might provide, a stimulus that has in the event proved sadly absent. At the time, Chancellor Kohl was rightly advised that the euro would prove to be a lame

First published as "The Sins of the Fathers and the Sins of the Sons: Economic Consequences of a United States of Europe," by Liberty Fund, Inc., at www.econlib.org on March 3, 2003. Reprinted by permission.

device, perhaps even a downright failure, unless the countries using it came under a common economic government "like in America." Kohl convinced himself that the mechanics of the common currency would eventually force Europe to organize itself as a single federal state, something it would probably never do otherwise. The euro was designed to make another European war forever unthinkable. (That the U.S. dollar did not prevent the American Civil War from taking place was, probably rightly, dismissed as a false analogy.)

The fiasco of the euro and the need to make it work as it was supposed to has led gradually to the participating states coming together, creating an economic supergovernment, soon to be followed by a full-fledged superstate, without anyone taking much notice of what was going on. But important as this creeping shift may be, it is being overtaken by a more rapid and more deliberate series of moves to endow Europe with a collective decision-making mechanism.

What started out as the four-nation Coal and Steel Community in 1952 (inspired by the naive Marxist notion that wars are caused by the need of steel barons to sell cannon and shells) became the six-nation Common Market in 1957 which was in theory to work by the principle of unanimity but which was run essentially by France. As such heavyweights as Britain (1973) and Spain (1986) entered and membership finally expanded to fifteen nations calling themselves the European Union with an executive arm in Brussels and a legislature in Strasbourg, majority rule was introduced to deal with some questions, but countries retained veto rights over what they chose to regard as their vital national interests. On issues where German submissiveness to French leadership persisted, decisions were reached by Franco-German arm-twisting, on other issues they were fudged or deferred. The feeling grew among the political classes that the system was just not viable. The single market was functioning reasonably well in manufactured goods, but in politically charged areas, such as agriculture, fisheries, financial services, and taxes, gridlock was created. Above all, no progress could be made on the supreme goal the believers in a really united Europe had set themselves, namely a common defense and foreign policy.

With the membership rising from fifteen to twenty-five states as of May 2004, and with further candidates crowding at the entrance, the existing makeshift ways of reaching decisions are judged to be hopeless. It occurs to nobody that decisions at supranational level need only be taken if there is a supranational agenda, and it is not a law of nature that there should be one.

This, then, is the great chance to put in place a powerful decision-making body that will do for Europe what the White House and the Congress have done for the USA—the same, only much better. Anxious to banish their fathers' sins, the sons are getting ready to commit a new type of sin for which future generations may have to pay dearly.

Two more or less rival projects are in the running. One, spearheaded by Romano Prodi, the president of the EU's Commission in Brussels, seeks to strengthen the Commission, to emancipate it from its present subjection to the member states and to transform it into a real executive branch of government. The Commission's budget is now barely 1.5 percent of European GDP, and even of that modest percentage two-fifths are preempted by farm subsidies which Brussels would dearly like to but cannot reform. There is clearly a long way to go before Brussels's spending power and patronage reach Washingtonian proportions, let alone the bite which the budgets of the separate European nation states take out of their respective GDPs. The Brussels executive is now a mere tadpole. For it to grow into a political toad, powers, revenues, and functions will have to migrate from the national capitals to Brussels just as they have migrated from the states to the federal government in the U.S. The central executive can grow not only by capturing money and functions from the states, but also by engaging in exciting new areas of activity which no one has done before—for there are so many useful things a government can find to do! To help achieve all this, this project would enhance the Commission's legitimacy by rendering it more responsible to the Strasbourg assembly and making its presidency elective rather than appointed as at present.

The other project is more solemn and formal. It is a constitutional convention guided by Valéry Giscard d'Estaing, a former French president who is to Mr. Prodi as a hornet is to a bumblebee. Prodi wants to be an elected president of the Commission; Giscard (who at seventy-eight cannot be faulted for lack of ambition) wants to be the president of a new "United States of Europe." This new entity, a republic modelled loosely on the United States of America, shall have the power to tax and to harmonize the fiscal policies of the member states. It is to be dedicated to "human rights" and to the fostering of the "European social model," a code word the great European center-left, allied to the labor unions on one side and the antiglobalization and anti-American opinion-makers on the other, will take for a discreetly friendly nod toward their political and economic agendas.

Acquiring the power to tax directly, instead of depending on the member states' contributions for its budget, is of course the decisive novelty. If eventually adopted, it will inexorably create a new top layer of government in Europe that will be destined to grow ever denser, ever heavier, as such layers have always done and always will. However, the constitution would also endow the new republic with powers to intervene in the fiscal, welfare, and labor legislation of the member states to prevent them from competing with each other by lowering corporate taxes and contributions to social welfare schemes. This healthy interstate economic rivalry, which goes by the unflattering name of "social dumping," is a practice which is jeered at by socialists and cheered on by the small but brave band of "neoliberals" because it frustrates the full flowering of the "European social model." What little tax and regulatory competition exists between the European states at present is what has prevented many European businessmen from throwing up their hands and shutting up shop, tired of rising payroll taxes and burgeoning regulations.

The road to Brussels is paved with good intentions and the framers of these new constitutional arrangements are motivated by the best political correctness one could desire. They are preparing something that will be neither Soviet Russia nor Nazi Germany. In fact, whether knowingly or not, they are creating a new European constitutional arrangement largely as a reaction to these very same horrors. It is such a pity that they do not see the unintended but very probable effects upon the next generation of what they are now creating. In politics and economics, and perhaps elsewhere too, you often avoid doing harm by refraining from doing anything very much or, in the words of the eighteenth-century French liberal Physiocrats, laissez faire, laissez passer. But how will the sons who strive to correct the sins of their fathers learn this important lesson?

A GIANT FREE-TRADE AREA OR A POLITICAL COUNTERWEIGHT TO AMERICA?

Nearly half a century ago, with the signing of the Treaty of Rome in March 1957, what is now the European Union (EU) started out as the European Economic Community (EEC) with six member states (France, West Germany, Italy, Belgium, the Netherlands, and Luxembourg). The unanimous aim of the founders, held at both the grassroots level and among the political elite, was that a future Franco-German war must never again happen. In the years immediately after the end of the Second World War the approach was gradual, confined to what were regarded, somewhat naively, as the industries which were thought to be the instigators of wars. Thus the European Coal and Steel Community was founded in 1951 by the same six nations which were later to form the EEC. In 1954 a bold attempt was made by the political elites to create a European Defense Community but this ran aground on nationalistic shoals. Advances continued to be made with the formation of the Common Market or EEC in 1957, the purpose of which was to create free trade inside its members' frontiers but which would be protectionist toward the outside world. Above all, as the price exacted by France for opening its own market to German industry, the EEC saddled itself with the economic monstrosity of the Common Agricultural Policy, whose most wasteful outgrowths are only now beginning to be trimmed.

The original six-nation EEC could not, in the longer run, shut out the rest of Europe and call itself European at the same time. Several countries were strongly pressing for admission. After de Gaulle's veto of British membership in the EEC, the European Free Trade Association (EFTA) was formed in 1960 by seven nations which had been re-

First published as "The Future of Europe: A Giant Free Trade Area or a Political Counterweight to America?" by Liberty Fund, Inc., at www.econlib.org on February 7, 2005. Reprinted by permission.

fused membership in the EEC—the United Kingdom, Denmark, Norway, Sweden, Austria, Switzerland, and Portugal. The EFTA differed from the EEC most notably in the absence in the former of any broader aspirations for political union, which created tensions with the more politically driven EEC. The federalists inside the EEC resented that the outsiders in the EFTA were getting all the benefits of free trade without shouldering the task of building a politically united Europe. Indeed there was a loudly voiced suspicion that some of them, notably the British, were doing their best to sabotage political unity. The upshot was that little by little all the EFTA members bar two entered the EEC. A northern tier came in with Britain, Denmark, Finland, Ireland, and Sweden and a southern one with Austria, Greece, Portugal, and Spain. The southern members and Ireland reaped huge benefits from the so-called structural funds which the EEC siphoned off from its richer members and distributed to the poorer regions to help them catch up with the European average. The richer members, in addition, had to put on the hair shirt of the Common Agricultural Policy. Margaret Thatcher, wholly unimpressed by Mr. Giscard d'Estaing's browbeating, secured for Britain a balance where the payments Britain made to the EEC nearly matched the benefits it received from Brussels. Germany and the Netherlands ended up as the main paymasters of the EEC budget, and every other country became a net gainer to a greater (Greece, Ireland, Spain) or lesser extent. With occasional crises and much friction, the new fifteen-member European Union has become an established concern, pushed along by the Franco-German alliance.

Then came the breakup of the Soviet bloc in 1989. All the former satellites asked to be admitted to the EU. Their political elites were motivated by the prospect of the structural funds and the charms of rubbing shoulders in the same club with the leaders of the richer Europe. At the grassroots, there was an innocent belief that what Russia could once do with impunity to a Poland, a Czechoslovakia, or a Hungary, it could never again do to a member of the EU. There was much quiet but bitter opposition among the federalists in France and Germany to the admission of ten new members on the grounds that many of them are in fact Trojan horses harboring Anglo-American ideals and purposes. Nevertheless, it was unthinkable to exclude what were practically founder members of the historic Europe, victims of

Yalta and of Western connivance in shameless Russian oppression. So seven ex-satellites and Slovenia were admitted in 2004, and southern Cyprus and Malta were slipped in for good measure as well. Romania and Bulgaria were virtually promised admission in 2007—in large part because none of the lead nations of the EU felt like turning the Romanians and the Bulgarians into bitter enemies by opposing their membership, and driving them into the arms of rival EU nations. Thus, as of 2007, there is to be a twenty-seven-member EU speaking twenty-three languages, with some federalists still hoping to turn it into a homogenous, socialist-oriented political entity, while others now believe that this has become a lost cause.

The EU is now committed to start negotiating full membership for Turkey in October 2005. Though virtually assured of an accord, the talks are planned to drag on for ten to fifteen years with the unspoken aim of giving hostile French and German public opinion time to get accustomed to the idea. Turkey, with over 70 million inhabitants compared to the present EU's 450 million, will be the latter's most populous member by about 2020. Because of the proposed constitutional treaty introducing weighted majority decision-making, it will be the EU's politically most influential state. However, it will also be its poorest member by far. Under present rules, it should be receiving agricultural and regional subventions of 30 billion euros, or 20 percent of the total EU budget. By the time Turkish membership is realized, these rules will no doubt be changed, but the economic benefit to the EU is still dubious. Free trade is in the mutual interest of the EU and Turkey, and is a largely accomplished fact. All other aspects of membership are in Turkey's interest alone. Turkey's professional classes and its army in particular expect that EU membership will prevent the country from sliding into Islamic excesses.

Throughout the EU the debate is raging about the wisdom of admitting Turkey to the club, even though the lead governments have already made up their minds and, in the case of Germany and France, are ruthlessly overriding public opinion. The main popular argument for Turkey is that if, after decades as an applicant, it were now turned down, the Muslim world would take the refusal as proof that the EU was a Christian cabal and a successor of the Crusaders. This in turn would lead straight to the "clash of cultures" and the "war of civilizations" touted by pop historians and sociologists. It seems to be forgotten that the Turks occupied all the Arab lands from Baghdad and Cairo to Marrakesh from the fifteenth century onward, and in the case of Iraq, Syria, and Jordan, down to 1918. Little love is lost between Turks and Arabs because of old wounds and because the former are regarded as allies of Israel.

The German government is championing Turkish membership with an eye to its own 2.5-million-strong Turkish immigrant population and the votes of its second-generation citizens. The determination of the French government to support Turkey, despite the polls that show 65–68 percent of French people are opposed to its membership, looks very strange. Its hidden mainspring is the craving to make the EU into a political, economic, and military superpower under undisputed French leadership, enabling France to stand up to America as an equal and a counterweight to U.S. "hegemony." Ever since the 1950s, this design never came anywhere near fruition, causing mounting frustration in Paris. Turkey has a standing army greater than any two of the largest national armies of the EU taken together. Bizarre as the idea may be in reality, the thought of half a million ferocious Turkish soldiers being added to the puny European forces seems to be too tempting to resist.

There is little doubt that hopes of enlisting the Turkish military to serve French design will be disappointed, as were similar hopes in the past. The addition of Turkey will make Europe even more like a free-trade area and even less of a political counterweight.

After Turkey, it will be Ukraine's turn. After the courage its people have shown in wresting electoral victory from the pro-Russian forces late last year, its entry with another 50 million people into the EU is a strong likelihood, and the dream of a homogenous and united EU capable and willing to act as one force is receding into some very distant future.

After Ukraine, whose turn will it be? A new doctrine is arising in educated opinion, which holds that it is not geography that qualifies a state for EU membership, but "shared values." On the strength of this doctrine, Europe is in for limitless expansion across North Africa, Central Asia, and the Middle East, because if Turks share European values, who does not share them? An ever-expanding Europe straddling three continents would be politically impotent and probably quite harmless. Economically, it would be a good thing, for the larger a free-trade area is, the more good it can do by trade creation and the less harm by trade diversion.

EUROPEAN CROSSCURRENTS AND THE FEDERALIST DRIFT

Imagine the following situation: some friends are jogging along together, the pace set to comfort the slowest of them. This, some economists would say, is a possible model of coordination. However, if each person starts to run as hard as he can, with some overtaking others, it seems that a race is taking place. The taker-overs can be styled as aggressors, the taken-overs as victims. The model is one of competition and conflict. Alternatively, it depicts progress of a sort.

A similar situation could be said to exist with the Franco-German "core Europe," in which French vanity in foreign policy and French fidelity to socialist economics set the direction while German subservience provides the driving force. This is a race for jogging, not sprinting. The embryo welfare state they created around the mid-1970s began to weigh the joggers down. As their pace slowed and as unemployment either side of 10 percent of the labor force became endemic, conviction and electoral necessity have combined to make them add ever more and ever heavier building blocks to the welfare edifice their economy was supposed to carry on its back. The end result was the much vaunted "European social model," economic stagnation, and the social strife which stagnation nearly always breeds.

Britain, which had set about building a welfare state three decades earlier than continental Europe, gave itself insane labor relations, narrowly skirted bankruptcy, and in 1979 was ripe for the Thatcher revolution. Some of the benefits of the Thatcher reforms are still being felt; unemployment is consistently low and the economy is moving forward, with national wealth per head having decisively outgrown the Franco-German level.

First published as "Jogging, Not Racing: European Cross-Currents and the Federalist Drift," by Liberty Fund, Inc., at www.econlib.org on July 5, 2004. Reprinted by permission.

Understandably, the British and half a dozen smaller European countries would rather go on with the race. France and Germany, just as understandably, insist that they must join the jogging party of "core Europe."

The latest collision of these two deep crosscurrents has shown up on the surface with the renewed Franco-German demand for "tax harmonization" and their attack on "social dumping."

Corporate tax rates are between 35 and 40 percent in "core Europe." They are 10 percent in Ireland. In Slovakia the corporate tax rate is 19 percent and so is, with disarming simplicity, every other tax rate from the personal income tax to the value added tax. In the newly joined member states generally, the effective tax rate is well below the nominal one. The German employers' association has been openly recommending that German companies should relocate eastward to the new member countries of the European Union to benefit from less onerous employment rules, lower corporate and payroll taxes (and has been castigated for its unpatriotic stance by Chancellor Schroeder). France and Germany are now seriously alarmed by the flight of enterprise and capital.

They insist that to avoid "distortion" of the market, both corporate taxes and social insurance charges must be "harmonized" across the Union. By harmonization they mean raising tax rates to the Franco-German level. "Social" charges, in particular, must rise everywhere not only because "social dumping" distorts the market, but more importantly because Europe must "fight inequalities" and live up to the "social model."

It is ironical that the Brussels Commission is a perhaps even more severe enforcer of antitrust and anticartel rules than the U.S. Justice Department when competition among companies is concerned. The strangling of the General Electric–Honeywell merger and the offensive against Microsoft bore testimony to the sternness of Mario Monti, the competition commissioner. However, the Brussels rule that companies must compete is now to be joined by a new rule that states must not compete. Cartels to fix prices and sales quotas are seen as wicked, while a tax cartel binding states not to undercut each other's tax rates would be regarded as virtuous, harmonious coordination. Arguably, prices are one thing, tax rates are another. But this does not mean that while prices may differ, tax rates must not. Uniformity of rates does not follow except perhaps if we are already in a full-fledged federal state where equality before the law may, *in extremis,* be thought to require equal taxation.

The tax controversy is but one example of how national crosscurrents induce a federalist drift. Any national difference that has a cross-border implication affects the operation of the single European market and as such (it is argued) must be moved from national to Union jurisdiction. This upward flow of matters from the state to the Union level has been going on for years and will apparently broaden still more under the new constitution. Since everything has some cross-border implication, however hypothetical or contrived, especially when borders are open, there is no evident limit to the federalist drift. The single-market clause is destined to play the same role in draining power from the states to Brussels as the interstate commerce clause played in draining power to Washington. The European Court of Justice will have to help this process along much as the U.S. Supreme Court has done.

In a recent report commissioned by Brussels, the former French finance minister and front-running socialist presidential candidate Dominique Strauss-Kahn has called for a European tax that would endow the incipient federal government with its own resources. The parallel with the earlier U.S. evolution is obvious enough. (True to form, French president Chirac has gone one better and is calling for a world tax, but that is a story for another day.)

None of this is meant to suggest that every single transfer of power to the center and every case where states are forced to jog along together rather than racing against each other separately is necessarily a bad thing. Trade commissioner Pascal Lamy, though a socialist and a French one to boot, created a sensation last May by offering to abolish all European subsidies on agricultural exports. This was a bold attempt to rescue the stalled Doha Round of trade liberalization bargaining. The attempt will probably fail, if only because the U.S. will not agree to scrapping its own export subsidies, but it is nevertheless a worthy try and may bear fruit after some delay. The Lamy initiative has unleashed the fury of the French farm and commerce ministers and of public opinion which sees it as another move to undermine that sacred pillar of French national interest and "rights," the Common Agricultural Policy. As the policy engenders idiotic and vicious side effects, undermining it would be the best thing that could happen to it.

However, even if every single part of the dismantling of national sovereignties and their concentration at a new federal level were a good thing—which is far from the case—the sum of the parts may yet prove to be a hard lump to swallow. Here again, the U.S. experience that so many Americans would love to undo if they could might serve as a lesson for Europeans.

HOW CONFEDERACY COULD TURN INTO A FEDERAL SUPERSTATE

It is a tenable proposition, supported by masses of historical evidence, that the main reason why any human society fails to attain the prosperity and material comfort that its endowments and culture should enable it to reach, is that its politics stifles and disrupts its economic potential. Moreover, it is likely that the gap between what would be possible and what is achieved tends to grow larger as technology advances and as political power expands and gets a grip on more and more aspects of people's lives.

Two polar cases illustrate this thesis. One is the average black African country. Its women and most of its men would till the land, engage in commerce, and peacefully go about their business. However, a fraction—the army, the police, lawyers, bureaucrats, and professional politicians—have got hold of the levers of a rudimentary government. They extort taxes from the rest "legally" and steal them blind "illegally," especially if the country produces cash crops, minerals, or oil. Some of the most able and energetic who are excluded from the stealing coalition and cannot get themselves co-opted have an incentive to form countercoalitions of "rebels." Militias of half-crazed adolescents, with machetes and submachine guns as their toys, will rampage across the country, massacring the villagers who have not fled to the misery and doubtful safety of refugee camps. Poverty and the shredding of the social fabric produce more teenage recruits for the militias, and so it goes on. At any one time in postcolonial Africa, an ample handful of countries are suffering from some version of this syndrome and the others are not far from falling victim to it. Arguably, none of this could happen if there were no rich prizes to be had from using the all too potent machinery of politics.[1]

First published as part 1 of "A Tadpole Constitution," by Liberty Fund, Inc., at www.econlib.org on December 1, 2003. Reprinted by permission.

1. The late Peter Bauer, one of the most clear-sighted of development econo-

The other polar case is the mature welfare state. Its government need not be corrupt and usually it is not, or not in a big enough way to make much difference. However, it is a prisoner of democratic politics. Unless it wants to commit political hara-kiri, it must fashion policies that will buy it a majority of votes. This involves it in selecting a variety of interest groups, necessarily including the poor, the unemployed, the sick, and the old, who all will vote for whoever best looks after them. It also involves a scattergun approach hitting most groups, whereby resources are taken from all strata and used to buy the votes the government needs to survive. It must stretch itself to the limit of the country's tolerance of redistribution, for if it left the least bit of slack in the system, its political rival could outbid it by promising to increase benefits by taking up the slack. The mature welfare state eventually ends up with a set of subventions, regulations, and entitlements to resource transfers to favored groups that is carved in granite and very difficult to change, let alone substantially to reduce. The net result is that mature welfare states tend economically to stagnate. Germany, France, and Italy are eloquent contemporary examples. The irony of this is that if they bore no excessive welfare burden, they would grow faster and be richer, hence a given welfare burden would no longer be so crippling.

Many economists have in recent decades come to be persuaded that there is a way to get the political incubus off the economy's back. All you need is to devise the right rules. The idea has been formally developed by the school that calls itself "constitutional economics." It maintains that if only society saw its best long-term interests and ignored short-term gains to be had from pressure-group politics, it would adopt a constitution that strictly limited the scope of collective choices, forbidding the government to go beyond the enforcement of law and order and maybe a welfare safety net to catch the genuinely helpless. Property would be secure from public covetousness, and full scope would be left for voluntary exchanges. Market solutions could not be interfered

mists, often insisted that foreign aid is actually harmful because it is given to, or distributed under the control of, governments, which increases the prizes to be had from sitting inside the stealing coalition. See P. T. Bauer, *The Development Frontier: Essays in Applied Economics* (Cambridge, Mass.: Harvard University Press, 1991).

with except to facilitate manifest Pareto-improvements, if any are left to facilitate.

Dissenters from this idyllic conception, including the present writer, suspect that such a constitution would not be adopted and that if it were, it would be circumvented and after a while twisted out of all recognition. They point to the American Constitution, in intent as close to the ideal as one can get, and what happened under it to states' rights, the freedom of contract, and the role of government at the hands of the Congress and the Supreme Court.

Another great test is about to start. The draft constitution of the European Union, elaborated over the last year and a half by a 105-member convention of delegates, is up for approval by an intergovernmental conference by mid-December 2003.

It will not be approved as it stands, and some wrangling will continue past the deadline, but the likely modifications will not greatly affect the central issues.

The final text will then have to be ratified by the fifteen existing and ten new member states of the Union. A few are also obliged to submit it to popular referendum and a few more will opt to do so. Barring a miracle, several of these will be lost and some fudge will have to be produced to get over this obstacle. A couple of states—Spain and Poland are bracing themselves for the role—may go to the brink, refuse to ratify, and hold out for special concessions. There will be many false and a few genuine alarms. In the end, however, the holdouts will be bullied into acceptance. Pressure of Europe's mostly pro-Union media, and the carrot-and-stick potential inherent in the Union budget by which a wavering state may be bribed or blackmailed, will presumably prove strong enough. Within two years or so, the Union will have its brand-new constitution ratified.

The text, absurdly long at 360 pages in the French version, bears the hallmarks of verbose French rhetoric and cautious English fudge. Its ambiguities will prove a gold mine for tomorrow's lawyers. However, for all its clumsy grandiloquence, it is bound to turn out to be a fascinating experiment for economists and political theorists to watch.

The constitution was expected by the hopeful to settle the issue between confederacy and federation. In fact, it did what the realists thought it would do, and produced a compromise neither side really likes. Of the two camps, it is the federalists who are the more disappointed. The text provides for no common defense, no common economic government, no tax harmonization among the member states, and no common executive branch of government. Worst blow of all for the federalist is that under this constitution the Union has no power to tax. For its budget, it must continue to look to the contributions of the member states, which are negotiated for four-year periods. The main channel through which power in federal structures is drained from the states and migrates to the center has apparently not been opened.

Confederate relief at this reassuring absence of the essential ingredients of a federal superstate is premature, to put it no higher. It is rather like seeing a tadpole and rejoicing that it is not a frog.

A tadpole, if it survives at all, is quite certain to turn into a frog. A confederacy may survive without turning into a federation, and not every constitution laying down the ground rules of a confederacy carries in itself the seeds of a future federal state. As in all historical processes, multiple causation is at work and the issue is more a matter of odds than of predictable certainties.

MAJORITY RULE BY ANY OTHER NAME

The new constitution equips the European Union with a new decision rule to replace the method used hitherto, namely unanimity assisted by arm-twisting and talking-to-exhaustion. Sheer cheek and nerve also had a role, often helping France to get her way when her case was seemingly hopeless.

Under the new system, three bodies reach decisions jointly. The Commission proposes, the Council of Ministers disposes, and the European Parliament approves.

The Commission is reformed, reduced to fifteen voting members but enlarged by another fifteen nonvoting ones. A total of thirty seats should permit each of the twenty-five member states to nominate one commissioner, which means that the latter will increasingly become the spokesmen of their home states and not the impartial servants of all. So far, so good—this is inefficient, but consistent with confederacy. The Commission will technically remain as powerful as before, for it retains control over what legislation is proposed. It has the executive staff to carry out eventual decisions. However, the Commission has but limited control over hiring and firing, hence the loyalties of the staff are in reality divided.

The whip hand is held by the Council of Ministers, which adopts, rejects, or modifies the Commission's proposals. The new constitution enlarges the breach the Nice Treaty of 2001 drove into the former unanimity rule. It provides for "double majority" rule; a decision is carried if at least 50 percent of the member states representing 60 percent of the Union's population vote for it. The 60 percent provision prevents three small members of the twenty-five-member Union from imposing decisions on twelve larger ones. In fact, as things now stand, the usual Franco-German coalition, by co-opting two small to middle-sized states, can always form a blocking minority of 40 percent of the population and use the block as a bargaining lever.

First published as part 2 of "A Tadpole Constitution," by Liberty Fund, Inc., at www.econlib.org on January 7, 2004. Reprinted by permission.

It is amusing, if that is the right word, that Europe's politically correct circles have convinced themselves that Asia Minor is in Europe, Islam is as consistent with human rights as Christianity (or, as the new constitution prefers to put it, Graeco-Roman and Enlightenment tradition), and it is politically correct to admit Turkey to the Union without much further delay. They are likely to achieve this by 2010 or soon after. On foreseeable demographic trends, Turkey would then be the Union's most influential member by midcentury.

Like any majority rule, the double majority rule, albeit less brutal, is inconsistent with confederacy. It has the irresistible force of a nuclear bomb to smash the ability of member states to decide matters for themselves. The very consciousness that the bomb is there helps steer the Union's agenda in a federal direction. Moreover, any likely majority under the 50-cum-60 rule is rose-tinted: it wants Union legislation to be more "social," to enshrine more "workers' rights," and make taxation more "equitable" by stopping member states from undercutting each other's taxes to attract young talent, entrepreneurs, inventors, research centers, and company head offices.

Recognizing the way the federal wind was going to blow, some states, notably Britain, the Netherlands, and Ireland, obtained "nuclear-free zones," areas where the majority rule would not apply. Defense and personal income taxes would remain "nuclear-free," i.e., member states would have a veto over Union intervention in their own armed forces and income taxes.

However, the wording of these exceptions is weak, showing the marks of compromise, and while defense may remain under national control in the foreseeable future, taxation is unlikely to be left "nuclear-free" for long. Corporate income tax should be the first to go, for it will be deemed contrary to the conditions of a single market for the Union that the total tax charge on corporate profits should be four times as high in Germany as in Ireland—and it is not hard to guess which rate will be adjusted to harmonize with the other. After corporate taxes, excise and value-added taxes should follow.

Two guiding principles of the constitution are supposed to determine whether a given issue is to be settled at the state or at the Council of Ministers level. One is subsidiarity. It means, roughly speaking, that everything should be dealt with at the lowest level capable of adequately handling it. If the principle had any objectively ascertainable meaning, it would safeguard against centralization and federal hypertrophy. Obviously, however, whether an issue is handled adequately at a local level is a matter of subjective opinion and not of fact. The second principle, cohesion of the Union, supersedes subsidiarity when the two conflict. If Madrid wishes to handle a Spanish problem in its own way, it would apparently be sufficient for a majority in the Council of Ministers to decide that cohesion demands that the matter be handled at their level in Brussels in harmony with the way it is handled elsewhere in the Union or, more radically, as it ought to be handled everywhere.

The constitution declares explicitly that Union law overrides state law. This gives enormous potential power to the European Court of Justice, which has the mission to interpret Union law. The Court is destined over time to swell to many times its present size. The primacy of Union law has first been established by judicial precedent at a time when the scope of Union law was limited to matters concerning market freedom. Union law has since been expanding and is obviously destined to expand over many new areas. The Court will, in terms of the constitution, extend its jurisdiction over all of them.

The European Court of Human Rights, even without explicit constitutional mission, has already been active in overturning decisions by member state courts. An incident that is now merrily burgeoning and billowing illustrates its impact. Two teenage Muslim girls in a French state school have after lengthy procedures been expelled because they refused to give up their veils, a religious symbol deemed incompatible with the lay character of a state institution, besides being awkward for taking swimming lessons. The girls' father, a lawyer, is appealing to the administrative tribunal, where he is predicted to lose, and will then appeal to the State Council, where he is also predicted to lose. His object is to be able at that stage to appeal to the European Court of Human Rights, where he is predicted to win. His victory is feared to give much encouragement to Islamic defiance of school authority, an encouragement France does not exactly need.

Judicial influence in a unifying, federating direction should gain further authority from the deep bow the new constitution makes to political correctness by declaring a Charter of Fundamental Rights. They include a curious ragbag of wishes, aspirations, and general directives, ranging from the right of workers to be consulted on major business decisions (without saying what is to happen if the consultation fails to produce agreement), the right of the unemployed to free placement services, the right of consumers to safe food, and other similarly "fundamental" rights that one is surprised to see as parts of a constitution. Perhaps the most baffling is the "right" to a job. Does your right to a job involve an obligation for me to employ you?—or merely your freedom to sue the government (of your state? or of the Union?) in the European Court of Justice for failing to ensure full employment? Dizzying perspectives are opened up by the Charter in this and other ways.

Next to the Council of Ministers and the Commission, the third leg of the decision-making tripod, the European Parliament, is not really rescued from its present and staggeringly expensive irrelevance by the new constitution. Power is divided between two contestants only, the Council and the Commission. The former is to abandon its half-yearly rotating presidency. It is to get a permanent president and, significantly, a permanent staff. There will then be two rival institutions, two presidents, and two bureaucracies.

It looks a safe enough bet that this structure will not survive intact for very long, except perhaps in form but not in substance. One president will reduce the other to some subordinate role, and one bureaucracy will gradually take over the other. Of the two, the Council is the more likely survivor, partly because it is destined to remain the Commission's paymaster and partly because the power to settle issues by the weapon of majority rule lends you more power than the putting of issues on the agenda, important as the latter may be. Whichever institution will absorb the other, one can already discern on the future horizon, maybe by the midcentury, the contours of a strong single federal legislative-cum-executive body holding together a superstate on top of the member states—the frog that started off as a tadpole.

WHAT NOW FOR "EUROPE"?

WHY THE PEOPLE FAILED THEIR MASTERS

France, one of the six founder members and the self-appointed leader of the European Union, has submitted to a referendum the proposed constitutional treaty, which is a four-hundred-odd-page effusion of verbosity. The political "elite," nearly unanimously supporting the text, blithely made it known that if it is adopted, there will be a "Europe" and if it is rejected, there will be none. The unthinkable happened. Fifty-five percent of the electorate voted "the wrong way," seconded a few days later by 62 percent of Dutch voters. Both electorates failed their political masters who had called a referendum in the confident expectation that it would endorse their goal of "building Europe" and give it legitimacy. By rights, the constitution is now dead, for its adoption is subject to unanimous ratification by all the member states. While states that ratify by parliamentary vote have approved, and will approve, it, states that submit it to popular vote now look likely to follow the French and Dutch example. Even if they did not, the French vote alone would suffice legally to kill it. I say "by rights," because desperate attempts are now being made to resuscitate the treaty in some disguise, of which more below.

The motives for voting "the wrong way" were kaleidoscopic, but two major ones stand out. One was the idea, encouraged by the authors of the document and the media which assisted its birth with loud applause, that a modern constitution is above all a list of what people have a "right" to get from their government (and never mind where the government gets them from in order to give them to the people). Despite the mouth-watering list of good things promised them in the "Charter of Fundamental Rights," which forms the most extravagant part of the document, the people were still disappointed: there were

First published by Liberty Fund, Inc., at www.econlib.org on July 4, 2005. Reprinted by permission.

not enough "social" promises of levelling upward. The list was not rich enough. "Europe" was not going to be sufficiently insulated from "inhuman," "blind" market forces. On the contrary, it was to be liberal or, as its critics insist, "ultraliberal," enshrining rules of free competition and thus undermining even the present level of "workers' rights." In particular, it does not require all member states, notably the ten new east-central European ones, to raise their taxes and social welfare entitlements to the Franco-German level, thus allowing free rein to "social dumping" and the luring of productive business and employment from West to East.

The other and perhaps deeper reason for "rejecting Europe" was the ever wider gulf between the common people and those in politics and the media who make a living and a name from purporting to lead and inform them. The "elite" has never ceased to pour out a torrent of rhetoric about the sacred goal of a politically united Europe, forcing it down the public's throat. A referendum on it was the perfect occasion for the common people to hit back at the Right without sparing the Left and to hit back at the Left without sparing the Right. Both halves of the political "elite" could be taught a lesson.

THE ECONOMY GOES ON MUDDLING THROUGH

Before the French vote, no less an authority than the prime minister announced that a "no" vote would lead to an economic crisis—a singularly irresponsible prophecy for a head of government to make. The crisis may come for all we know, but it is not likely to, and if it does, it will not be due to the "no" vote. Without the new constitution that would have given greater influence to common institutions including the Council of Ministers and that citadel of political correctness, the European Parliament, most of the important economic decisions now remain subject to state veto rights. While European economic policy cannot, for this reason, do much good, thanks to the sanity of the veto-bearing British, Irish, and the northern Protestant belt, it cannot do much harm either.

There is every prospect that the European economy will continue to underperform, dragged down by the near-stagnation of Germany,

France, and Italy. Without quite radical structural reforms, these core countries will continue their decline relative to the rest. There is some chance of reforms starting in Germany with the foreseeable change of government in the autumn, a weaker chance in Italy next year, and no chance at all in France at least for the next two years until the presidential term of the "republican monarchy" runs out.

Some sections of opinion in Italy and Germany would like to shed the euro, returning to their original national currencies in the hope that this would raise their performance to the British, Danish, and Swedish level, countries that never gave up theirs. However, though a majority in Germany and a strong minority in Italy would welcome a return to the mark and the lira, there is no support for this among decision-makers, and it would in fact be a tricky undertaking with a high short-term risk of shocks to the dissident countries' new exchange rates and bond markets.

"LITTLE MAN, WHAT NOW?"

Little Man, What Now?—the title of a popular German novel of the interwar years—would fit a book about the present predicament of the minor politicians, journalists, lobbyists, international functionaries of all kinds whose influence, income, creature comforts, and, above all, sense of self-importance have hung on the political "Europe" that the French and Dutch referenda seem to have now dispatched down the drain.

It is not only old-fashioned honest selfishness that drives them. If that were the case, they could all be installed at public expense in luxury somewhere in the South of France or Portugal to play golf and discuss Europe. Compared to the European budget of about 116 billion euros, let alone some national ones, the cost would be minute and probably worth it. The problem is that most of these people passionately believe in the dream of their "Europe" becoming a superpower "able to stand up to America" (though apart from flattering their pride, it is not clear what good such "standing up" would do anyone). This ambition cannot be bought off and is dangerous even if it remains a mere dream, let alone if steps are taken to realize it.

The "political class" is not taking its defeat at the hands of the people lying down. Instead of accepting that the European Union is destined to remain a free-trade area with some common regulatory bells and whistles and that the proposed constitution destined to transform it into a political entity is dead, they are busily trying to salvage something from the wreck. The plan seems to be to scrap the November 2006 deadline for ratification, have a pause in the process to allow the memory of the French and Dutch "wrongheaded votes" to fade out, and have some kind of fresh start in the expectation that some ingenious formula or other will be found and adopted to get round the obstacle of unanimous ratification. A modified formula, avoiding the ill-fated name "constitution" and sweetened with "fudge," could eventually be concocted so that only the European Parliament's vote would be required to pass it. The parliament would be as sure to approve it as mice are sure to eat the piece of cheese put before them. This is a longer-term plan that cannot be rushed, and it may not succeed. However, at least for the next couple of years we will not know that it has definitively failed.

FREE-RIDING ON THE EURO

In most places around the world, it is still usual that parents look after their small children and grown children look after their elderly parents. The looking after is unpaid work and is not counted in the national product. Sweden has passed that stage. In Sweden, the lookers-after look after other people's small children and elderly parents, while their own small children and their own elderly parents are looked after by yet other people. The state pays everybody for the looking after. The total of this pay is added to the national product. It also gets added to the budget deficit unless taxes have meanwhile been increased.

It is a commonplace that Sweden runs what is probably the world's most extensive welfare state, and suffers from the absurdities that welfare states usually generate. It is tempting to blame the obtuseness of the electorate for voting with absolute consistency, in election after election, for the extension or at worst the maintenance of the welfare system and a sharp egalitarian bias in tax policy at the cost—a cost most do not recognize—of reduced material wealth.

It is arguable that with its high level of education, exemplary civility, and admirable technological leadership in many fields, Sweden should be much richer than it is. Nevertheless, it is also true (though less of a commonplace) that if they really must have a welfare state, the Swedes manage it less wastefully and more intelligently than most. Since the reforms put in place over the last few years, the country's overall economic performance has improved markedly. Moreover, while until the late 1990s Sweden's "social" spending as a share of national income was the highest in Europe, this share has since been reined back a little and is now exceeded by that of France, whose welfare system is not quite as comprehensive but is more wasteful.

Sensible Sweden has now taken a sensible decision; in a referendum on 14 September, it has by a majority of 56 percent rejected the

First published by Liberty Fund, Inc., at www.econlib.org on September 17, 2003. Reprinted by permission.

proposal to adopt the euro as its currency. Two things are remarkable about this outcome. One is that government and opposition, large corporations, the media, and all the chattering and scribbling classes have joined forces in a sometimes quite frantic campaign for a "yes" vote. Outlandish claims were made about how the euro will speed up economic growth and reduce the cost of living—the exact opposite of what has happened in the euro-zone since its formation. The electorate has remained deaf to these extravagantly un-Swedish promises. Nor did dire threats of being "shut out of Europe" impress it.

The other remarkable feature of the referendum was that according to the pollsters, the chief reason for rejecting the common currency was the fear that as a member of the euro-zone, Sweden would be obliged to curtail its welfare system—a misperceived threat if ever there was one. However, the upshot is that Sweden is staying out, Denmark is less and less likely to reverse its earlier rejection of the common currency, while the present British government's ambition to persuade the country to adopt it looks for the time being utterly hopeless.

Maybe the euro is rejected for all the wrong reasons, but the choice is probably right: the euro is a trap. It is an unintended one, but no less cunning for that.

Each member state of the euro-zone is caught between two alternatives: to engage in fiscal free-riding or to be the sucker, the victim of free-riding by the others. The reason is easy to grasp. When a country has its own currency, fiscal profligacy carries its own punishment. Interest on the national debt rises more than proportionately to the debt, both because the country's own capital market gets overstretched and because the risk attaching to its currency increases. Default on the debt and devaluation of the currency (coming after a flight into inflation to water down the debt), though perhaps still remote, start looking less improbable. The repercussions render a loose fiscal posture more and more difficult to hold, and in due course tend to impose some discipline on the government.

As a member of the euro-zone, the same government running a large deficit is spared most of these disciplinary consequences. No member country, with the possible exception of Germany, is big enough in the zone as a whole for its deficit financing to represent a significant strain on the zone's capital market. Currency risk subsists only relative to currencies outside the zone, in practice only the dollar and the yen, but it is eliminated within the zone; there is no Greek euro and no Spanish euro, so one cannot weaken relative to the other. Fiscal irresponsibility by one country still has adverse consequences for the zone as a whole, but only a small fraction of them is borne by the irresponsible country in question, with the bulk spread over all the other member countries. This is the classic breeding ground for free-riding.

Under these circumstances, fiscal vice is not punished but fiscal virtue is. Today, Spain maintains a balanced budget, while both Germany and France are running deficits that hover around the mark of 4 percent of GDP. According to all serious forecasts, their deficits will exceed 3 percent of GDP for four years or more in a row, not dipping below that level before 2006 at the earliest. One result is that Spanish borrowers have to pay higher medium and long rates of interest than they would do if Germany and France also had balanced budgets. This is not to say that budget deficits are always evil if some of their negative consequences are shifted to other countries, as they in fact are in the euro-zone. In the short run, occasional deficits may be justified—or would be if they were not habit-forming. However, it is clear that in a euro-zone-type arrangement, defense against the free-riding of others consists in becoming a free-rider oneself.

Where the markets do not automatically provide deterrents to overspending, can "constitutional" rules do so? Germany, with its strong anti-inflationary, sound-money leanings has tried to inject such rules into the euro-zone when it got its partners to adopt the so-called "growth and stability pact," as part of the Maastricht treaty. The rule sets an upper limit of 60 percent of GDP on the national debt and 3 percent of GDP on the annual budget deficit of euro-zone countries.

The debt limit has no "teeth"; in fact, the average share of the national debts of the euro-zone countries is now 71.5 percent of their GDP, with Italy and Belgium the chief offenders with over 100 percent and both France and Germany now over 60 percent and rising. The deficit limit has "teeth" but very weak ones. The offending country is summoned to take remedial measures, and if it fails to bring its deficit down to the limit, it may be fined. However, few observers seriously believe that the Brussels Commission would dare to fine an influential member country, nor that the fine, if by miracle it were imposed, would change that country's fiscal policy. To make doubly sure, a strong movement is now afoot to take the "rigidity" out of the pact.

If the pact is not kept when it is not convenient to keep it, what remedy can the euro-zone find against fiscal free-riding that looks capable of undermining the euro? In the United States, the vast bulk of public spending is decided in Washington at the federal level. The states might have an incentive to free ride but have little or no scope to do so. In Europe the central budget is only about 2.5 percent of the member states' combined GDP, and each member state has both incentive and scope to free-ride at the expense of the rest.

The conclusion is obvious: to throttle back fiscal free-riding by the member states and protect the euro, taxing and spending decisions have gradually to move from the states to Brussels. Whatever it may be called, in practice it means a move toward a more politically centralized Europe—a move the new European constitution, now in the final negotiating phase, would surreptitiously facilitate.

SOME DEMOCRATIC ECONOMICS

The sordid affair between the European Parliament and money that has been going on for the last quarter century became turbulent last December and promises further turbulence ahead of the European elections in June, all of which prompts some evident and some not so evident conclusions about what we might call democratic economics.

At first sight, the affair is a simple illustration of what happens when lawmakers can legislate about the money taxpayers must pay them. The 626 MEPs (Members of the European Parliament) elected by the voters of fifteen member states of the Union each get a "basic" salary equal to what they would get if they were members of the parliaments of their home countries. Thus a Spanish MEP earns a "basic" salary of about 36,000 euros a year, a British one about 70,000, a German 100,000, and an Italian a bit over 110,000 euros. MEPs from some of the new member countries joining on May 1, 2004, will under present rules have to make do with as little as 6,000 euros a year.

These salaries are "basic." They are richly supplemented by a rule on expenses which is an open invitation to fiddling. At French insistence, the seat of the parliament is in Strasbourg while the committee work is mostly done in Brussels and all MEPs have to go to Luxembourg as well. An assiduous MEP is therefore theoretically travelling all the time between these cities and his hometown, though many are far from assiduous. They could also have a wide variety of other expenses that may or may not be necessary to incur in order properly to represent the people. They can claim any and all of these regardless of whether they have incurred them: no vouchers are required. The result is that an MEP can make up to 40,000 euros a year "profit"—that is to say, steal 40,000 euros—by padding his expense account.

There are honest MEPs who do not steal. That the majority do is proven by the fact that for twenty-five years all attempts by the honest

First published by Liberty Fund, Inc., at www.econlib.org on March 1, 2004. Reprinted by permission.

ones to reform the expense account system have been voted down by a majority. Such brazen insistence on their right to fiddle, and oblige taxpayers to put up with the fiddle, has gradually led to the European Parliament falling into disrepute. Polls indicate that at the elections next June, voter participation will average no higher than 25 percent and may be as low as 18 percent in Britain. There is clearly a tendency for the EU Parliament to sink into utter irrelevance, and in the long run there is a threat to the 626 jobs that provide those luscious perks.

To face this threat and to launder their reputation, last December a majority of MEPs finally agreed to a deal introducing properly substantiated expense accounts. In exchange, MEPs were all to have the same "basic" annual salary of about 110,000 euros, subject to a most favorable tax rate. In addition, they were to get a "special" lump sum allowance of 43,000 euros, a daily attendance fee of 257 euros, and no less than 144,000 euros a year for secretarial and office costs. The deal was vetoed in January by the Council of Ministers as being "bad PR" ahead of the elections, and may or may not be resuscitated in the near future. If eventually it is concluded on anything like these terms, it will be proof that in representative democracy, he who pays the piper does not necessarily call the tune, for the piper may have powers to extort the pay without having to play the paymaster's tune.

However, it is not really the sums extorted that matter from an economic point of view. In underdeveloped countries, they are indeed very large if we include the proceeds of outright corruption. In places like Kenya, Nigeria, and perhaps above all Angola, they may run into high single-digit percentages of GDP. But in Western Europe and in the United States, the amount the political class as a whole pays itself both in "legally" provided incomes and in illicit graft over and above the total amount the same people could probably earn in private life is a negligible fraction of national income. The popular (and populist) belief that we are poorer than we need be because politicians are thieves and steal our money is naive. Democratic economics very likely makes us poorer, but it does so in a more roundabout way, and not because politicians are more dishonest than most other people—though they very likely are.

In 1906, the French National Assembly voted a law raising the salary of deputies at a stroke by 67 percent. Prior to this watershed law, politics was mostly the domain of "notables" with private incomes and professional men, such as lawyers and journalists, who practiced it part-time. After the law, there was a sea change. The composition of the Assembly changed radically, in came the schoolteachers, and the part-time amateur was replaced by a new breed of professional politician fully maintained by the taxpayer. However, with universal suffrage, he was not chosen and installed in his seat by the taxpayer, but by voters in general, whether they paid much tax or little or none.

Setting pay so that politics as a career is opened up to men and women without private means is by all accounts a step toward greater democracy. If lawmakers as a class have no vested interest in inequalities of income and wealth, the chances are that they will make laws that promote greater equality because in an electorate with one-man-one-vote and secret ballot, there is a natural majority in favor of making an unequal distribution more equal, for any majority will gain more by taking from the rich than from the poor. The result of legislation generated by the democratic process is more progressive taxation, greater welfare entitlements, and a larger share of GDP absorbed in government spending than would otherwise be the case. Politicians who would oppose this trend run a high risk of being voted out of office and being replaced by others who are no more dishonest but are better at attracting the majority vote—which it is the politician's business to seek if democracy is to be competitive.

However, attaching an adequate income to elective office is not enough. The politician must not depend on particular interests for his campaign financing and for the running expenses of his party. In the United States, he does so depend. The largest sources of money for presidential and congressional campaigns are called AT&T, the public employees' unions, Microsoft, Philip Morris, the American Bar Association, and so forth. Federal contributions are hardly material; in the perspective of a presidential campaign costing from $100 to $200 million, and congressional districts costing tens of millions to win or lose, federal aid is of little interest. In Britain, both campaign and party financing is wholly nonstate.

As opposed to the Anglo-American systems, in continental Europe there are widespread attempts severely to limit private financing of elections and parties. In France, a 1994 law places an outright ban on campaign financing by private business, while contributions by individuals are limited to 4,600 euros per donor. A 10,200-euro limit per individual donor is fixed by the 1999 German law on party financing. In both countries, there is a complicated system of subsidies paid to candidates and parties according to votes gained, with a ceiling of 57 million euros to any one party and a threshold of 5 percent of the total vote in Germany. In France, the state subsidy is sufficient to keep even no-hope candidates and splinter parties in reasonable comfort from one election to the next. Large parties do trade the odd favor to some private interest against under-the-table contributions, but do not strictly need to in order to get by. These state-financed systems are, in brief, as independent of moneyed interests as one can expect in real life. Significantly, they are legislated by the legislators for the legislators. The piper has emancipated himself from the money that pays him.

The effect of moving toward a more perfect, more completely democratic political system where politicians are not beholden to particular interests stares us in the face. The economics of democracy reveals one reason why government policies in much of continental Europe are more egalitarian, more welfarist, and more statist than in the Anglo-American world, and why the latter is economically more successful than the former. Many other reasons may also be acting in the same direction, but it would be a delusion to forget that democracy, whatever its merits, is no recipe for the growth of riches.

THE SOVIET LEGACY

The countries that eked out a dismal existence behind the Iron Curtain between 1945 and 1989 were colonies of an unprecedented kind. Every colony in modern history was colonized by a power that was its superior in crucial aspects of civilization, technology, organizing and governing ability. The European colonies of the Soviet Union had the unique misfortune of being subjugated by a power that was their inferior in all but brute military strength. It was a bit like Belgium becoming a Congolese colony. That might happen yet, but not in our lifetime.

Unlike most others, the Soviet colonies had nothing to gain and nothing valuable to learn from the occupier. What the peoples under Russian rule did learn was misbehavior, cynicism, mendacity, dissimulation, and mutual mistrust. They refused to learn the supposed virtues of socialist man, the exemplary behavior of the good Soviet citizen who devotes his life to serving the noble goals set before him by the Communist leadership. They did not end up all bad; they developed capacities of self-defense, ingenuity in the face of need, resistance in the face of force, and rapid grasp of opportunities.

Common to all these colonial subjects was silent contempt for the Soviet people, the Soviet state, and the native authorities who acted on the Russians' behalf. Contempt for the authorities entailed contempt for their laws. Stealing from the state became a sport, not misbehavior. There was deep contempt for the judiciary and the police that administered what was seen as a mockery masquerading as the rule of law. Disrespect for state law, however, was not offset by greater respect for society's own unwritten conventional rules of decent behavior, mainly because the ties that would normally bind workmates, colleagues, and even mere strangers had been frayed so thin by the maniacal tugging of a perverse dictatorship that ruled by intimidation, make-believe, and the destruction of all relationships except loyalty to the state.

First published as part 2 of "Misbehavior, Punishment, Prosperity," by Liberty Fund, Inc., at www.econlib.org on September 3, 2007. Reprinted by permission.

Every society in the Soviet bloc was horizontally sliced in two. The top slice consisted of the *nomenklatura,* the party rank and file that supported it, and the secret police that had to protect the tenure in power of the whole upper slice, including first of all its own secure tenure. Comically enough, the secret police in nearly every satellite country was called the "security" police or service, though the only security it cared for was the secure enjoyment of its own and its accomplices' place on top of the ordinary people.

Like everywhere else, the ordinary people formed the bottom class, with one difference. Everywhere else, there is some upward mobility driven mainly by ability, effort, and luck. In the Soviet colonies, upward mobility from the lower into the upper slice of society depended first and foremost on proofs of loyalty and usefulness to the party. Proof more often than not included denunciation and betrayal of one's fellows and hypocritical play-acting and flattery of the mighty.

A really striking feature of the postwar history of this part of Europe is that nowhere were the *nomenklatura,* the party hacks, and the secret police called to account. When Hitler's Germany collapsed, the Western allies in their zones of occupation initiated a large-scale "denazification" process, screening out and banning from certain public posts or sending to prison those who played an active role in Nazi misdeeds. Many of them fled to the Soviet zone, where the Russians and later the "German Democratic Republic" found useful collaborators among them. But when in 1989 the Soviet colonies regained their independence, party bosses and secret police officers, let alone minor functionaries, all went scot-free, the more so as they have all declared that they had always been social democrats at heart. Apart from those guilty of murder and torture (difficult to prove), they were tacitly forgiven for the humiliation and misery they had inflicted on their own people while they enjoyed the power, prestige, and privileges that accrue to members of successful criminal conspiracies. The watchword was "no witch hunt." When in early 2007 a new Polish government started a belated campaign of screening former secret police agents and their civilian helpers (most of whom collaborated under duress), large sections of Polish opinion protested and were loudly echoed by intellectuals in Western Europe who invoked the infamous memory of McCarthyism in the USA. Screening might or might not have become a nasty witch hunt, but dispensing with it was to confirm the widespread conviction that unless you actually rob the bank or mug an old lady in front of several reliable witnesses, you never have to pay for wrongdoing and can always walk away with its fruits.

Thanks to "no witch hunt," when privatization began, ex-secret-police officers, ex-leaders of the Young Communist movement, and ex–"red directors" were all there in the starting blocks, ready to jump and appropriate state property. They had the advantage of their own ready-made network of ex-comrades who "knew all the ropes" and who could smooth each other's little ways. The present Hungarian prime minister, an ex–Young Communist and member by marriage of a powerful Communist clan, now a billionaire, made his first millions by buying state property for a symbolic peppercorn and then losing little time selling it back to the state for many millions. The extreme case is Bulgaria, where practically all industry and commerce have come to be owned and run by former secret police officers. It is in Bulgaria that contract killings of business rivals are the most frequent, and one wonders whether there is some causal relation between the ownership structure and this muscular kind of competition.

Could it be said that while the Soviet legacy is not pretty, it has not done real harm, for the European ex-colonies of Russia are now all champions of economic growth? Despite near-total fiscal irresponsibility (that bought the present government its election victory) even Hungary is managing to grow at 4 percent, 6 percent is normal in Poland and the Czech Republic, while the Baltic states have been beating the 10 percent threshold for several years. In the face of such performance, does endemic and shameless corruption really matter?

It is easy to forget the depths of poverty, dilapidated infrastructure, and near-insane investment planning to which these countries had sunk during Soviet rule and socialist management. Some large industrial complexes were actually running at negative value added, meaning that at world prices their bought-in inputs cost more than their output was worth; this in turn meant that, had they been closed and their workers sent home, the national income would have increased. The present high growth rates in these countries are mostly the combined result of the gradual elimination of such absurdities, of the rush of new technologies being borrowed from the West, and of inflows of capital and management induced by the cheapness of local labor—in that order of importance. All these growth-boosters are welcome but almost by definition temporary. Some current economic policies in the ex-Soviet satellites are interesting and promising, provided they are persevered with; radical tax reform and the move from complex tax structures to a flat tax is one of them. Nevertheless, the catching-up phase of easy growth is unlikely to last longer than fifteen to twenty years.

The role of corruption that became endemic in the colonial era is the big question mark. Some economists argue that it is a method of rational resource allocation, for it is the most efficient supplier who can offer the highest bribe to get a government contract, and it is a good thing that he gets it. To say this is to forget that bribing is not an open auction but a clandestine transaction that, in addition, has such non-price aspects as confidence and relationships. Moreover, even in open auction the less efficient might be able to offer a higher bribe than the more efficient if he could furnish cheaper, shoddier work thanks to protection offered by the bribe-taker—an option not open to the high-quality, high-cost competitor. Reams could be written about the effects of corruption, and no incontrovertible conclusion may be available in economic theory. One's gut feeling, though, is that whatever corruption may do to costs and quality in a particular transaction, its wider effect upon the behavior and willingness to play by the rules of an entire people who watch corruption thriving cannot but be seriously damaging. Prosperity does, after all, depend on the punishment of misbehavior.

A WAR OF ATTRITION BETWEEN ECONOMIC REALITY AND POLITICAL DREAMS

The international economic scene, like a good Western, is populated by white hats and black hats and is enlivened by tests of strength and endurance between them. The white hats are fighting for the prosperity of the ranch and they have nature and economic realities as their ally. The black hats try to get control of the ranch as a means of realizing political dreams and are backed by mass shortsightedness and gullibility. For the last decade or so, despite some lost battles such as the capitulation of the French government in the great transport strike of 1995 or the failure of the Italian government to force through essential pension reform, the white hats were quietly winning the war. Markets were becoming more free, welfare systems less extravagant, and governments a little less demagogic. After a series of disastrous presidents from Jacques Delors to Romano Prodi, the Commission of the European Union gained a more enlightened leadership under José Manuel Barroso and a more "northern," more freedom-oriented team of commissioners. They are now the target of bitter attacks by socialists of all countries and all parties for their "Atlanticist," "ultraliberal" leanings—a sure sign that they are doing some good work for the ranch. The "Yukos affair" in Russia and the "Bolkestein Directive" in the EU are two campaigns in this ongoing war of attrition.

THE YUKOS AFFAIR

In Russia, after his reelection President Putin announced a sensible economic program, encouraging hopes that after two failed attempts in 1861 and 1905, that potentially rich country might be third time lucky and finally extricate itself from the wet, cold mud in which it

First published as "A War of White Hats and Black Hats: A War of Attrition Between Economic Reality and Political Dreams," by Liberty Fund, Inc., at www .econlib.org on March 7, 2005. Reprinted by permission.

seemed to be forever mired—thanks mostly to the caprice and perversity of its own governments.

Now, however, a stalemate in the war of attrition seems to exist where neither side is really winning and the black hats give as good as they get. President Putin, despite protestations to the contrary, has abandoned his avowed policy of establishing secure tenure for property with freedom and light taxation for enterprise, both indigenous and foreign. The Yukos affair bore spectacular witness to this U-turn. The company, the country's biggest privately owned hydrocarbon producer, was hit by a series of claims for taxes in past years that could not even pretend to be founded on the tax code; for 2001 and 2002, the back tax claimed exceeded the company's total sales. To satisfy unpaid tax demands of $21 billion, the government put up Yukos's largest productive asset at public auction and sold it to the sole bidder, a letterbox company, for $9 billion; the letterbox company then sold it on to state-owned Rosneft for the same amount. The sinister aspect of this comedy is that the Russian government asserts with a straight face that Yukos was not nationalized, let alone confiscated; the transaction was a perfectly normal case of recovering a debt owing to the state. There is much apprehension in Russia that other, albeit less spectacular, cases will follow.

The running is made by a squad of gray eminences around the president, many his former colleagues in the KGB, some holding high rank in its successor, the FSB. They are nationalist and not corrupt by Russian standards, but not literate in economics. Government ministers are mainly gray bureaucrats with the possible exception of finance minister Kudrin. The intellectual cream is represented by two liberal (in American English, "classical" liberal) economists: Germain Gref, the economy minister, and Andrei Ilianorov, Putin's personal economic adviser. Ilianorov openly called the Yukos affair "a swindle" and was reduced a notch in rank but kept his place. Gref declared that the government will not meet the president's 7 percent p.a. ten-year growth target "by banging the table." He warned that the scarcest factor of production in Russia is an honestly functioning court system, without which the country, intoxicated for the time being by the high oil price, will sink back into the perennial mud.

A delegation of Western economists was received by Mr. Putin and castigated him for not pressing on with his original economic reform program. He told them with a rare sign of real humor: "Everybody wants to go to heaven, but nobody wants to die." Political expediency and short-termist compromise must prevail over the virtue of doing the right thing.

THE BOLKESTEIN DIRECTIVE

The Bolkestein Directive is not the title of the latest thriller you find in the airport kiosk. It is the last major administrative act of the outgoing EU commissioner for the internal market. It is designed to make the market for services within the EU as free as the market for goods. Its particular sting is a country-of-origin clause which permits a Polish, Baltic, or Hungarian person, say an architect or a market research agent, to sell a service in Germany or France while only paying the (low) social insurance premiums and taxes due in his home country. This is taken in Western Europe as a quite flagrant license to practice "social dumping," the undercutting of decades of socialist achievements, and is political dynamite. President Chirac of France promptly "vetoed" the directive and was joined, though in less peremptory style, by German chancellor Schroeder. Brussels says the directive was issued under existing powers, cannot be "vetoed," and will stand. The French government of course will do as it pleases. It will not be the first time that it refuses to apply a directive or honor a treaty; its contempt for the deficit limit it signed up to in the Maastricht stability pact is eloquent proof that the EU cannot force a major member country to do what it really hates doing.

THE LISBON REFORM PROGRAM

The Bolkestein Directive, like the Yukos affair, is symbolic of wider conflicts. In 2000, the EU countries solemnly adopted the Lisbon Program of economic reforms that were to make Europe "the world's most competitive, knowledge-based economy": education was to be reformed, regulation simplified, and above all labor laws were to be eased to enable labor markets in the most sclerotic of euro-zone countries, Germany and France, to start functioning.

In the universities, regulatory agencies, and the unions, the black hats were, and still are, sitting in heavily fortified positions. For nearly five years now, they did not permit the Lisbon program to move forward. After he took office last November, and after he survived attacks by the left-leaning European Parliament and other socialist bodies, Mr. Barroso proposed to revive the Lisbon Program and tried to rally member countries to it. He was told in barely veiled terms by some major euro-zone governments that they were more concerned with safeguarding the "European model" than with initiatives that would make waves.

Germany, independently of the Lisbon Program, did carry out one immensely important reform of unemployment benefits that will almost certainly produce a speeding-up of economic growth later this year, though things will first have to get worse before they will get better. France relaxed the ceiling of permitted overtime under the infamous 35-hour-workweek laws from 130 to 220 hours a year. The new upper limit would permit a "legal" workweek of 39 hours, though they would be quite expensive overtime hours. However, true to form, the government made this extension of authorized overtime subject to the agreement, not of the workforce at a plant or office, but of the union supposed to represent them. This was yet another step in the government's continuing effort to build up the unions and give them an importance by means of legislation that their sparse membership (only 8 percent of the labor force, and that almost entirely in the public sector with negligible membership in private industry) would not justify. However, according to the European model the unions must be important and if they are not, the government will give a helping hand to make them so.

A BRIGHTENING OF THE ECONOMIC SKIES OVER BRUSSELS?

There is a new Commission of the European Union in Brussels. It is taking office next month. Nearly every member of it is new. The well-meaning but bumbling and often confused-looking president, Romano Prodi, has been replaced by the former Portuguese premier José Manuel Barroso, who is not only smoother, younger, and more articulate, but also a man largely freed from the numbing intellectual ballast of Latin social ideology. For someone who was a Maoist in his student days, he is modern and economically literate. His tactical skill in allocating portfolios in a way that radically reduces the influence of the French and to some extent also of the German commissioner has earned applause from lovers of judo.

Each of the twenty-five member states has one commissioner, compared with two for the larger members and none for some of the small ones in the previous Commission. Many of the member states habitually nominate commissioners to reward politicians who for one reason or another must be put out to grass. Barroso on the whole managed to give such people portfolios of minor, in some cases only of symbolic, significance. The half dozen really important portfolios have gone to men and women of high caliber and liberal convictions. (The confusion of tongues between American and English English calls for making sure the reader remembers that an American liberal is a European social democrat.)

Moreover, given that some portfolios matter far more than others, the influence of northern Europe—Britain, the Netherlands, the Scandinavian and the Baltic states—has grown and that of the "core" states, especially France, has diminished. To French indignation and dis-

First published as "Weather Forecast—A Brightening of the Economic Skies over Brussels?" by Liberty Fund, Inc., at www.econlib.org on October 4, 2004. Reprinted by permission.

may, Brussels looks less and less like an administrative annex of Paris. Though there are individual exceptions, the shift of influence from the center to the north is by and large a shift from the viscerally socialist to the viscerally liberal mentality.

The Prodi, and before it the Santer, and especially the Delors commission presided over a Europe that was in many respects deeply suspect; suspect, that is, when seen from the politically liberal and economically rational point of view. It was fond of regulating, uniformizing, and harmonizing. It sought to promote "workers' rights" and a formal machinery of worker participation in management. It was often protectionist in practice even as it condemned trade barriers in theory—in this insincere stance it was a worthy rival of the United States. It fought against the insidious attempts of liberals, mainly the British, to "reduce the Union to a mere free-trade area." Above all, it administered and often helped to defend the monstrous Common Agricultural Policy that brought to Europe dear food, an unpardonable waste of farm inputs, an endless succession of "crises" due to the overproduction of butter, milk, sugar, wine, pork, fruit, beef, and whatever else you care to think of, and untold environmental damage from the deluge of farm chemicals and manure upon the land, groundwater, and the sea. It must in fairness be said that in latter years the Commission has placed itself on the side of the angels and fought for a rational reform of the Common Agricultural Policy in the face of ferocious French, Spanish, Greek, and even German opposition.

There is, of course, no prospect of an immediate and radical sea change in European Union policy merely because the top men of the Commission have been replaced and the changes are mostly for the better. The Council of Ministers holds the whip hand over the Commission. The Council is still what it has always been, a committee where the voice of the powerful usually prevails even when majority voting is supposed to decide an issue. However, the Commission largely controls the cogs and wheels of the administrative machine, and the influence of the machine, mute as it is, should not be underestimated.

It is at the level of the machine that big changes that had been fermenting for several years seem now to have matured. For at least three decades, the Brussels administration had been something of a

French fief. It was France that proclaimed which policy would qualify as "truly European." The important directorates were mostly headed by Frenchmen, and the French administrative spirit and the French language dominated the Commission's "culture." Ten years ago, the bulk of draft directives and other working documents were originally written in French. Today, over 80 percent are drafted in English—with all the change in the spirit of a text that such a change of language involves—even if the English in question is sometimes merely Eurospeak. All commissioners but one speak an English of sorts, but only seven speak some French.

There remains in one corner of the Brussels sky the dark cloud of the new constitution. Several states, including France and Britain, have already announced that they will submit it to referendum, and others are likely to follow. Referendums will be held over 2005 and 2006. Other states will have recourse to ratification by their legislatures. Even if none of the twenty-five member states balk, the process is unlikely to be completed before 2007. At least some states—Britain, Denmark, Poland—may well balk, and some formula or other will have to be negotiated to sweep their opposition under the carpet.

For these reasons, the threat represented by the constitution (as it now reads) is not imminent. All the same, it is a serious threat. Nominally, it removes certain vital areas, notably income taxation, criminal law, and "social rights," from the competence of the majority, so that any member state can veto pan-European legislative proposals in these areas. Britain, at whose insistence these issues were removed from the rule of the majority, is tipped to be prepared to veto both tax harmonization and advances in welfare provisions, as well as more restrictive labor laws. Ireland, perhaps the Netherlands, and some of the new member states from east-central Europe might also use the veto. For this reason, parts of the European Left are now agitating against the constitution, which they accuse of giving free rein to "savage liberalism." They interpret it as blocking all progress toward a "social Europe" where no state would be allowed to lag behind in the provision of welfare and the widening of "workers' rights."

This is a bit like accusing the padlock, with its keys attached, for blocking access to the beautiful garden. The constitution furnishes the keys. They are wrapped in the Charter of Fundamental Rights and the cross-border implications of the common internal market. The latter has even wider potential effects than the commerce clause of the U.S. Constitution, while the former is so vast, so woolly and vague that under it the European Court of Justice would probably be willing, or could feel forced, to overrule British or other vetoes of proposed "social" measures. If ratified, the constitution would open the gates, not to "savage liberalism," but to politically correct social "rightsism" with the economic stagnation and unemployment that are its concomitants.

It seems clear that the new Commission is not keen to go in this direction and would drag its feet if pushed. It is already doing so on corporate taxation. Left-leaning governments might go on pushing it, and so might the demagogy of the European Parliament. But by the time the proposed constitution becomes law—if it ever does—several years will have passed. The economic enlightenment and the better grasp of realities that have brightened up the sky over Brussels might, with a little luck, have made some more headway. As the saying goes: the worst is not certain.

TURKEY KNOCKING ON EUROPE'S DOOR

So Turkey is knocking again at Europe's door, though this time it is not about to break it down with a battering ram. As things stand today, the odds look in favor of the door being opened to it, though negotiations are bound to be arduous and a protracted transition period may be imposed on the free movement of people.

Admitting Turkey is no routine matter, the less so the more the Union moves from single market to political federation and perhaps superstate. Five percent of Turkey's territory is in Europe, 95 percent in Asia. Nearly 100 percent of its population of 67 million is Muslim, and 15 million of those are Kurds who refuse to believe that they are "just mountain Turks" and who still dream of self-determination. With present trends, by 2020 the country's population should grow to 90 million, 15 percent of the Union's projected 600 million. In numbers, it would be by far the biggest member, leaving Germany with its present 82 million and projected 78 million well behind. At the same time, Turkey, with an average income of about $3,000 per head, would be twice as poor as the poorest members. Turkish traditions are in harmony with the direction the EU is taking toward a strong role for the state in the economy and the imposition of a "social conscience." In all other respects, however, the fit between the club and the candidate is not obvious, to put it with due restraint.

Making their way into Europe has been the main and constant objective of their history ever since the Ottoman tribe started nibbling at the Greek colonies of Byzantium along the coast of Asia Minor in the thirteenth century. A century later the tribe had the beginnings of an empire. In 1352 the sultan took Constantinople that was to become Istanbul, and went on to subjugate Serbia, Bosnia, Bulgaria, and Wallachia (the bulk of the area that in 1878 was constituted as Rumania). Except for the slave trade that moved people south to the Turkish slave

First published by Liberty Fund, Inc., at www.econlib.org on April 7, 2003. Reprinted by permission.

markets (along with a countercurrent of Turkish migration northward from Anatolia), Turkish rule over the Balkans was not harsh by the standards of the age. Unlike the Spanish persecution of Muslims and Jews and the religious wars in France and Germany, the Turks were tolerant of other religions, treating the Greek Orthodox church quite well, regarding Protestants as allies against the Habsburgs, though there was always mutual hostility with the Roman Catholics.

After the defeat of France by Charles V in 1525, France and Turkey concluded an alliance that was to last nearly two hundred years and greatly hindered the coalition of the Habsburgs and the papacy to halt the Turkish advance into Hungary, then one of the major European powers. Suleyman the Magnificent annexed most of it in and after 1541. There were a few more westward pushes till late into the seventeenth century, including another great siege of Vienna, but the steam was by then going out of the Ottoman drive.

Like the British Empire that was acquired in a fit of absence of mind, the Turks also picked up, without really trying, an empire in the south and east, Baghdad, Mecca, Damascus, Cairo, and the whole North African coast of the Mediterranean falling like ripe plums into the sultan's lap, though his sovereignty was not enough to give him effective control. It is hard to avoid the impression that the non-European parts of the empire were but a sideshow.

The decline of European Turkey was as steep as its rise. Hungary and the Balkan countries were liberated, or liberated themselves, between the seventeenth and nineteenth centuries. After World War I, only Constantinople and a bridgehead around it were left of the European possessions.

Apart from the exhaustion caused by too much conquest in too many wars, the causes of the Turkish decline were socioeconomic and they are still at work under the surface today. As a result of its system of land tenure, there was never a Turkish landed nobility and aristocracy. Unlike most European states that moved through feudalism to unitary kingdom, the Ottomans simply missed the feudal stage and moved directly to a highly centralized absolute monarchy on the model of her Persian neighbors. The high officials were the sultan's slaves, often Greeks on the civil and Albanians on the military side. Between them and the lowly *reaya* who paid the taxes, there was nobody with an independent power base on the land or in trade who did not closely depend on the central government's grace and favor. Society was, and in a way still is, classless, for the meritocracy of officials and state-sponsored businessmen does not generate a class structure that is entrenched in civil society and stands on its own legs economically.

Endemic corruption is in no small measure a consequence of the servile meritocracy. Economists sometimes contend that it makes no difference whether officialdom is decently paid or underpaid and makes it up by taking bribes. For this to be true, the bribes must not affect the allocation of resources, and for that to be anywhere near the truth, the bribe-taking itself must be a competitive process, the business that can make the best use of a state permit or most efficiently fill a state order paying the highest bribe and getting the permit or the order. There are complex reasons, going way beyond the scope of this article, why this benign result fails to be produced. For one, theft trumps competition. If a state bank's directors siphon off the depositors' money to their associates and blandly mark its trace as a "nonperforming loan" in the books, the return on the directors' "investment" is infinity and no legitimate borrower could outbid and outbribe that, no matter how productive the project he seeks to finance. It is along such lines that the misallocation of resources and the poor performance of the Turkish economy much of the time between the eighteenth century and today can find an explanation.

By the early twentieth century, Turkey went by the name of "the Sick Man of Europe." It is a sad irony that some Turks, indignant at the tendency to classify Turkey as an Asian country that ought not to try and elbow its way into the European Union, cite this unflattering sobriquet to prove that even when it was down and out, Turkey passed for being European. After dethroning the last sultan in 1922, Kemal Pasha and his successor Ismet Inonu ruled a benevolent quasi-dictatorship with a strong lay, Westernizing, and modernizing tendency, a drive that has had a good deal of success, considering the morass from where they started. Inevitably, however, a deep rift in society opened between lay and Western on one side, Islamic and Oriental on the other. The dread of the lay and Westernizer minority of being sucked into Islamic backwardness by the majority is the reason why Turkey has lately come close to gate-crashing in its insistent demand to be admitted to the European club.

Democratic mechanics tend to produce Islamic governments. The army, as the guardian of Kemal's lay tradition, tends to remove such governments. It has done so four times since World War II, the last time in 1997. Until last November, Turkey was governed, if that is the right word, by weak and teetering lay coalitions presiding over runaway expenditure, ballooning public debt, galloping inflation, and a paroxysm of corruption. Nominal interest rates ranged from 40 to 150 percent p.a., and the price index in the last three years rose by 54.9, 54.4, and 45.3 percent, respectively. In 2001, the dams burst, the Turkish lira was allowed to float downward, and the national product fell by 7.4 percent—a crisis of Argentine dimensions.

The new, moderately Islamic government of the "AK" ("clean"—a play on initials) Party has a stabilization program sternly supervised by the IMF that has had a measure of success. Inflation has slowed to about 30 percent, the depreciation of the lira in inflation-adjusted terms to about 10 percent; GDP in 2002 has risen by 3.7 percent and might manage to keep up this rate this year and next. Unemployment at over 8 percent is average by European Union standards. However, tales of official incompetence and corruption are flying as thick as ever. The task of pulling through is heroic, mainly because of the dire state of the public finances. The public debt is either short-term, floating rate, or dollar-linked, so that inflation does not lighten it. Its service is so onerous that in order to keep the debt constant, the state is supposed to generate a budget surplus before debt interest of 6.5 percent of GDP, and it is far from evident that a nondictatorship in Turkey can politically long survive such fiscal rectitude. The army and the electorate must be satisfied, and in addition too many eager hands are trying to fill too many empty pockets for the accounts to balance.

The biblical camel would find it hard to pass through the eye of the needle, but it is not much easier for a democracy to reform a statist, politically controlled economy along liberal, competitive lines. Truly, the Turkish case seems to be one of scarce means in vain pursuit of self-contradictory ends. Note that the EU, while no doubt wishing to see the Turkish economy in better shape, has set two imperative conditions for their membership: democracy and the abolition of the death penalty. As of last year, Turkey has done both, more or less. The rest, far less important for political correctness, is in the lap of the gods.

TURKEY AND THE EU CLUB

It is often thought not worth belonging to a club that would accept you, and imperative to belong to one that hesitates to accept you. Judging by her insistent demands made over the last two decades, Turkey finds it vitally important to belong to the European Union, and the EU has not been awaiting her coming with open arms. It has held up several hoops Turkey had first to jump through. She had, as it were, to learn how to use a knife and fork and how to sit with her knees close together. She had to enshrine "human rights" in her legislation and stabilize her wildly seesawing economy.

Now good manners have largely been legislated for, the currency has been redenominated by knocking six zeros off it on January 1, and after a shaky two years in 2000 and 2001 and a spectacular forward jump of 9.9 percent in 2004, the economy has this year settled down to moderately high growth of over 4 percent and just under double-digit inflation—both very creditable achievements provided there is no backsliding. Lip service to "human rights" is not the same as embedding the rule of law in tradition, and one year's very decent economic performance does not wipe out the rocky record that goes back to the '70s. Nevertheless, while the peoples of the EU member states remain dubious, reluctant, or downright hostile, the political leadership has decided that Turkey is now ready and eligible for membership. Negotiations on terms formally started in October 2005. They are irreversible and will not be allowed to fail; despite much hedging on both sides, refusing entry to the Turks has become unthinkable. According to the Turkish side, a membership treaty will probably be signed in 2012, according to the EU sometime between 2015 and 2020. Under present rules, ratification and/or popular referendum in member states would then still be needed, but nobody seems seriously to expect that they will derail the project.

First published by Liberty Fund, Inc., at www.econlib.org on December 5, 2005. Reprinted by permission.

DOES TURKEY NEED TO BELONG?

Two obvious questions arise at this stage. Why does Turkey want to belong to the EU, and why should the EU take her in? Neither answer is obvious.

There is already free trade between Turkey and the EU except in farm products and some services. Membership would yield little additional commercial benefit. Capital movements are also free. Movements of labor would probably not become much freer for many years than they are at present if the treatment of Poland, the Czech Republic, Hungary, and the other states admitted in 2004 is any guide; only Britain freely accepts workers from these countries, and Turks are not likely to fare much better initially.

Because average income per head in Turkey at under $7,000 is less than a third of the EU level, the country should receive "structural funds" from the EU, and because she is more agricultural than the average, she should be a large net beneficiary of the Common Agricultural Policy. Under present rules, she should receive an annual total of 13 or 14 billion euros from these sources, comparable to what Spain and Ireland used to get and more than the 9 billion euros France is still managing to draw from the CAP. There is no serious prospect of Turkey ever getting anything like this sum. Even a fraction of it would be hard to squeeze out of the EU budget.

Adopting unified EU rules and regulations to ensure competition, honest accounting, and the policing of financial and product markets might prove to be useful for Turkey, and if EU regulations could curb corruption (which may be too much to hope) the benefit would be great. On the other hand, it has been argued that what gives the Turkish economy much of its vigor is the mass of small family businesses with a foot in the "black" economy, free of minimum-wage, maximum-workweek laws and social charges that the labor union and socialist influences in Brussels seek to impose on all EU member countries.

On balance, the economic case for Turkey seeking admission to the club is not proven and the judgment may go either way. The real spur driving the Turkish application is political. The business and professional classes and much of the officer corps are dreading a slide of the country into Islamic obscurantism and bigotry. They strongly feel that membership of the EU would be a safeguard against this danger. In fact, they see it as the sole available safeguard. Though their pride is offended by the lukewarm welcome they are getting in Brussels and by all the hoops they are asked to jump through, they seem ready to swallow it all for the sake of "being in Europe."

DOES THE EU NEED TURKEY?

In a recent Europewide poll, people were asked whether the cultural differences between the EU and Turkey are too great an obstacle to Turkish membership. In the twenty-five member states, an average of 54 percent "agreed" or "tended to agree" that the obstacle was too great. Country percentages were 73 in Austria, 66 in Germany, 62 in France, 55 in Italy and the Czech Republic, 50 in Holland, 44 in Spain, 43 in Poland, and 42 in Britain. (Turkey is now spending 25 million euros on a public relations campaign to soften these attitudes.) Out of the EU's 450 million people, only about 16 million are Muslims, but the aggressive assertion of their religious identity makes the number seem and feel many times larger. Adding 72 million Muslim Turks really rouses alarms about the coming Islamization of Europe, especially in view of Muslim birthrates being so much higher than white European ones. Austria, in particular, is not ready to forget that the Ottoman conquering drive up the Balkan peninsula and into central Europe after the capture of Constantinople in 1453 was only stopped by the luck of arms under the walls of Vienna in 1529 and again in 1683.

Contrary to the popular sentiment, and typical of the widening cleavage between the two, the political elite is largely favorable to bringing Turkey into the Union. The reasons are manifold. There is the unformulated feeling that raising Europe's population at a stroke to over 500 million will at last give her superpower status, "equal to America." After all, the Turkish army is bigger than any other in Europe, and it would do wonders for the self-confidence of certain political leaders if its command could somehow be made to pass into their hands. A "European foreign policy," so much lamented for its absence, would then finally be born, to the greater glory of Europe's political masters.

There is also a vague feeling abroad that integrating more closely a young emerging economy into Europe will wake up and shake up the latter's somnolent capacity for growth. There is little doubt that the catching-up factor, and particularly the continued borrowing of European technology and organization, will go on stimulating Turkey's rate of growth and, by a ricochet effect, growth in Europe, too.

However, the strongest motive for ignoring that 95 percent of Turkey lies in Asia is to kill two birds with one stone: it is to affirm Europe's secular (rather than Christian) character and to appease Islamic hostility to Europe by taking in a Muslim country as an important member of the club. Whether the latter effect can thus be achieved is a question only time will answer.

On a trip to Rome a quarter century ago, Mr. Chirac told a group of French journalists that while the ruins of Rome are "sweating death," those of Mesopotamia are breathing life; the great Oriental religions are superior to ours; and it is "an *imposture*" to pretend that our culture descends from Athens and Rome. Though he seldom shows much constancy of ideas, in this respect he seems not to have changed them. A strong advocate of Turkey, he is still suspicious of Christianity and would still embrace "Mesopotamia," in line with the French revolutionary heritage and the traditional pro-Muslim policy of the country. To a lesser extent, the latter also plays a role in the official attitudes of Britain and Spain.

Be that as it may, the progress of Turkey toward full membership in the club is now gaining momentum. It is very unlikely to stop short of its designated terminus. Europe will then begin to look and feel substantially different. With a bit of luck, it might not become a worse place than it is now. It could even be a better one.

EUROPE
MORE SECULAR AND MORE ISLAMIST

Long-range thinking is a fairly safe pastime. By the time your forecasts turn out to be wrong, nobody remembers what they have been and your reputation remains intact. The present essay will take advantage of this agreeable circumstance.

Our subject is Turkish membership of the European Union, or more precisely how such membership will shape the Union a few decades down the road. As is well known, Turkey has been insisting on admission as a full member for the last half century; the peoples of Europe have been lukewarm or frankly hostile to this, and their politicians, mostly favorable, had to stage a balancing act consisting mainly in keeping the negotiations for Turkish membership moving forward as slowly as was decently possible, while telling their public that membership is too far off to worry about. Realistically, it looked that a treaty with Turkey could be signed some time around 2015 and ratified by the members over the ensuing three to five years. The Greek part of divided Cyprus, surprisingly enough a full member of the Union, kept threatening to veto this process, and though they were legally entitled to do so and used their veto right as a bargaining lever to obtain unification of the island on their terms, nobody really believed that they could make their veto stick to the end.

However, causing surprise in Brussels and anger in Ankara, during his presidential election campaign in 2006 M. Sarkozy flatly declared that if he is elected, France will oppose Turkish membership. A French veto could hardly be brushed aside. The negotiating process, touching only a fraction of the tens of thousands of pages of small print, came to a standstill, and when M. Sarkozy was duly elected, nobody pretended to know what turn the events would take. However, only a

First published by Liberty Fund, Inc., at www.econlib.org on October 1, 2007. Reprinted by permission.

few months later France quietly announced that she is not opposed to membership negotiations being fully resumed. The long-range forecast was reinstated, for it was unthinkable that once Turkey made all the concessions, promises, and legislative reforms Brussels demanded, the club could end up blackballing it.

The economic implications of Turkish membership would be modest. Trade between it and the Union is almost completely free anyway, as are capital movements. Turkey is already enjoying the windfall of European technology transfers without bearing the cost of developing it and ironing out its early shortcomings. There would be two additional benefits to Turkey. By rights it ought to become one of the chief recipients of farm aid under the Common Agricultural Policy, or what will be left of it by 2020 or so. It should also get massive allocations of "structural funds" designed to improve the infrastructure of poor regions of the Union. Turkey's income per head, despite nice progress in the present decade, is still only about 40 percent of the average of the twenty-seven current members. Guesses about the annual aid Turkey might get under these two headings range as high as 30 billion euros, though it could not really complain if it got half that amount.

The economic effects are dwarfed by the political and indeed the long-term historical ones. Turkey now has a population of about 75 million, 60 million Turks and 14 million Kurds, all Muslims. On present trends, soon after 2020 Turkey would become the most populous country of the Union. Under the double majority rule incorporated in the European miniconstitution that might be agreed by end-2007, it would become the most influential, weighing more than Germany, at least in terms of voting power.

Out of Europe's present 450 million people, an estimated 15 million are Muslims. This is but a statistically puny 3 percent, yet London is coming to be called Londonistan, parts of Marseille and the northeast rim of Paris look and sound as if they were in North Africa, and some Cassandras profess to see Europe becoming Eurabia. Both demographic trends and clandestine immigration favor the relative growth of the Muslim population. However, what makes the Muslim presence look so prominent is not their still-modest numbers but their conspicuous effort to remain apart and the fervor with which they affirm their Islamic faith.

After Turkey becomes a member of the EU, the latter will have a population of about 540 million, of whom maybe 95 million, or 18 percent, will be Muslims. Most of the latter will stay put in Asia Minor and never come to join the Arab, Pakistani, Bangladeshi, and Turkish diaspora in western and southern Europe. Despite their low visibility, their political weight will count nonetheless. A minority of them will no doubt sooner or later flee the poverty of Anatolia and settle in other countries of the Union, intensifying the alarm many there feel about the progressive Islamization of Europe.

At first sight, it looks strange that it should be religion, widely written off as a spent force in the modern world, that should pose such a threat, or at least the apprehension of a threat, to Europe's identity. The explanation is that as modern-day Europe is gradually shedding the Christian, transcendent, and metaphysical tradition of its culture and defiantly professes to be secular, the Muslim world (or at any rate the most vocal, most active and influential elements of it) is becoming more passionately religious. It puts Islam at the center of its consciousness. Islam fills the life of contemporary Muslims as fully as Christianity once did the life of medieval Europeans. In Iran, a theocratic state has firmly established itself. In Iraq, a civil war is raging along a religious divide. In such secular states as Egypt, Pakistan, and Algeria, only dictatorship could so far resist the rising Islamist tide. In nearly every Muslim community, there is a clamor for Sharia law. In Turkey, despite warning growls of the army, an Islamist president has just been elected, and the governing party is having a hard time reconciling the secular policies imposed by the army, the business classes, and the exigencies of Brussels with the strongly Islamic leanings of its own electorate.

One explanation that is no worse than many others is that rising religious fervor, coupled with feelings of spiritual superiority and an aggressive, conquering posture, are due to Muslim societies being sad failures in a worldly sense. The Arabs ruled much of the Middle East and North Africa from the seventh century onward, occupying the Iberian Peninsula and penetrating deep into France before decline set in. Decline has been almost continuous ever since. Arab mathematics, philosophy, and medicine are but proud memories. The one source of Arab riches and prestige is the oil Western petroleum engineers find and pump out from under the sand.

At its peak, the Ottoman Empire was as glorious as the Arabs had been before it. It became the overlord of the Arab lands from the Persian Gulf to Morocco; it owned the Balkans and nearly captured Vienna in 1683 before it sank into impotence and withdrew to Anatolia, keeping only a toehold in Europe around Constantinople. Its greatness in architecture, handicrafts, and military science became a thing of a nostalgic past.

It should perhaps not surprise nor shock us that peoples conscious of great achievements in their history, conscious of past power and riches, and acutely conscious that power and riches have perhaps irretrievably passed into Western European and North American hands, should take their failure to keep pace very badly. Hatred of the West and its ways must come naturally to Muslims who see their own societies bogged down while others are barrelling ahead. It heals the wounds of Islamic self-esteem to proclaim, and indeed sincerely to believe, that Western values are contemptible, Western materialism, greed, indecency, and immorality disgusting and a provocation to right-thinking men. Islam by contrast is a refuge of spiritual purity and a guardian of the true values.

In the secular world, there is a social hierarchy that, like it or not, puts the successful above the unsuccessful. Thus it comes about that Muslims, too many of them unsuccessful individually and all of them unsuccessful as nations, have a hard time adopting Western standards of success and preserving their self-esteem at the same time. This is why nationalism—a modern movement pursuing modern aspirations with archaic means—is taking such weird forms in Muslim countries. Outright rejection of Western secularism and utter devotion to the service of Islam are psychologically the easier options.

This is emphatically not to say that every Muslim is a potential suicide bomber, nor that there is no remedy to their serious problems of self-esteem. Time, a modicum of personal and national achievement, and time again hold the homeopathic remedy. The fifteen or more years that Turkey will have to spend in the waiting room of the European Union are long, but in the best interest of Europe perhaps none too long.

A BILL OF RIGHTS EUROPE DID NOT NEED

The British government will not submit it to a referendum, the new government in Poland welcomes it, everyone wants to turn the page. The 2007 Lisbon Treaty giving Europe a constitution it has supposedly so badly needed is now assured of ratification.

Compared to the original draft constitution the French and Dutch referendums threw out in 2005, the "simplified" treaty is still a weighty book (256 pages in the English version). It does most of the things the original was meant to do, though it leaves out much of the federalism that has proved offensive to many. Its most important practical provision is the extension of the double majority rule (majority of states and majority of populations) to new domains. In "social" and fiscal affairs, though, each state retains the power temporarily to opt out of majority decisions. The six-monthly rotating presidency will be replaced by a president elected for two and a half years. The number of commissioners will be appreciably and the number of members of parliament insignificantly reduced. None of this is an earthshaking change and none looks like doing more harm than good.

Even with the best of goodwill (which it would hardly deserve), no such benign verdict could be passed on the Charter of Fundamental Rights. The original draft had it as part of the main text; the simplified treaty puts it in an annex but states in the main text that the Charter is binding on the signatories. There is an apparent contradiction between some "social" provisions of the Charter and the "opt-outs" granted to states in the text, but this is dwarfed by graver blunders, ambiguities, and risks of twistable interpretation.

Ultimately, the Charter transfers part of the power of shaping "social" and economic policy from national governments to the judges of the European Court of Justice. There is an albeit imperfect parallel here with the gradual transfer of policy-making in the United States

First published by Liberty Fund, Inc., at www.econlib.org on December 3, 2007. Reprinted by permission.

from the Congress to the Supreme Court. We cannot argue that elected governments make better policy than unelected judges. But we cannot argue, either, that it is a good thing that constitutions, and bills of rights in particular, do have the unintended effect of giving the judicial interpretation of poorly drafted texts the upper hand over politics. There must be less erratic ways of reducing the scope of politics.

In the matter of poorly drafted texts, the Charter would be hard to surpass. Consider Article 14: "Everyone has the right to *education* and to have *access* to vocational and continuing training. This *right* includes the *possibility* to receive free *compulsory* education" (my italics). Every italicized word is either open-ended, ambiguous, or meaningless, and "right to be compelled" takes the prize for stark fatuity.

A text of this quality inspires derision and would embarrass the courts if they were petitioned to grant ever fuller exercise of these rights. Other rights laid down in the Charter should leave them just baffled. Article 3: "Everyone has the right to respect for the integrity of his or her physical and mental integrity." Article 6: "Everyone has the right to liberty and security of person." Article 9: "The right to marry and the right to found a family shall be guaranteed in accordance with the national laws governing the exercise of these rights." That is, the Charter confirms that national laws shall be kept—but since affirming the contrary would be sheer nonsense, what is this "right" supposed to do? National laws must be kept anyway because they are laws. To single out some and "guarantee" them throws suspicion on the others that are not so singled out.

Another example of sloppy drafting that is more than just a lawyer's quibble is the right to strike. Article 28: "Workers *and employers* or their respective organizations have, in accordance with Community law and national laws and practices, the right to negotiate and conclude collective agreements at the appropriate levels and, in cases of conflicts of interest, to take collective action to defend their interests, including strike action" (my italics). If this clause simply means that national laws and practices must be respected, it is redundant. If it is trying to say more, large open questions arise. If employers have the same rights as workers, are lockouts as sacred as strikes? Do strikebreakers have rights and do pickets have rights to stop them in certain ways? What about "secondary" picketing? If the Charter cannot go into these details, it would do better not to proclaim the right to strike and leave it at that.

At a more fundamental level, the Charter confuses freedoms and rights, and dispenses rights with an open hand as if it were oblivious that when it grants rights to some, it must impose obligations on others.

Freedoms are acts that under the rule of law (or, more deeply still, under the conventions and customs spontaneously adopted by a society and embedded in its practices) violate no prohibition. Sitting down and standing up are freedoms, as are myriads of other acts that do not interfere with the freedoms of others. If they did, they would violate a prohibition. Speaking your mind is a freedom because others would run into prohibitions if they forced you to keep still by threats of doing you serious harm. Article 15 grants you the right to engage in freely chosen or accepted work, Article 17 the right to own, use, and dispose of property. All these acts are freedoms, for they violate no prohibition. It is curious to grant a "right to a freedom"—that is, a right to do what you are free to do.

If the Charter is nevertheless handing out "rights to freedom," it is tacitly conveying one of two things. Either the freedoms not enumerated as "rights" in the Charter matter less than those that are enumerated; or it does not suffice for an act to violate no prohibition if the Charter does not also declare it to be a "right." Planting either of these ideas in the public mind—a mind already heavily influenced by the "rightsism" of modern political thought—is an excellent means of stifling the idea of freedom. The framers of the Charter no doubt meant to achieve the opposite, but they clearly failed to grasp what a Bill of Rights is liable to do.

Unlike freedoms that define relations between your own acts and a set of publicly accepted prohibitions, rights define a relation between you, another person, and acts you have the option to require the other person to perform to your benefit. If you have the right to work, there must be another person somewhere who is under an obligation to offer you work. If you have a right to unemployment pay, somebody is obliged to pay it. The whole welter of welfare rights must be matched by obligations of the public authorities (and ultimately the employer or the general taxpayer) to provide the means without which these rights would remain empty humbug.

However, just like electoral manifestos and books on social justice, the Charter is voluble on rights and mute on the obligations they entail. It is mute, probably not out of cynicism, demagogy, or shrewd calculation, but more likely because its framers were not clearheaded and tough-minded enough to see through the implications of what they were doing.

Some of the rights the Charter grants not only place a burden on an unseen, unmentioned obligor, but may actually end up by harming the rightholder to whom the Charter meant to do a good turn. The prohibition of organ transplants involving financial gain, thus reducing the supply of organs available for transplants, may be a case in point. One with a wider impact on material welfare is "labor market flexibility" or rather its opposite. Article 30 gives every worker protection against "unjustified dismissal." Under the freedom of contract, employment can be terminated on terms provided for in the contract (e.g., notice, severance pay). The Charter now chisels into constitutional granite what the International Labour Office has just claimed to be "international law," namely that termination of employment must be justified. Whether it is or not can only be finally settled by legal action in the courts, and subject to an appeals procedure. We now know well enough that if the employer cannot fire, he will not hire, so that it is the worker who loses out from "job protection." However, an article reading "Every party to a labor contract has the right to terminate it on terms previously agreed" would not at all look good in a Bill of Rights—besides being unnecessary, for contracts are freedoms and do not require a "right" before they can be concluded and performed.

EUROPE'S SOCIAL-DEMOCRATIC "GOVERNMENT"

If national-veto rights are eroded at the European Union's summit in Nice this week, those who gave in to France will present Paris's victory as a compromise. The veto—it will be said—has been saved for such important national decisions as the setting of personal income tax rates; qualified-majority voting will be used in other, less important areas. But such claims should mislead no one, least of all students of history. Qualified-majority systems have seldom resisted the pressures that in time turned them into the rule of simple majorities. In Europe, this will mean socialism for everyone, in fact if not in name.

France, the current holder of the rotating EU presidency, and the Commission maintain that with enlargement from fifteen to nineteen members, and then to perhaps twenty-four or more, decision-making will become as good as hopeless unless we do away with the veto.

But if today we won't let one country stop fourteen, one day soon we won't have seven stopping eight, or twelve stopping thirteen. Once things start being decided by a count of votes, they nearly always end up with bare majorities imposing their will on the rest.

Among leaders currently in office, only Germany's Joschka Fischer is knowingly in favor of a European superstate, but he is way ahead of the more cautious official government position. At the other end of the spectrum, Britain's Tony Blair is looking over his shoulder at his wavering electorate and talks of a Europe whose building blocks will remain sovereign states. (One could ask how sovereign are blocks once they are cemented in a wall.) The British public suspects that a mistrusted French bureaucratic grip over Brussels will be permanent, and it resolutely repudiates being governed by an unelected technocracy.

First published in the *Wall Street Journal Europe,* December 5, 2000. Reprinted by permission.

BETWEEN EXTREMES

But the decision will probably fall between these two extremes, where one finds most European governments. They still harbor the hope of having it both ways—retaining sovereignty where it matters and refusing supranational rule where it hurts, but making European cooperation "more effective."

This is, alas, little more than a pipe dream. Once a government loses the ability to veto a decision, it is gone forever. And as the areas where qualified-majority decisions hold sway are gradually extended, we would also see a subsequent drift toward bare-majority rule. Power would slowly be drained from the states and flow to a superstate level in Brussels. This drift of power toward the center would increase the distance between government and citizens.

The EU powers that be, from President Romano Prodi on down, say they're aware of this problem, which they see as a "democratic deficit." Their suggested remedy is "more democracy." So they propose transforming the European Parliament from a sinecure for politicians who failed to make it on the national stage into a body with real functions. This body would then elect a president of Europe (Jacques Delors, of all people, is already being tipped), and he would form a government from within parliamentary ranks.

Unlike the present Commission, such a European government would have the legitimacy that the expression of the popular will would have bestowed upon it. The "deficit" would thus be eliminated.

The threat is obvious. Libertarianism, or what remains of it, survives in Europe episodically. In large measure, it is kept alive by the fact that this continent is a decentralized, diversified place, where different laws and different political arrangements coexist. But there is no electoral majority for liberalism in Europe as a whole, and there is plainly no hope for one in the foreseeable future. An elected European government could only be a social-democratic government (even if it called itself something else), and this would likely remain so for as long as it took irreversibly to mold a European superstate in its image.

Electoral majorities are formed by offering various interest groups benefits whose cost will mostly be borne by those who remain outside the majority. After the election, democratic government is under almost permanent pressure to expand welfare provisions and entitlements, create new tax breaks, and generally intensify the redistribution that is the staple of all state activity in any case.

At present, the heavily distributive "European model" is deeply rooted in France and Italy, is somewhat less dominant in Germany and Spain, prevails in a rather antiseptic form in Scandinavia, and is in tatters in most of the formerly Communist satellites.

But an all-Europe government would, almost by necessity, have to be as generous as it is in France and Italy. Any party that sought to form a European majority would have to outdo rival bidders by offering ever more generous programs to all kinds of groups from Greece to Portugal and from Poland to Ireland. Current interstate redistribution programs—such as the Common Agricultural Policy and the structural funds—would pale when compared with what a democratic superstate would feel induced to do.

MEAGER TANGIBLE BENEFITS

There is a belief across most of Europe that progressive taxation, extensive social insurance, and strict labor laws (with, for good measure, a compulsory shortening of the authorized workweek) are good for the poor and the weak, and good even for prosperity and employment. Most of the poor and weak believe this because they see some meager tangible benefits but do not see the cost. But they bear this cost nonetheless in the form of high unemployment and a dependency culture.

Many of the not-so-poor and highly educated classes also believe in the value of these programs, partly because a strong welfare state provides them with roles they covet. Thus, a European federal government, pushing through one "social charter" after another, would have a ready-made constituency waiting for it.

Much of this sounds as though I believed that a conspiracy is being hatched somewhere. That's not the case. The EU is not all bad. It often does useful work, such as in stopping anticompetitive policies by the members. The reality is that if anyone or any group were consciously trying to make any of what I have described happen, little of it would really take shape.

What makes it plausible—nay, likely to come about—is precisely that hardly anybody is planning it, but all but a few are moving toward this socialist superstate with their eyes wide shut.

POWER CORRUPTS, SO LET'S MAKE IT LESS ABSOLUTE

Party-financing scandals seem destined to be Europe's new plague, cropping up here and there with increasing frequency and never really abating altogether. In the last ten years or so, illicit party funding has become the prime detonator of public scandals in Italy and France and has moved to center stage even in Germany. France now seems to be the country most shaken, with recurring allegations that President Jacques Chirac accepted millions in kickbacks for his Gaullist Party, though few of France's neighbors have remained immune. Is any of this new?

Using dubious means to raise the money political parties need to keep themselves in the style to which they are accustomed is not a fresh invention. Former British prime minister Lloyd George sold peerages the way a grocer sells pound packets of sugar; across the Atlantic, "Boss" Richard Daley of Chicago and the legendary chiefs of New York's "Tammany Hall" were masters at fortifying their power bases by "judiciously directed" public spending. Across much of continental Europe, professional politicians have seldom missed opportunities to enrich themselves or their parties. As democracy spread and mandates to govern came to depend on electoral swings, competitive vote-getting has come to depend on often-ruthless fund-finding tactics, involving anything from legitimate fund-raising to outright graft.

So why pay attention to the current incarnation of this old phenomenon? The difference this time is that this established practice is, unusually, prompting indignation and disgust from the population. The scandals, spun out by the media in teasing detail, are generating contempt for politicians and increasing a popular refusal to be led by the "chattering classes." The Danish rejection of the euro in a referendum last

First published in the *Wall Street Journal Europe,* October 17, 2000. Reprinted by permission.

month, despite the near consensus for it among mainline politicians and editorial pages, was more than anything an example of people no longer willing to be led by the political class. Europe seems to be fed up with politics as usual.

SUDDEN BACKLASH

It would be nice to believe that this newfound indignation has come about because our standards of public morality have suddenly risen. But in the absence of any visible evidence that they have, we should look for an explanation elsewhere. I would suggest that the sudden backlash has to do more with the size of the corruption than with its nature. As government has steadily grown in recent years, so has politics, and so has corruption.

To see why, we should analyze the three broad ways of financing politics. The first is the Anglo-American one. In Britain and in the United States, substantial differences notwithstanding, individuals, businesses, labor unions, and other associations make voluntary contributions to parties and candidates. The amounts and their disclosure may be regulated, but as long as the system remains transparent, it appears fair enough. It involves no theft of public funds; the donors give their own money.

While the front end may look honest, however, the back end is not always so. While some donors no doubt act out of a sense of public duty, many expect to be noticed and remembered by the party or candidate they have supported. Once elected, the politician must pay for the support one way or another, on pain of getting no support the next time round. There is no more tangible manner of saying thanks than the diversion of public spending or the twisting of the regulatory framework in favor of the benefactor. The bargain may most often be tacit but is no less immoral for that.

In countries where voluntary donations are not the custom, outright graft is the unpalatable alternative. Here, the party controlling a city, regional, or national budget will award public works or supply contracts, issue building permits or licenses for new supermarkets to the enterprise that offers the right kickback in the right manner. Public payrolls will be padded with party stalwarts, this being the carrot; the stick will often be tax audits.

The broad public has long suspected that these exchanges were taking place, but they had seldom seen them come to light, due to the complicity of politicians and the subjection of magistrates and the press to the powers-that-be. Things began to change in the 1990s, when first Italian judges and then their French counterparts staged a veritable insurrection. Their dogged investigations uncovered scandals of Byzantine complexity. Ironically, the culprits were often surprisingly innocent, in that they had stolen millions for their party without much, if any, of the money sticking to their hands.

The third way (growing in political acceptance on the Continent) attempts to solve the moral dilemmas of the first two. The only way to stop parties from working out tacit or explicit exchanges with donors in their search for funding is to give it to them openly and publicly, subsidizing parties subject to some threshold of electoral support, reimbursing campaign expense subject to some ceiling, and so forth.

Advocates of this approach argue that it removes the need to sin. But they fail to notice that it is, if anything, more immoral than the corruption it attempts to stamp out because it forces taxpayers to subsidize the cost of gaining and holding on to power. Not only are taxpayers made to pay for parties whose programs they may abhor, but worse, it makes the whole political class—not just elected politicians, but unelected ones too, as well as a whole host of campaign advisors, party workers, and general hangers-on—a ward of the state.

ALL ARE IMMORAL

Anyone reviewing the three methods could easily conclude that all manners of financing democratic politics are corrupt in some vital aspect. All are immoral, and it is hard to say which is more so. The despair itself suggests a solution, however.

All three flawed formulas would be tolerable, and tolerated the way fleabites or other minor irritants are suffered, if only politics had not assumed such an overwhelming, absolutely dominant role in recent decades. Roughly half of what the average European country produces is consumed in ways decided by national and local governments. A supranational government is starting to take a rising share, too. It is no use saying that all these governments are, in turn, elected by the same individuals who work to create the national product. The connection, tenuous at the best of times, no longer functions. The share of gross domestic product taken by the stewards of the collectivity has simply become too large, while the individual's influence on the collective's choice has become too remote, too hypothetical.

The trouble with politics is not that it is corrupt, but that it is too big. Its essentially competitive nature pushes it to expand, to preempt for itself more and more of the space individual choice used to fill, until it reaches the limit of tolerance fixed by each society's history and state of mind. In most parts of Europe, we are now probably straddling that limit. The disgust with politics is one symptom that we've gotten there. The remedy, if there is one, must lie in reversing the expansionary drive of the democratic state. Government must be put in its place. We are paying too dearly for the collective "benefits" the modern state professes to shower upon us.

PART 7

Economics, True and False

WHAT PRICE PRIDE?

ON THE HIDDEN COSTS OF ECONOMIC ILLITERACY

In eight years of arduous haggling, the last major effort at dismantling trade barriers, the Uruguay Round, completed in 1994, is now estimated to have reduced the average trade-weighted import tariff and nontariff obstacles of the European Union by a mere 2 percentage points, from 14 to 12 percent. The remaining protection of domestic food and manufacturing output is estimated to raise consumer prices by 6 percent. As a result, employment in agriculture and in the main protected industries of the Union is now 3 percent higher (and in the nonprotected sectors of industry and the services presumably 3 percent lower) than it would be under free trade. Employment in the protected sectors was boosted by an average annual cost to the European consumer that roughly amounts to the annual wage of ten average European semiskilled workers. In other words, the hidden cost of keeping one more worker employed in the protected (and probably one fewer in the unprotected) sector of the European economy is the output that ten currently unemployed workers could have produced. The rise in the real incomes of consumers upon the fall in food and other prices would have been just about enough to purchase this additional output. But this staggering cost is not a levy, not a tax anyone has to pay. It is merely forgone income the average voter is totally unaware of and that does not hurt him.

After the Uruguay Round, it is now the turn of the Doha Round. To obtain the participation of the less developed world, the European Union and the United States had to agree to reduce their farm subsidies radically in exchange for more liberal trade mainly in services.

The Brussels Commission must negotiate the Doha Round on behalf

First published by Liberty Fund, Inc., at www.econlib.org on April 7, 2003. Reprinted by permission.

of the European Union, and it cannot do so unless it manages to get the member states to agree to a thorough reform of the famous, and infamous, Common Agricultural Policy (CAP). However, last October in a daring preemptive move, France obtained Germany's agreement to a freeze of the CAP until 2006 in exchange for capping CAP expenditure at the 2006 level until 2013. France is the chief beneficiary of the CAP and Germany the chief paymaster, so that both parties thought to have done a nice enough deal. The other member states acquiesced.

Despite the Franco-German move to postpone CAP reform till 2006, the Commission must under the Doha commitment try and press on with it. It is therefore once again putting forward, in a slightly modified form, a plan that was far too sensible and sophisticated to be acceptable last year.

Stripped of its complex details, the essence of the plan is that farm subsidies should no longer be linked to farm output. Instead of benefiting from price supports on grain, dairy products, wine, and olive oil, farmers would get roughly equivalent payments in recognition of their putative contribution to keeping the countryside inhabited and looked after. They would get these payments even if they greatly reduced the output of their farms—something they would almost certainly do as farm prices fell and it became uneconomic to farm intensively with high inputs of chemical fertilizers, weed-killers, pesticides, and brought-in animal feed.

Total value added by agriculture in the EU at the last count was 146 billion euros,[1] produced on 6 million farms by a labor force, including owners, of 14.7 million. (Many of the "farms," especially in Spain, Portugal, Italy, and Greece, are very small, under 1 hectare and do not provide full-time occupation.) Value added includes the reward of labor, rent, debt interest, and profit (if any). On this basis, the average annual income of farmers and farmworkers appears to be 10,000 euros. Needless to say, this average conceals many six-figure incomes in Britain, France, and northern Germany. Nevertheless, it is clear that

1. This and subsequent data are taken from *Eurostat Yearbook 2002: Statistical Guide to Europe—Data 1990–2000* (Luxembourg: Office for Official Publications of the European Communities, 2002).

it is quite insufficient to keep up the farm population, stop the drift to the towns and the abandonment of marginal farms.

However, in addition to what appears in the statistics as the value they produce, farmers also get EU subsidies of 42 billion euros a year, which makes the lot of the average farmer look a little less grim. Since these subsidies are linked to production, in order to earn them he engages in intensive farming. European consumers spend about 800 billion euros a year on food at retail prices. The on-farm value of this food, allowing for net exports, is of the order of 350 billion euros, which exceeds value added in agriculture by about 200 billion euros. This, then, is the cost of the inputs European agriculture buys from the chemical and farm-machinery industries, from overseas producers of feed grains, and from service providers of all kinds. Though such estimates are hazardous, it is a fair guess that at least half of this expenditure serves only to earn the 42 billion of production subsidies and would be uneconomic if subsidies were stopped or decoupled from production—which is precisely what the CAP reform proposes.

Merely by shifting the farm subsidies from a pro rata to a lump-sum basis, perhaps 100 billion euros of wasted inputs could be saved. Admittedly, realizing the saving would require adjustments in the pattern of industrial output and in foreign trade, with an increase in both industrial exports and food imports, but such adjustment would be perfectly feasible.

Or rather, it would be feasible if farmers had no pride and politicians had no incentives to excite their pride to fever pitch. Farmers, notably in France, Spain, and Ireland, now swear that the switch from production subsidies to lump-sum payments will take place over their dead bodies—and the dead bodies of many riot policemen.

The subsidy on cereals, dairy products, or meat, they angrily exclaim, is an act of justice pure and simple; what it does is to bring the farmer's receipt for his produce up to his cost of production, which—as everyone must see—is only fair. It would be monstrous to expect farmers to make Europe self-sufficient in food and be out of pocket for doing so. Many politicians repeat, as a self-evident truth, that Europe must be able to feed itself if it wants to safeguard its independence. The man in the street cannot be bothered to think too hard about whether this is really self-evident. He also accepts, without a second thought, that farmers must get prices that will cover their costs of production.

It takes a little economic literacy to see that costs of production are as high as they are because prices, topped up by farm subsidies, are what they are. It should be obvious that grass-fed cattle cost less to fatten than cattle stuffed full of Brazilian soybeans, fish meal, hormones, and vitamins.

The force of the farmers' argument, and the driver of their present fury, is that they find the CAP reform proposals humiliating. From producers, they feel they would be reduced to national pensioners, recipients of alms, with only a lame face-saving function as keepers of the countryside. Much of that function, they shrewdly foresee, would be sheer make-believe.

Much of their concern is understandable. It is doubtful, though, whether it weighs enough to justify the extravagant cost of dressing up their subventions as rewards for much-needed production. The saddest aspect of this whole inglorious dilemma is that public opinion is almost completely oblivious of the hidden cost that must be paid to comfort the farmers' pride.

ON THE ECONOMICS OF PROTECTING EMPLOYMENT

Karl Popper once advised a student that if he wanted to reap intellectual fame, he should write endless pages of obscure, high-flown prose that would leave the reader puzzled and cowed. He should then here and there smuggle in a few sensible, straightforward sentences all could understand. The reader would feel that since he has grasped this part, he must have also grasped the rest. He would then congratulate himself and praise the author.

The misfortune of Bastiat was that he never spouted endless pages of obscure prose. He wrote with such impeccable, jargon-free clarity that his readers thought he was simply stating the obvious that they knew anyway. He was, and still is, widely taken for a mere vulgarizer, clever with his pen but not a great thinker. In his own country, where obscure and high-flown writing is often prized above simplicity, Bastiat is as good as unknown. Yet it is there that heeding his words would do the most good.

In one of his most pathbreaking essays, "What Is Seen and What Is Not Seen,"[1] Bastiat writes:

> There is only one difference between a bad economist and a good one: the bad economist confines himself to the *visible* effect; the good economist takes into account both the effect that can be seen and the effects that must be *foreseen*.
>
> Yet the difference is tremendous, for it almost always happens that when the immediate consequence is favorable, the later con-

First published as part 1 of "The Seen and the Unseen: On the Economics of Protecting Employment," by Liberty Fund, Inc., at www.econlib.org on December 6, 2004. Reprinted by permission.

1. Frédéric Bastiat, *Selected Essays on Political Economy,* ed. George B. de Huszar (1964; reprint, Irvington-on-Hudson, N.Y.: Foundation for Economic Education, 1995).

> sequences are disastrous, and vice versa. Whence it follows that the bad economist will pursue a small present good that will be followed by a great evil to come. (p. 1)

What is politely called "employment policy" or the "fight against unemployment" in much of continental Europe today is a classic example of how the visible good conjures up an invisible evil. Job protection, in particular, stands out.

Today, in Germany and France, divorcing your spouse is easier, and in most cases cheaper, than dismissing an employee under due observance of the provisions of the contract of employment. The administrative hurdles can be a long nightmare. Court approval may be required and, failing it, the employees in question must be reinstated. The labor union representing a majority of the employees must agree to the "social plan" by which the employer company undertakes to assist the employees who lose their jobs. Nestlé, losing vast sums of money year after year at its French mineral water firm, Perrier, and made to jump through hoops by the radical labor union CGT, which kept rejecting one "social plan" after another, could tell a tale about this. So could many others who often spend the best part of their management time trying to obtain permits for job cuts.

Lately, a French draft bill, redefining the conditions under which job cuts could be permitted, included the "safeguarding of competitiveness" as one of the grounds for authorizing such cuts. The CGT cracked the whip, President Chirac heard the crack, Mr. Raffarin the premier heard that Mr. Chirac had heard it, and the provision about competitiveness was tactfully scrapped.

It is too obvious for words that when firing is very difficult, very expensive, and takes long to accomplish even if it is eventually allowed, hiring will look a much more dubious proposition than it would otherwise do. The potential employer will think twice before creating a new job or filling one that falls vacant by natural wastage. Having thought twice, his third thought is quite likely to be not to hire.

Perhaps there is something to be said for making companies think twice about hiring, for while costless and riskless hiring and firing may make for an ideally efficient labor market, it does not make for loyalty and stability, nor for the employees' peace of mind. But their peace of mind suffers more when faced with long-term unemployment.

With the exits from a hall blocked by formidable legal devices and extraordinary privileges granted to labor unions, it is surely fatuous to stand at the entry, wave a program called Employment Policy at the potential employers dithering outside, and tell them to "come in, come in all the same." How many would come in, knowing that they could not get out as and when they wished?

It may be, though it is hardly certain, that "blocking the exits" does preserve some jobs. Volkswagen has recently accepted to block its own exit by agreeing to maintain present employment levels till 2011 in exchange for a wage freeze to 2007—an astonishingly audacious undertaking. Perhaps it will work out. Be that as it may, the jobs that are saved by one means or another are "what can be seen." The jobs that fail to get created, or fail to get replaced, because of the very justified fear the blocked exit raises in the employer, are "what cannot be seen." As Bastiat would have it, the small but visible present good must be followed by a greater but invisible future evil. Surely, however, not everybody is a complete idiot? Surely, many or most people must see that this is so? In fact, many do see it, but this does not necessarily prevent the few but visible jobs from being preferred to the many invisible ones that may be lost as a result.

The peoples of East and South Africa suffer heavily from AIDS but are reluctant to talk about it. They prefer to regard it as a malevolent act of Nature, rather than to admit that its spread had something to do with their own free and easy practices. The "political classes," if not the peoples, of continental Europe display much the same attitude in the face of endemic unemployment. It is a malevolent circumstance beyond their control. The social regime they have put in place is not responsible for its spread. In no way is it the consequence of the "European model," which is blameless in the matter. They will readily praise the European model for its purported humane dispositions, including its concern for protecting employment, but will not admit that the spread of unemployment owed anything to these concerns. Much of this is just fake innocence and whistling in the dark, for it is impossible honestly to believe that chronic unemployment is in no way the "model's" fault.

Behind the fake innocence, a powerful political mechanism is at work, forcing attention to be confined to "what can be seen"—a mechanism that Bastiat in the 1840s did not account for, because in his time it did not yet exist. It developed after World War II along with the rise of the welfare state, and its systematic study was left to the "public choice" branch of economics to undertake from the 1970s onward. Job protection is an instructive case study.

"Blocking the exit" in a country the size of Germany or France may well abort each year 200,000 or more jobs that would have been created. A company trying to cut 200 jobs at its plant in a smallish provincial town will set off 200 furious and desperate screams insisting on protection. The despair and fury are perfectly understandable. They could hardly be mitigated by telling the protesters that overall job protection will cost the country as a whole 200,000 jobs. The local screams will be transmitted to the capital, and multiplied in volume, by the labor unions and the news media, frightening the wits out of a government worried about its score in the polls and the next election. It takes more self-confidence and "long-termism" than most governments possess, to rise above such worries.

Once the state has moved into the economic sphere and taken responsibility for propping up the well-being of its citizens with the money it takes from them, it can hardly stop them running to it for help when their well-being needs propping up. The process, of course, becomes cumulative, for "what is not seen" must systematically be sacrificed for the sake of "what is seen." Bastiat's great discovery, opportunity cost, that evaluates a chosen alternative against the forgone alternative that could have been chosen in its place, must then lose its edge.

THE COSTLY MISTAKE OF IGNORING OPPORTUNITY COSTS

Projects involving major expenditure and intended to produce future benefit are usually assessed in terms of expected payback. Comparing expected yield to the interest rate, or discounted cash flow to the capital cost of the project, is the standard way of judging whether it is worthwhile. In an accounting sense, the cost is straightforward. It is seen as and when it is incurred. "What is the cost of a million-dollar project?" is a silly question. The answer is in the question: it is a million dollars.

This is a fair enough way of looking at cost as it appears in a competitive market. Raising a million dollars from the market for a given project will not noticeably hinder further millions being raised for other projects. If we said billions in place of millions, the relation would probably still hold, though perhaps only just. With ever more general "globalization," the supply of resources is getting so elastic that even preempting a significant chunk of them for one purpose may not seriously jeopardize the fulfilment of other purposes. Resource scarcity is correctly measured by the cost of capital. The capacity to cover that cost is the sole test of a project. No concern arises about one project "crowding out" another.

Yet "crowding out" is inevitable, for the same million cannot be spent on two alternative projects, each of which costs a million. The crowded-out alternative is not seen. It is quietly ruled out by the market because it is not judged capable of meeting the test of at least paying for itself. The project that is carried out meets the test, or is believed to do so. Its opportunity cost is the forgone alternative that does not get carried out. It does not meet the test, or is not believed to do so, hence it is

First published as part 2 of "The Seen and the Unseen: The Costly Mistake of Ignoring Opportunity Costs," by Liberty Fund, Inc., at www.econlib.org on January 10, 2005. Reprinted by permission.

worth less than the project that has crowded it out. In the competitive market, the visible accounting cost and the invisible opportunity cost perform the same work of selection.

This happy coincidence abruptly ceases to hold in a nonmarket environment, where the cost may be raised from the taxpayer, where the expected benefit is most often unpriced, nontraded, and intangible, and where resources move from one use to another in response not to profitability but to legislative and regulatory commands. It is in this environment of public policies that Bastiat's pioneer teachings about opportunity cost[1] become strikingly timely again, just as they were during the 1848–49 socialist episode when he wrote them down.

Public expenditure is seldom totally useless; its usefulness, however modest, is "what is seen," and this is one reason why even such expenditure can be so popular. The public tends implicitly to believe that "what is not seen" does not even exist—that when a new opera house or stadium is built, it is all a net gain of national wealth, for nothing else would have been built in its place. In the limiting case, even useless outlay can be "useful" if it provides employment. Bastiat has a tale about the broken window that gives the glazier a job of work: "what would become of the glaziers if nobody ever broke a window?" He also relates that when Napoleon had ditches dug and filled in again, he was convinced of doing good, by causing "wealth spread among the laboring classes."

The belief that even useless activity is good if it provides work and income for the glazier and the ditchdigger, instead of leaving them idle, and thus by a ripple effect stimulates demand and employment throughout the economy, has been lent intellectual respectability by the good old Keynesian doctrine that the cause of unemployment is lack of effective demand. After the experience of recent decades, this belief is no longer widely held. Bastiat, of course, never held any such belief. Indeed, he seems to have been quite unaware of the possibility

1. The concept of opportunity cost was first formally defined by one of the founding fathers of the Austrian school of economics, Friedrich von Wieser, in 1876. A generation earlier Bastiat made it clear to the ordinary reader in his brilliant essay "What Is Seen and What Is Not Seen," in Frédéric Bastiat, *Selected Essays on Political Economy,* ed. George B. de Huszar (1964; reprint, Irvington-on-Hudson, N.Y.: Foundation for Economic Education, 1995).

that if resources are idle, their opportunity cost may in fact be zero. However, the bitter and stubborn failure of make-work schemes in Western social democracies to lure idle resources out of unemployment into work shows that in practice zero opportunity cost, like Milton Friedman's free lunch, just cannot be had.

Perhaps the most important area where public policy tends to overlook opportunity cost is in the defense of "what is seen." Bastiat takes issue with the poet and revolutionary deputy Lamartine over subsidies to the arts and the theater. Maintaining these activities by state aid serves a worthy aim, including employment for artists, actors, and artisans, but Lamartine sees only what is thus preserved. He does not see the opportunity cost, namely that the resources devoted to the arts would have served other aims that corresponded to what people actually chose rather than to what the state induced them to choose by subsidizing a particular branch of activity. Bastiat does not deal with the idea of "merit goods" that ought to be produced whether the public wants them or not. But he stresses that promoting the fine arts can only be done at the cost of cutting back other things—a loss we do not see. It is, he notes, impossible to promote everything at the expense of everything else. This echoes his famous definition of the state, "the great fictitious entity by which everyone seeks to live at the expense of everyone else" (op. cit., 144).

There is great anxiety today about the migration of jobs from high-wage to low-wage areas. Western Europe and North America are supposed to lose in this process, and there is great agitation to stop it and preserve the employment "we see." A massive regulatory apparatus, notably in Germany and France, makes it difficult and expensive to dismiss employees. The obvious effect is to frighten employers, for who wants to hire if he may be unable to fire? However, while the opportunity cost of thus defending existing employment is to suppress new job creation, the latter is "not seen."

Migration of work across geographic frontiers obeys the same economic logic as its migration across technological ones. The basic case of the latter is when work is taken from men and given to machines. This classic symptom of rising wealth has long been accepted as such by modern man, whose concern today is with other symptoms of progress in productivity, such as "outsourcing" and "delocalization" to low-cost areas. However, in the middle of the nineteenth century, the machine was regarded as the chief enemy of the working man and of all traditional activity.

In the same tongue-in-cheek manner that he adopts when speaking of the broken window, the candlemakers who must be protected from the unfair competition of the sun, and the "negative railway" that, by not being laid, will keep all the carters and their horses in business, Bastiat finds that only "stupid nations" can enjoy wealth and happiness, for only they are incapable of inventing the machines that destroy prosperity.

Much regulation has been inspired by the same kind of reasoning. "Outsourcing," "delocalization," and other ways in which firms respond to the high cost (aggravated by high social charges) of low-skill labor are rendered difficult and sometimes impossible by government action. This is tantamount to suppressing the opportunities for the improved, more profitable use of all resources—including the labor that is released from poor jobs and is induced to move to more skilled, more productive ones. There are clearly industries and occupations that highly industrialized countries should simply not engage in. Defending them by passing legislation in favor of what we have and against what we could have is not unlike the long-forgotten attempts to legislate against machines.

"Good Lord," Bastiat sighs, "what a lot of trouble to prove in political economy that two and two make four; and if you succeed in doing so, people cry: 'It is so clear that it is boring.' Then they vote as if you had never proved anything at all."

"GLOBALIZATION" AND ITS CRITICS
MUTUAL GAIN VS. CLOUD-CUCKOO LAND

It is an old truth that lack of understanding and sheer stupidity cause more harm and suffering in the world than wickedness and self-seeking. This is particularly the case when politics holds a broad sway over individual lives, when a large proportion of the national income is spent by government, and when a few major collective decisions can make the difference between prosperity and penury; for in such situations the obtuse and the stupid have immense leverage to spoil things while intending to improve them. To aggravate matters, they also possess a mode of discourse that has a more potent and immediate impact on popular opinion than the cooler voice of lucid good sense.

Much of the passionate criticism of "globalization"—perhaps even the very use of this woolly term—can be best understood by bearing these factors in mind. So can the truculent nature of many of the hodgepodge of antiglobal policy measures adopted to combat it. Both the criticism and the policy amount to a protest against the intrusion of reality into a fairyland where everyone had the "right" not to get hurt.

"Globalization" is blamed on many things, of which two stand out. The more naive of the two is a conspiracy theory. Capitalism, personified by the multinationals and especially by the oil majors and the makers of some famous consumer brands, are everywhere busy sacrificing humane values for the sake of profit. They locate production where wages are the most miserable. They pressure gutless governments to condone their destructive practices, to allow them to evade taxes by tricky transfer pricing, to speculate in currencies and commodities, and to steamroll national industry into the ground. In short, they quietly build worldwide capitalism. (It is amusing to note that if multinationals

First published by Liberty Fund, Inc., at www.econlib.org on November 1, 2004. Reprinted by permission.

did do all these things, the almost exclusive beneficiaries would be present and future pensioners, very much part of the common people, who own all but a fraction of these sinister multinationals. Exxon Mobil and Coca-Cola do not pay dividends to themselves. Their dividends go mostly to "ordinary people.")

The other supposed culprit in bringing about "globalization" is the rise of market liberalism and in particular the gradual freeing of trade and capital movements that began in the 1950s and which is, albeit slowly and jerkily, still going on. The freer trade is, the more limited is the sovereignty of states over their own economic destiny. "Globalization" rubs out national identities, smothers diverse national cultures under an American layer, and undermines the primacy of politics over economics, a primacy that is sacrosanct to democratic ideology. Anti-globalizers want to ward off these by-products of freer trade by reverting to cozy protectionism. At the same time they tacitly assume that one can have it both ways and the riches created by the free movement of goods and capital can somehow be preserved.

A Kennedy Round, a Uruguay Round, an EFTA or a NAFTA, the GATT, and the WTO have undoubtedly made trade more free and global. But they did not invent free trade. Instead, they have restored a situation of few or low barriers that had prevailed more than once in history, the last time in the final third of the nineteenth century. In fact, free trade and protection have usually alternated in a complicated geographical and time pattern in which it is hard to discern a bias one way or the other.

Deep underneath these ups and downs, however, there has been a great trend for as long as we can look back: the trend of a steeply improving transport technology at sea, on inland waters, on the road and rail, and lately in the air, evolving from such basic devices as the wheel, the sail, the oar, the spring, and the engine that transforms energy into motion.

The effect of improving transport technology was, of course, that the movement of goods and also of persons became progressively less costly in both time and other resources. The scope for the division of labor and mutually profitable exchange steadily widened. This manifested itself in the steep fall of transport cost as a proportion of the delivered value of merchandise—an effect that, over the centuries, far outweighed any effect the raising or lowering of trade barriers may have had.

It was by historical standards only recently, in the sixteenth and seventeenth centuries, that long-distance trade was still practically limited to spices, tea, silk, dyestuffs, and precious metals—goods with a high value-to-weight ratio. Today, even lowly cement and scrap metal will travel thousands of miles. In Goschen's day, half a percent on Bank Rate was supposed "to draw gold from the moon." Today, a single-digit basis point rise will do it.

The long decline of transport and communication cost, and hence the declining relevance of location, has in our own age reached a point where competition is never far away. Business and labor can no longer get away with comfortable practices. In the post–World War II period, even in some of the more advanced economies, workers used to "own" their jobs, wages could only go up and hours worked could only go down. Everybody had a "right" to make a living in his chosen occupation or, failing that, draw earnings-related unemployment pay almost indefinitely. If winemakers or shoe manufacturers could no longer make their business pay, they nearly always managed to get state aid and carry on. Structural change in the economy, that would force many to adapt and suffer damage in the transition, was powerfully retarded by the political will not to let anyone get hurt.

This was Cloud-Cuckoo Land, and rather abruptly it is proving to be unsustainable. Welfare reform is in the air, working hours are getting longer again, and instead of the unions blackmailing the employers as has been the case for decades, it is now the employers who start blackmailing their workers by the threat of relocating, outsourcing, or straightforward job cuts. There is of course fierce political gesticulation to stop these developments, but what is politically desirable is no longer necessarily practicable. Reality is back with a vengeance. And reality, when it takes people by surprise, is not uniformly tender.

If globalization throws the doors open to reality, and reality is harsh, what is the point of globalizing? If it could be halted or reversed, should it be?

The short answer is that since transport and communications technology cannot be disinvented, reversing globalization cannot be done. However, such an argument will not stop wishful thinking.

In a public debate with antiglobalizers, Frits Bolkestein, arguably the clearest mind in the outgoing Commission of the European Union, once innocently asked them: "Why do you want to keep the poor countries poor?"

One elegant achievement of economic thought is the Factor Price Equalization theorem proved by Paul Samuelson. It states that if trade in goods is free and transport costs are zero, the rewards of factors producing tradable goods will in equilibrium be equal everywhere. More realistic assumptions used by Olin and Heckscher yield the result that factor prices will at least tend to converge. The significance of the theorem is that people do not have to migrate from poor to rich countries to achieve higher incomes; free trade will do it for them even if they stay at home. The point of globalization, then, is that both the rich and the poor countries gain, but the poor ones gain more, faster. Lovers of equality and worldwide "social justice" ought to welcome it, and not begrudge the transfer of less skilled jobs from the richer to the poorer countries.

They contend, instead, that in practice the opposite happens and social justice is flouted. The rich gain more than the poor; indeed, the poor may actually lose. Statistics can be made to say almost anything. They are made to say that the majority of third-world countries have been losing ground to the rest of the world in the course of trade liberalization. The International Labor Office has in a recent report held globalization responsible for this.

The majority of third-world countries that have grown more slowly than the world average are mainly African and mainly small- or medium-sized. They suffer cruelly from their incompetent governments, which are often engaged in shameless thieving. Two countries in the third-world minority, which is growing faster than the world average, are China and India. With a combined total of close to 2.5 billion inhabitants, they account for nearly a third of the world's population between them. Their recent growth rate has been twice to three times that of the first world. If globalization was at least partly responsible, it certainly does seem to prove the point.

ARE HIGH OIL PRICES A FORM OF EXPLOITATION?

No day passes without the news offering a neat economics lesson or two. No tuition fee is payable; only a little thought is needed to absorb the lesson.

It is in the nature of news that much or most of it is bad, for good news is no news and commands neither much airtime nor many column inches. In democracies, where everything ultimately hinges on the popular vote and the polls report almost day by day which way the popular vote would go if it were cast then and there, governments need nerves of steel not to lean the way the polls go, and few governments have nerves of steel, especially when they have election dates to think about. Nondemocracies have other reasons to be concerned about popular discontent.

One recurrent piece of news is about shamelessly high, and rising, oil company profits. Latest broker consensus estimates put the 2005 net earnings of the ten oil majors at over $100 billion. Exxon Mobil alone is expected to earn $31.6 billion, with Royal Dutch Shell, BP, and Chevron each making over $20 billion. Such numbers make the lay public feel dizzy and furious, especially when the moment comes to fill the car's tank and pay painfully more than one did last time, or three months ago.

Governments find it imperative to be seen to be doing something to get the price down. In Western Europe, between two-thirds and three-quarters of the retail price of gasoline is tax and the easiest way to reduce the price would be to cut the tax. Nearly every government has so far resisted the pressure to do this. Keeping the tax high is the main way to keep European consumption below the American level and put an obstacle in front of the triumphant advance of the "sports utility"

First published by Liberty Fund, Inc., at www.econlib.org on October 3, 2005. Reprinted by permission.

behemoths. The remaining way to appease the angry public is to attack oil-company profit margins. Though high profits curb consumption no less than do high taxes, cutting the former does not hurt government revenue, while cutting the latter does.

Last month, both the Austrian and the French governments threatened to put an excess-profit tax on oil-company profits unless they reduce gasoline prices at the pump. (They duly did so to a minor extent, though some of the reduction was due to an easing of crude prices after the International Energy Agency organized a release of 2 million barrels/day from government stocks.) France in addition invited the companies to make greater efforts to develop renewable energy sources.

WASTING RESOURCES ON RENEWABLE ENERGY

Renewable energy deserves a digression. Seven kilometers offshore from where I live on the Channel coast, the French powers-that-be have just given the go-ahead for a German company to build the country's biggest wind farm, from which twenty-one windmills, tall as forty-story skyscrapers, will deliver 105 megawatts of power into the national grid when the wind blows. To attract the investment, a price equal to 2.2 times the Western European average had to be guaranteed. Although 105 megawatts is about a tenth of the capacity of an average-sized thermal power station, both will have the same initial capital cost.

If oil companies have not so far put more money into renewable energy, it is because, short of a technological miracle, they thought it would be a waste of money. Some miracle of an unexpected kind will very likely occur one day to make some renewable energy source economical, but until it does, responsible oil companies will make haste slowly toward biomass, solar, or wind power beyond the research stage. They can hardly invest in anticipation of technological miracles, and to invest in existing technology is to waste two units of hydrocarbon energy to produce one unit of renewable—as is the case with hydrogen as a fuel and ethanol of vegetable origin.

WILL OIL GO TO 100 DOLLARS A BARREL?

Hydrocarbon reserves are supposed to start running out around 2020–2030, and go to $100 a barrel or more before they do. These conjectures need to be put in perspective.

Crude oil reserves have been supposed to be running out for the last forty years, yet have remained remarkably constant as a multiple of annual production, rising as production rose. There is no guarantee that this will go on being the case indefinitely. But contrary to the somewhat simplistic argument that "like everything else, oil in the ground is a finite quantity," there is no presumption of the reserves-to-production ratio falling in the foreseeable future. For all we know, it may rise. The headlong progress of seismic search and drilling technology is likely to permit exploration to depths undreamt-of a mere five years ago. After all, over 90 percent of the world's sea bottoms remain wholly unexplored. Deep drilling in very deep water used to be unthinkable; now it is just very expensive, but as the practice spreads, it will become less expensive.

Currently, about 30 billion barrels of oil a year are taken out of proved reserves and about the same amount put back due to new discoveries and transfers from probable to proved reserves. At an average price of $50 a barrel, this oil will fetch $1.5 trillion, of which $500 billion accrues to OPEC countries and $1 trillion to non-OPEC producers. At a "ballpark" figure for finding costs of $12/barrel, it takes $360 billion to add back the same quantity of oil to the reserves. The difference between the finding cost and the selling price is accounted for by amortization of production installations (in fiscally generous countries, by a depletion allowance as well) by lifting costs, royalties, and taxes, and the upstream profits of the operating companies. Downstream profits are earned from much thinner refining margins. Raising the finding cost by, say, 50 percent to replace reserves would raise the total cost of crude, and of refined products, by much less than 50 percent. There seems to be no good reason for crude to cost $100 for any length of time. If it did, a glut of crude might well follow a few years later.

It is the upstream profit that acts as the tail that wags the dog. Its expected level determines the finding cost the oil company will be willing to incur to replace (or raise) reserves. Until two years ago, the French oil company Total had a policy of not undertaking an exploration-and-development project unless it could at least pay for itself at a world oil price of $10 a barrel. This severe cut-off level would hardly allow spending more than $3 a barrel on finding costs. However, what determines the finding cost that an oil company will be willing to risk is not the expected price of oil, but the expected profit it can make at that price. If the price goes from $50 to $70 or even $100 a barrel but the company is not allowed to make any more money at $100 a barrel than it did at $50, it will not be prepared to incur higher finding costs. The deep ocean bottoms will remain unexplored and known world oil reserves will start to run out. Then will biomass and wind farms come into their own, at a vastly higher cost than would have been necessary if oil company profits had not been threatened with excess profit taxes and publicly pilloried as shameless if not downright criminal.

BUT OUGHT EXPLOITATION NOT TO BE STOPPED?

One lesson to be learned from the high price of oil is that it acts as a lure, inducing oil companies, from Exxon down to the small wildcatter, to explore prospects that did not look economic before, thus to increase probable and proven reserves and—perhaps to their own dismay—get the oil price down again. We call this economics, and it takes cool heads to let it work itself out. Most of the voting public lacks cool heads, and poll-watching politicians cannot afford to stay cool if they want to keep their influence and their seats. They will feel a need to reject the workings of oil economics for being "exploitation of the defenseless consumer" that ought to be stopped. Hence the threat to confiscate "excess" profits—a threat that will discourage some of the very investment that would in time raise oil reserves and deflate the "excess" profits that called it forth.

Behind this easy lesson looms a larger one about labor and capital, wages and profits. A self-correcting mechanism inherent in contractual freedom helps push up low wages because low wages permit high profits and high profits lead to more rapid capital accumulation, hence higher demand for labor. The mechanism works in the opposite direction if high wages squeeze profits and curb capital accumulation.

In his *Journeys to England and Ireland*[1] the sociologist and historian Alexis de Tocqueville was appalled by the miserable living conditions and low wages of workers in early-nineteenth-century English industry and noted that the mill owners were bringing starving men over from Ireland to have a large and docile labor supply and prevent wages from rising.

It is a fact that the Irish were made better off by being brought to work in the Lancashire mills, and it is a fact that the English were flocking to the mill towns because their life as farm laborers was more miserable still than as cotton spinners. Nevertheless, to observers like Marx and Engels, exploitation was flagrant. If it had been stopped by legislative fiat and regulation, capital accumulation would have stopped and the spectacular industrial expansion of England would not have taken place. It was thanks to this expansion that by the latter part of the nineteenth century the English worker was arguably the best paid and generally best off in the world and the Irish immigrant to northwest England and west Scotland could share in this relative prosperity. Without "exploitation" and the corrective mechanism of capital accumulation that it sets off, much of the developing world would still be stuck in utter misery.

1. Alexis de Tocqueville, *Journeys to England and Ireland,* trans. George Lawrence and K. P. Mayer, ed. J. P. Mayer (New Haven: Yale University Press, 1958).

IMMIGRATION

WHAT IS THE LIBERAL STAND?

Poverty is the chief bane of the greater part of the world, especially of Africa, much of Southeast and Central Asia, and Central and other parts of South America. A variety of local causes are blamed. A common cause, however, is government that is either downright vicious or at least incompetent to handle and employ without causing harm, the power with which it is endowed. A common remedy is on its way, operating in some areas—most spectacularly in China and India—and rising on the horizon in others. It is popularly called "globalization," and in the economist's language it is the falling relative cost of transport, transaction, and trade barriers. "Globalization" promotes the progressive equalization of productivity-adjusted wages all over the world. If their governments are not getting worse (and some are in fact getting marginally better), it is only a matter of a few decades for the poorer two-thirds of the world to rise above absolute poverty.

The reduction of relative poverty—what sociologists call relative deprivation—looks far more difficult, if not impossible. Demography will see to it that real income per head in the poor world will increase only a little faster than in the rich world, where indigenous population will be stagnant or falling. At the same time, television and its ilk will keep undermining social stability and will see to it that people in the poorer regions of the world should see their own standard of life more and more by the yardsticks of how the other half lives. They now seem to feel more miserable even as their physical circumstances become less appallingly bad.

The upshot is that the pressure to immigrate to the fairylands of Western Europe, the U.S., and the white ex-British dominions is rising and is destined to go on rising perhaps for several decades. Economists may be tempted to say that free trade will serve as a safety valve, for

First published by Liberty Fund, Inc., at www.econlib.org on August 7, 2006. Reprinted by permission.

where goods and capital move freely, people need not move to make themselves better off. But as the depressing story of the Doha Round shows, trade is not getting free enough fast enough, and capital movements will never be broad and sweeping enough as long as Bolivian, Russian, or Zimbabwean governments can lay their hands on it in the hallowed name of national sovereignty or social justice.

WHAT HAS CHANGED

Immigration, of course, is nothing new. During the great migrations after the fall of Rome, entire peoples moved from Asia to Europe, though this was not a movement into settled countries across defined frontiers. From the eighth century onward there was a broad stream of involuntary migration from Central and East Africa, with Arab traders catching or buying from tribal chiefs black Africans to be sold into slavery. Estimates of black African slaves moved to the Middle East over the thousand years to the seventeenth century vary from a low of 8 million to a high of 17 million. (It is claimed that the great majority of male slaves were castrated, which would explain why there is next to no black minority population in Arab lands.) After the seventeenth century, demand for slaves from the Caribbean, Brazil, and the southern United States priced the Middle East out of the market, and the slave trade passed into white hands. Until the abolition of slave trading (though not of slave owning) in 1808, 8 to 10 million more black Africans were shipped across the Atlantic.

There have since been two radical changes. Immigration ceased to be involuntary. People moved from Europe to North America and other lands with temperate climates of their own free will, attracted by economic incentives. Entry to these lands was unrestricted. The second great change, coming roughly with World War II, was when the entrance gates started to close. Immigrants were no longer admitted as a matter of course, but as a selective privilege granted sparsely. More and more immigrants turned into intruders, slipping in through porous frontiers and living and working with no legal status.

There are now an estimated 8 to 12 million illegal immigrants, mostly Hispanics, in the U.S. Europe's illegal immigrants are ethnically far more mixed, coming as they do from black Africa and the Caribbean,

Arab North Africa, Pakistan, Bangladesh, Ceylon, Indonesia, Turkey, and the Balkans. An estimated 570,000 live in the United Kingdom. French guesses range between 200,000 and 400,000, though the reality is almost certainly higher. The annual influx into both countries may be about 80,000.

The economic effect of illegal immigration is on balance probably positive, though it is controversial in countries with high unemployment, such as Germany, France, and Italy. It can hardly be disputed, though, that without illegal immigration from Mexico, the U.S. would not have had its spectacular growth of recent years, and the notion that illegal immigrants steal the jobs of whites in Europe comes from voodoo economics. Illegal immigration hurts, not economically, but because it is resented as a loss of control by a society of whom it will admit into its midst—a loss that is easily accepted when the colored immigrant population is yet small, but becomes fearsome when the cumulative weight of decades of uncontrolled illegal entry starts to change the ethnic and cultural profile of a country. The Netherlands is arguably the most tolerant country in Europe, but with 1,700,000 nonwhite inhabitants, it has recently become violently nervous about the future and slammed on immigration controls that are draconian by Dutch standards.

The European Union is budgeting to give 18 billion euros over seven years to help African economic development (a flagrant example of hope prevailing over experience for the umpteenth time), on the understanding that African governments will do their share in reducing the flow of illegal migrants. Many other initiatives are being taken to strengthen frontier controls, to restrict the legalization of illegals, and to deport some to their countries of origin as a deterrent to would-be illegals. None of these attempts seems to have much of an effect seriously to reduce the influx of unwelcome immigrants. Only quite radical measures might stem the tide, for whose severity current European opinion has, understandably enough, no stomach.

NO-MAN'S-LAND OR FAMILY HOME?

Classical liberals have a bad conscience about immigration controls, let alone severe ones. The liberal mind has always disliked frontiers and regards the free movement of people, no less than those of goods, as an obvious imperative of liberty. At the same time, it also considers private property as inviolable, immune to both the demands of the "public interest" (as expressed in the idea of the "eminent domain") and the rival claims of "human rights" (satisfied by redistributing income to the poor who have these rights). Private property naturally also implies privacy and exclusivity of the home.

One strand of libertarian doctrine holds that it is precisely private property that should serve as the sole control mechanism of immigration. Immigrants should be entirely free to cross the frontier—indeed, there should be no frontier. Once in the country, they should be free to move around and settle in it as if it were no-man's-land, as long as they do not trespass on any part of it that is someone's land, someone's house, someone's property of any sort. They can establish themselves and find a living by contracting to work for wages and to find a roof by paying rent. In all material aspects of life, they could find what they need by agreements with owners and also by turning themselves into owners. Owners, in turn, would not object to seeing immigrants get what they had contracted for.

A very different stand can, however, be defended on no less pure liberal grounds. For it is quite consistent with the dictates of liberty and the concept of property they imply, that the country is not a no-man's-land at all, but the extension of a home. Privacy and the right to exclude strangers from it is only a little less obviously an attribute of it than it is of one's house. Its infrastructure, its amenities, its public order have been built up by generations of its inhabitants. These things have value that belongs to their builders and the builders' heirs, and the latter are arguably at liberty to share or not to share them with immigrants who, in their countries of origin, do not have as good infrastructure, amenities, and public order. Those who claim that in the name of liberty they must let any and all would-be immigrants take a share are, then, not liberals but socialists professing share-and-share-alike egalitarianism on an international scale.

MORE NONSENSE ON STILTS

MR. BENTHAM IS AT IT AGAIN

There is no right which, when the abolition of it is advantageous to society, should not be abolished.
—Jeremy Bentham[1]

"Nonsense on stilts" was about the least rude of the many rude expressions Bentham used to pour scorn and contempt on the newfangled "rights of man" that were proclaimed at the end of the eighteenth century. These were not the contractual rights, backed by obligations which parties to contracts had assumed to honor, that figured in common and civil law and helped commerce to flourish. Rather they were flights of rhetorical fancy and pious wishes—as he put it, the letter was nonsense and beyond the letter there was nothing.

However, in promoting his rival notion of utility, which he thought was hardheaded, down-to-earth, unsentimental, and amenable to cool calculation, Bentham acted much like the pot that had called the kettle black. His "greatest happiness of the greatest number" is a model of strictly meaningless rhetoric if ever there was one. Nevertheless, his utilitarianism had a century-long run of intellectual dominance until it was toppled in the 1930s by Lionel Robbins and others, and even after losing its academic prestige, it remained politically influential to our day. It is its amazing ability to bounce back in unexpected forms that this article is about.

The great point of utilitarianism was that it raised "practical reasoning" to near-divine rank with final authority over what was to be or not to be. It treated it as agreed, established truth that an impartial observer can tell whether the utility gain of one person is greater or

First published by Liberty Fund, Inc., at www.econlib.org on April 24, 2003. Reprinted by permission.

1. *The Works of Jeremy Bentham,* Edinburgh, 1833, William Tait, vol. 2, 53.

less than the utility loss of another. Hence he can also tell whether a policy—say, taxing Peter and giving the money to Paul—is a good thing or not. Goodness was the vernacular for utility maximization. The calculus of utility opened up a glorious vista for endless policy changes, each of which would increase the utility of the gainers by more than it reduced the utility of the losers. Coupled with the supposition that the marginal utility of income was diminishing, this doctrine provided the "scientific" justification of progressive taxation.

Bentham himself was perfectly aware that aggregating the utilities of different persons, e.g., to subtract from the gains of some the losses of others, is just as nonsensical as taking four apples out of seven oranges. He privately conceded that such arithmetic was really impossible. Yet he pleaded for its use, because without it "all practical reasoning is at a stand."[2] Clearly, it would have been unbearable for him to stop telling society where to seek its advantage and how to procure the greatest happiness for the greatest number, for he had no doubt that this was what he was dong.

The thought is unbearable to the modern economist, too, except that the last two generations of them are sophisticated enough to handle "interpersonal comparisons" (or, more accurately, interpersonal aggregation) with care. Most will now say that when they recommend a policy, they do not mean to say that Peter's utility gain would be greater than Paul's loss, hence society's total utility would demonstrably increase. They would instead allude to a sort of value judgment they share with most right-thinking and informed observers, a more modest stance that disclaims science, though its modesty is sometimes a sham, meant coyly to convey that science in fact cannot be far behind.

Now and again, however, dyed-in-the-wool utilitarianism does make a comeback where it is least expected. Progressive taxation, once universally approved by all thinking men on the ground that getting a dollar gives more happiness to the poor than losing it causes unhappiness to the rich, has in recent decades lost some of its intellectual su-

2. Elie Halevy, *The Growth of Philosophical Radicalism* (London: Faber, 1956), 495, quoted by Lionel Robbins, *Politics and Economics: Papers in Political Economy* (London: Macmillan, 1963), 15.

premacy. Some of its side effects—perverse incentives, brain drain, capital flight, a wasteful cult of tax avoidance—have begun seriously to blur the nice calculation of Peter's utility gain exceeding Paul's utility loss. Top rates of income tax have been reduced in practically all developed countries. It was time for Bentham's spiritual successors to mount a counterattack. The most recent one is of stunning audacity.

Lord Layard, the distinguished British labor economist, has now moved to the borderland between welfare economics and ethics and produced a theory relating taxation to happiness that is a classic of confident utilitarian reasoning Bentham himself could not surpass.

Layard's opening salvo is that neuroscience now gives us sufficient knowledge of what goes on in our heads to enable our happiness to be objectively measured. He insists that what he can measure is not passing sensations of pleasure and pain, but lasting contentment, overall satisfaction with our lives—well, in one word, happiness. He then, plausibly enough, explains that one source of unhappiness is not poverty, deprivation, unsatisfied wants, but rather a relative worsening of our condition compared to that of our peers. What irks and depresses us is not that we are not rising fast enough, but that our neighbor is rising faster than we do. This, of course, is reminiscent of the theory of poverty as relative deprivation, i.e., as something that cannot be cured by the whole society getting richer without getting more egalitarian. It also recalls the well-known argument that the pain suffered by the envious is a legitimate reason for levelling down, for chopping off the heads of the "tall poppies."

The novelty of Layard's twist is the parallel he draws with pollution. A fast-rising man's success saps the happiness of the plodder just as surely as the polluter's pesticide, exhaust gas, or noise saps the happiness of those around him. Pollution is a "negative externality" that imposes a cost, i.e., reduced happiness, on the victims. Everybody agrees that to "internalize the externality," the polluting activity ought to be taxed. The tax forces the polluter himself to bear the cost, inducing him to lower pollution to the socially optimal level. If this is true of pollution, it must also be true of getting richer or being promoted faster than the rest of us. The man who is doing too well for our peace of mind shall be discouraged by a tax on success.

Anyone can spin a tale from this auspicious beginning. Successful

Jones is punished for his zeal by a tax. This reduces his happiness. It also reduces his zeal, making him less successful, which decreases Plodder Smith's unhappiness. One of them supposedly gains more than the other loses. Layard would have us believe that it is Plodder Smith who gains more, and after all he can check this by sounding the brains of both. Moreover, the new tax paid by Jones can be used for many good purposes, adding to Everyman's happiness which, too, can be measured by interrogating certain receptors in his brain. The result must be added to the score so far. The story then goes on; while Jones's reduced zeal relieves some of Smith's unhappiness, it also puts a brake on the growth of GDP, and Mrs. Average will enjoy fewer goods than she could otherwise have done, which might well make her a little less happy. However, the interpersonal score is still incomplete.

All agree that pollution by smoke, chemicals, or noise is bad, hence all should accept that pollution by success is bad by analogy. All agree, too, that drug addiction is bad. Layard tells us, again quite plausibly, that shopping and buying ever more expensive consumer goods is addictive. To feed the habit, we work too much. A tax on effort would make it more expensive to indulge our addiction to consumer goods we do not really need, and would make work less attractive and leisure more. "Kicking the habit" altogether by giving up excess consumption would help us adopt the balance between work and leisure that would be most conducive to happiness.

That increment, too, must be added to the score. However, the bottom line may still be some way off. For leisure, let alone idleness, may be addictive, too. Some of the characters in this story might end up growing lazy, doing less work than the amount that would make them happiest. And some people would have to go without the goods these characters would have produced if they had not been idling. That, too, must be duly accounted for.

Once all these entries are made, the stocktaking of happiness can move on to the echoes and the ricochets, the secondary and tertiary effects of primary changes engineered to enhance that most bizarre of entities, aggregate social utility. Second only to God, the latter-day Benthamite is all-seeing and up to the task. After some passing discouragement, he is confidently at it again, and as long as he is, there is hope for our greater happiness.

RISK, VALUE, AND EXTERNALITY

The "social" in social justice would always deserve to be put in quotation marks, for on close inspection it is far from evident that the adjective really fits the noun and "social" justice is really justice in any but a sloppy sense of the word. However, I will resist the temptation of the quotation marks, which could well be accused of subliminally prejudging the issue.

This essay is a bird's-eye review of some attempts to make social justice intellectually respectable by reconciling it with justice in general. I cannot explain why, but I find it truly striking that all these attempts massively resort to economic theory of one sort or another. With the exception of orthodox Marxism, they all aim at performing an almost acrobatic feat: justifying the placing of the burden on the better-off of redressing an alleged injustice suffered by the worse-off, without making any sort of case that the better-off are guilty of it.

1. CHARITY AND OBLIGATION

There is a moral intuition, strong in some and weak in others, that tells the better-off to give to the worse-off. The same sort of intuition sometimes tells some people to persuade, browbeat, or force the better-off to give to the worse-off. The result is charity. The donor may be wholly voluntary, wholly coerced, or in-between, but the recipient is not *entitled* to what he gets; the matter is not one of justice in any proper sense of the word.

Justice is a property of acts. Just acts conform to certain rules, unjust ones violate them. A state of affairs is just if it is the outcome of just acts. If we want to claim that a state of affairs, say, a particular distribution of material advantages, is an injustice, it is incumbent upon us to show that it results from unjust acts. Otherwise, talk of injustice is just talk.

First published as part 1 of "Economic Theories of Social Justice," by Liberty Fund, Inc., at www.econlib.org on May 3, 2004. Reprinted by permission.

This is where the problem of the identification of social justice as supposedly a branch of the general body of justice must be faced.

Stripped of rhetoric, an act of social justice (a) deliberately increases the relative share (though it may unwittingly decrease the absolute share) of the worse-off in total income, and (b) in achieving (a) it redresses part or all of an injustice. (Note that "income" is used in a broad sense to include stocks and flows of all material goods or claims on same that are transferable.) This implies that some people being worse-off than others is an injustice and that it must be redressed. However, redress can only be effected at the expense of the better-off; but it is not evident that they have committed the injustice in the first place. Consequently, nor is it clear why the better-off should be under an obligation to redress it, even though if they do not, no one else is left to do it.

We seem to have stepped between the horns of a dilemma. Either the better-off are under an obligation to help the worse-off although the unjust condition of the latter is no fault of theirs. Clearly, it would be defective justice to place the obligation of redressing an injustice on those who have not committed it. Or no obligor is found, no obligation is imposed, but then the right of the worse-off to redress turns out to be empty verbiage; there is no social justice, only a recommendation of charity. Yet if charity must be made compulsory by brute force on donors (though the recipients are not entitled to claim it), the weight of another injustice will press upon the situation.

It is to extricate social justice from this type of dilemma that fragments of economic theory that we would not normally expect to be incorporated in theories of justice find a part to play.

2. THE MISDEEDS OF LUCK

The better-off are better-off for a reason, or indeed a long string of reasons. Genetic endowments may be responsible for native intelligence, tenacity, cunning, and will. Upbringing may foster a sense of duty, discipline, effort, thrift, the respect of rules, the capacity to adapt one's conduct to that of others and to the facts of life. Education may teach the art of acquiring knowledge. Inheritance may provide capital, social position may attract the influential friends one needs, and so forth. All this is a matter of luck, directly or at one remove. On top of it all comes sheer fluke, chance encounters, being in the right place at the right moment. If the better-off have an above-average income, it is because they have above-average luck in the widest sense, and the inverse must be true of the less-than-average income of the worse-off.

It is thus possible both to profess the neoclassical theorem of income distribution—that incomes are determined by marginal factor productivity and factor ownership—and at the same time to hold that when social justice is fully satisfied, all incomes are equal. For if all differences in productivity and ownership are ultimately due to luck, a distribution purged of luck is an equal one. The acts of injustice that make some better off than others are the acts of Nature, who spreads fortune and misfortune blindly, randomly across the economy. The better-off bear no responsibility for the injustice that strikes the worse-off. Nature is the guilty party. It is her misdeeds that cause the injustice that social justice must rectify. However, putting the burden of redressing the injustice on the better-off who have not caused it is not doing them an injustice for the simple reason that it only deprives them of the excess income, the lucky windfall they would never have had if it had not been for the injustices committed by Nature.

Since Nature never stops throwing good luck at some and bad luck at others, no sooner are such injustices redressed than some people are again better off than others. An economy of voluntary exchanges is inherently inegalitarian (even if economies of a more regimented type may conceivably but somewhat improbably be less so). Striving for social justice, then, turns out to be a ceaseless combat against luck, a striving for the unattainable, sterilized economy that has built-in mechanisms (or, as some like to put it, "framework institutions") for offsetting the misdeeds of Nature.

3. SHELTERING FROM RISK

Two contractarian theories seek to show that no injustice is being done to the better-off by asking them to help the worse-off, because they have agreed, in a hypothetical but prima facie sane contract, to bear this burden in their own interest.

One of these theories is Rawls's "justice as fairness," whose huge popularity must be a perpetual source of wonderment. Since ultimately all income differences are due to luck, the better-off shall in fairness enter into a hypothetical position where they wish to conclude the contract of permanent distribution that would seem rational to them if they ignored how luck has in fact served them so far. Under these conditions they would agree to a distribution that always favored the worst-off, because their dread of risk was so great that they would prefer "maximin," the distribution that favored the worst-off, just in case that they happened to find themselves in that unlucky position. (We may note that people must have a very peculiar motivation to make them adopt a "maximin" strategy, i.e., to maximize the worst outcome at the cost of all the better alternatives, no matter how much better they might be.)

The other, far less convoluted, theory is the contractarianism of Buchanan and Tullock. Here, the better-off agree to bear the burden of at least partly redressing what is widely, but contestably, called social injustice. They do this because they see their future through a veil of uncertainty, and fear the risk of some turn of the wheel of fortune that would put them among the worse-off. Since they think that a distribution that improves the relative position of the worse-off may at some future time turn out to be in their interest, they voluntarily assume the cost of bringing about such a distribution. This, for them, is the cost of sheltering from risk.

For this sort of insurance to be rational, the expected "utility" of their and their heirs' risk-sheltered future income must exceed that of the unsheltered one, and this after allowing for the "cost of the shelter" (i.e., the extra taxation on the better-off that is needed to improve the share of the worse-off to the extent agreed in the hypothetical contract). Needless to say, this condition is wholly formal. The only way to ascertain the likelihood of its being satisfied is to have recourse to revealed preference: if the better-off vote for tax and welfare laws that transfer their income to the worse-off, the theory is at least not falsified. It is of course not verified. (The Rawls version of contractarian social justice, which has arguably no descriptive content, is not subject to any such validity test.)

4. ORTHODOX MARXISM

The theories reviewed in Section 2 enlist the economics of prudential choice to try and justify a view of social justice (and not of charity) that will make sense even without imputing unjust acts to anyone (except implicitly to Nature). In this view, it need not be the fault of the better-off that the worse-off are worse-off. The former find it in their interest to offer redress for an injustice that in a strict sense is not one. It should cause no surprise that theories constructed in this way are to some degree tenuous and rely on eccentric assumptions.

Orthodox Marxism is in its essentials simpler and blunter. Since all value is created by labor, the share of the product appropriated by capital accrues to the better-off as a result of unjust acts of exploitation. Justice requires that all income should accrue to the workers. This is accomplished by expropriating the capitalists and taking the means of production into some, albeit poorly defined, form of common ownership. This theory hardly calls for further discussion, except to remark that despite (or is it rather because of?) the appalling economics that underlies it, the idea of surplus value rightfully belonging to the workers and due to be returned to them still has a strong hold on the popular subconscious.

5. NEOSOCIALISM: FRAMEWORKS, NETWORKS, TISSUES

What I here call neosocialist thought either ignores or rejects the marginal productivity theory of factor rewards. Incomes are not determined by what a competitive market is willing to pay for factors that promise a given marginal contribution to the product. The reason proffered is that the market is not competitive, and even if it were, no one would have much idea of what a factor could contribute to the product. Under complex division of labor, the marginal product is a fictitious mental construct that lacks proper meaning. Nevertheless, the distribution of incomes is not simply indeterminate. Rather, it is systematically shaped in ways that render it unjust, opening the way to arguments about social justice and redress.

Neosocialism is somewhat formless and often less than lucid. One can discern several strands of thought within it, some of which could be condemned for double-counting.

One such strand puts forward the idea of the "framework" to which everything else is owed. Property and contract exist and markets function only if and when the economy is solidly embedded in an institutional framework upheld by a collective will and effort. Without a political authority that is both lawgiver and law enforcer, society would be a shambles and its total product derisory. Hence the product really belongs to society as a whole and not to its individual members. Its distribution among them is ultimately a matter for the political authority to decide. If some get more than others (perhaps because their group or class has undue influence), a question of justice arises.

The idea of the network is at the center of a rather different strand of neosocialist thought. Success and income are to a large extent the fruits of membership in networks. The successful have better access to better networks, therefore they become even more successful. Income differentials deepen in a cumulative process. The greater are the inequalities of income and of network membership, the greater is the inequality of opportunities. This gives the cumulative process another push. Finally, distribution today is largely prejudged by distribution yesterday, for those who are already better-off have greater bargaining power and can negotiate bargains that make the already worse-off even worse-off. It is not that the rich actually act unjustly, yet their advantage inflicts injustice on the poor.

Perhaps the simplest, and also the most radical, of neosocialist notions appeals to the "social tissue." Each individual is part of the "social tissue," not only of institutions, frameworks, and networks, but of an infinitely elaborate matrix of inputs and outputs. Whatever he achieves and produces is in reality achieved and produced by all his ancestors and all his contemporaries, each of whom has contributed something to enable the efforts of others to bear fruit. (Neosocialism blandly passes over the fact that everyone has already been remunerated for what he has contributed, so that to say that they are owed for what they have brought to others is double-counting.)

Everything is produced collectively by one great holistic entity, i.e., the entire society. None can claim any particular share in it, because nobody has contributed a particular share. Everyone has contributed to every part of the total product; everyone is a beneficiary of a general externality generated by everybody else.

In this perfectly socialist scheme of things, there is by definition one just distribution of incomes: that which society collectively chooses. Any redistributive measure decided by the democratic political process must, also by definition, count as the redress of a social injustice—not because it conforms to some objective criterion of justice, but because just is what society decides. Here, a shaky notion of social justice converges to a woolly notion of collective preference.

INDEX

The typeface used for this book is ITC New Baskerville, which was created for the International Typeface Corporation and is based on the types of the English type founder and printer John Baskerville (1706–1775). Baskerville is the quintessential transitional face: it retains the bracketed and oblique serifs of old-style faces such as Caslon and Garamond, but in its increased lowercase height, lighter color, and enhanced contrast between thick and thin strokes it presages modern faces.

The display type is set in Adobe Walbaum.

Printed on paper that is acid-free and meets the requirements of the American National Standard for Permanence of Paper for Printed Library Materials, Z39.48-1992.♾

Book design by Richard Hendel, Chapel Hill, North Carolina
Typography by Tseng Information Systems, Inc., Durham, North Carolina
Printed and bound by Edwards Brothers, Inc.
Ann Arbor, Michigan